FAMOUS CRICKETER

TOM GODDARD

by

Gerald Hudd

Published by the Association of Cricket Statisticians and Historians, West Bridgford, Nottingham
2006
Typeset by Limlow Books
Printed by City Press, Leeds
ISBN-10: 1 905138 37 7
ISBN-13: 978 1 905138 37 1

Gloucestershire 1951
(back): D.M.Young, C.A.Milton, G.E.E.Lambert, T.W.Graveney, C.J.Scott, C.Cook, L.M.Cranfield
(front): G.M.Emmett, J.F.Crapp, Sir D.T.L.Bailey, T.W.J.Goddard, A.E.Wilson

THOMAS WILLIAM JOHN GODDARD

Thomas William John (Tom) Goddard was born in Gloucester on 1st October 1900. Receiving his first cricket coaching from Arthur Paish, the former Gloucestershire player, he joined Gloucestershire County Cricket Club in 1922, initially as a pace bowler. Standing 6ft 3inches tall, the Gloucestershire authorities saw him as possessing all the necessary attributes of a successful fast bowler. But he was not a conspicuous success as a fast man. Although he took sixty eight Championship wickets in the 1926 season, he managed altogether to take only 153 at an average of 34 runs each in his first six seasons. At the end of the 1927 season the County decided he would not make the grade although he was offered terms for 1928 Goddard felt he was getting nowhere and declined them. He was determined to prove Gloucestershire wrong. Joining the groundstaff at Lord's and having unlimited opportunities for practice, Goddard started to experiment with off-spin. He had always been able to spin the ball, his long,strong fingers being ideally suited to this form of attack. The presence of three outstanding spin bowlers in the Gloucestershire side, Parker, Dennett and Mills, in the early to mid-Twenties had meant that no attention had been paid to Goddard's ability as a spinner. But in 1928, the Gloucestershire captain, Beverley Lyon, watched Goddard bowling off-spinners in the Lord's nets and was so impressed that he persuaded the County to re-engage him as a spinner for the 1929 season. The results were sensational. He took 184 wickets that season at 16 runs apiece including a haul of 9 for 21 at Cheltenham against Cambridge University. His career was well and truly launched.

Goddard had already taken one hat-trick as a fast bowler, against Sussex at Eastbourne in 1924. In 1930 he took his first as an off-spinner, against Glamorgan at Swansea. He made his Test match debut that season against the powerful Australian batting side at Old Trafford. He took two wickets for 49 runs in 32 overs, by no means a failure against batsmen of the calibre of Bradman, Woodfull, Ponsford, and McCabe, but he was not chosen for the final Test at Kennington Oval. He might have been excused a sigh of relief as he heard that Australia had notched a total of 695 in their only innings of that match. He did play against the Australians again, though, in what was probably the most exciting match of his career. The game at Bristol between Gloucestershire and the Australians ended in a tie with Goddard taking 7 wickets for 106 in the match including the final wicket, that of P.M.Hornibrook, leg-before-wicket to probably the loudest appeal that even Tom Goddard ever made.

It is a minor mystery as to why Goddard played in only eight Test matches in his entire career. He appeared once against Australia in 1930, twice against New Zealand in 1937, three against South Africa in 1938/39 and twice against the West Indies in 1939. In 1937 he bowled England to victory at Old Trafford , taking 6-29 in the second New Zealand innings. At Johannesburg on Boxing Day, 1938, he did the hat trick against South Africa, his victims being A.D.Nourse (caught and bowled), N.Gordon (stumped), and W.W.Wade (bowled). His Test record shows that he took 22 wickets at that level for 26.72 runs each. He was amongst the thirteen selected to play in the Old Trafford Test against Australia in 1938 but the match was abandoned without a ball being bowled and he was not chosen again in the series. It is fair to say that off-spinners were not exactly "flavour of the month" with the England selectors in the years that Goddard was in his pomp. The first choice spinner was the orthodox left-hander, Hedley Verity of Yorkshire and when a second spinner was played it was usually a leg-spinner such as Ian Peebles, Walter Robins or T.B.Mitchell of Derbyshire. Not until the arrival of Jim Laker and Tony Lock of Surrey in the 1950s was the combination of off-spinner/ orthodox left/arm considered an effective method of attack. There is no doubt at all that an off-spinner with Goddard's destructive strike-rate would have been welcomed in any Test attack of recent years. It is probable, too, that the arrival of the Second World War at the end of the West Indies series in 1939, deprived him of a number of international appearances in the early 1940s.

In all first-class cricket Goddard took 2,979 wickets at an average of 19.84. Only four bowlers have ever taken more career wickets. He finished with six hat-tricks, the same number as his

Gloucestershire colleague, Charlie Parker and only one less than the all time record of seven held by Douglas Wright of Kent. On sixteen occasions he took 100 wickets or more in a season; four times he passed 200. His most successful season of all was 1937 when he claimed 248 victims and was named as one of the Cricketers Of the Year in the 1938 *Wisden*. Ten years later, in 1947, at the ripe old age of 46 he almost bowled Gloucesterhire to the County Championship taking 238 wickets that year. In 1939 he took 17 Kent wickets in a day at Bristol , 9 for 38 in the first innings and 8 for 68 in the second. Only two other bowlers in history, Hedley Verity of Yorkshire and Colin Blythe of Kent, have performed this particular feat. In his *annus mirabilis* of 1937 he took all ten Worcestershire wickets at Cheltenham for 113 runs in the second innings. In the first innings he had merely taken 6 for 68. For Gloucestershire, alone, he took 2862 wickets at 19.58 runs apiece. In his career he took five wickets or more in an innings a staggering 252 times. On 86 occasions he took ten wickets or more.in a match.

Bowling usually round the wicket to a posse of short-legs he puzzled batsmen whenever the wicket took spin and, even when it was friendly, those long fingers had a menace all their own. He once clean bowled Patsy Hendren with a ball that pitched more than a foot outside the off stump and spun enough to hit the leg. He used his 6ft 3 inches to vary his flight. As he normally bowled round the wicket Tom would cover the area around mid-on himself and so effective was he that he took 118 catches off his own bowling. In all he took more than 300 catches, those big hands easily swallowing anything that came within reach. His close catchers helped him as well; Hammond alone took more than 100 catches off Goddard's bowling. He had a reputation as an appealer, his "How were 'ee then?" echoing round the ground whenever the ball struck the batsman's pad. The volume of his appeal and his fierce accompanying looks belied a gentle character, one who often felt hard done to by umpires who tended to think "It's only old Tom letting off steam again". Away from cricket Tom liked nothing better than a Sunday afternoon's fishing as relaxation after a long, taxing week on the cricket field.

Tom Goddard was granted two benefits by Gloucestershire. The first, in 1936, raised £2097 and the second in 1948 brought him £3355. There is a marvellous story concerning his benefit match at Gloucester in 1936 against Nottinghamshire. Notts were bowled out in the first innings for 200 (Goddard 4-49). At the end of the first day's play Gloucestershire had passed 100 with only three wickets down and a third day's play was looking unlikely. Goddard sat in the pavilion, for once bemoaning his own success. "Don't worry", said Wally Hammond. "I'll bat all day tomorrow and ensure you get a third day crowd". He did too, scoring 317 runs in the process. Gloucestershire duly wrapped up the match on the third day.

Another Goddard/Hammond story may be of interest. It concerns the Kent match at Bristol in 1939, the match already referred to in which Goddard took 17 wickets in a day. In the pavilion suggestions were flying about that Goddard was unplayable on that particular wicket. "Rubbish", said the listening Hammond. "I could play him out there with the edge of my bat". Hammond's bluff was called and the Gloucestershire team trooped out again and took up their fielding positions. For several overs Hammond played Goddard comfortably using only the edge of his bat. It should be said that Hammond, in this match had scored 153 not out in Gloucestershire's only innings in a match in which no other batsman passed 40. Like many a tail-ender, Tom fancied himself as a batsman. In 1932 when Gloucestershire were playing Essex at Southend-on-Sea, Farnes and Nichols had blasted out the top order but they could not remove Goddard who stayed for two and a half hours to hit a career best 71. He made three other fifties and many other useful contributions, usually when the County most needed them.

During the Second World War, Goddard obtained a commission with the R.A.F. It is interesting to speculate as to how many wickets he might have taken has he not lost these six seasons when he was at the height of his powers. Would he have finally become a fixture in the England side and visited Australia in the tour scheduled for 1940/41? Goddard's two overseas tours were both to South Africa, in 1930/31 and 1938/39. How many more wickets might he have taken, too, had he started his career in 1922 as an off-spinner and if he had not missed a complete season in 1928? He might well have become the greatest wicket-taker of all time. The respect in which he was held is illustrated by the fact that when Bradman's Australians toured England in 1948, Bradman advised his own off-spinner, Ian Johnson, to study and try to copy Goddard's methods.

Tom Goddard retired from the first-class game at the end of the 1952 season. He was 51 years old and the off-spinning succession at Gloucestershire was secure in the hands of John Mortimore, Bomber Wells and David Allen. For many years he ran a furniture business in Barton Street, Gloucester where he also sold me my first cricket ball. Tom willingly signed an autograph whilst I was mesmerised by the size of the man's hands. It was easy to understand how 300 odd catches had been swallowed up in hands that size. Tom Goddard died on 22nd May 1966, aged 65. He left a widow, Flo, and a host of memories and he will always be remembered by a generation of cricket lovers. He set figures that will never be surpassed.

1922

Goddard made his debut for Gloucestershire at the Spa Ground, Gloucester on June 7th 1922, against Middlesex, the reigning County Champions. It was a disastrous match for Gloucestershire with Middlesex winning by an innings and 165 runs inside two days but Goddard took his first first-class wicket, a good one too, that of J.W.Hearne caught by M.A.Green at mid-on. Goddard was the fifth bowler tried and it should be said that Hearne had scored 201 at the time. The County did rather better in Goddard's second and only other match in 1922, beating Worcestershire by an innings and 92 runs also at the Spa. Goddard did not get on to bowl in this match

	Own Team Total	O	M	R	W		Opp Total	Ct
1. Gloucestershire v Middlesex, Spa Ground, Gloucester, June 7, 8 (Middlesex won by an innings and 165 runs)								
not out	20	122	18	5	48	1 J.W.Hearne c M.A.Green	408-9d	
not out	2	121						
2. Gloucestershire v Worcestershire, Spa Ground, Gloucester, July (8), 10, 11 (Gloucestershire won by an innings and 92 runs)								
not out	6	202					58	
							52	

SEASON'S AVERAGES

Batting and Fielding	M	I	NO	Runs	HS	Ave	50	Ct
Season	2	3	3	28	20*	-	-	-

Bowling	O	M	R	W	BB	Ave	5i	10m	Strike	RunR
Season (6b)	18	5	48	1	1-48	48.00	-	-	108.00	44.44

1923

Goddard took part in sixteen of Gloucestershire's Championship games in 1923 taking 25 wickets at 29.12 apiece, figures which put him in fourth place in the County's bowling averages behind Parker, Dennett and Mills who took 299 wickets between them. As these three were all spin bowlers it is not surprising that Goddard's off-spin was not considered necessary. He took 6 for 41 against Lancashire at the Wagon Works Ground, Gloucester in June and 5 for 19 against Surrey at Bristol in May but he rarely opened the bowling and with Parker, especially, in outstanding form his opportunities were limited. As a batsman he scored just 44 runs in 26 innings and he took the first six of his career catches.

| | Own Team | O | M | R | W | | Opp | Ct |
| | Total | | | | | | Total | |

3. Gloucestershire v Surrey, Bristol, May 9, 10, 11 (Match drawn)
```
b R.F.Lowe              0   359       11    4   19   5   J.W.Hitch    lbw           174
                                                          P.G.H.Fender c E.G.Dennett
                                                          W.J.Abel     b
                                                          H.A.Peach    b
                                                          H.Strudwick  b
did not bat               -  213-6d   14    1   46   2   A.Sandham    lbw           292-7
                                                          T.F.Shepherd lbw
```
4. Gloucestershire v Essex, Leyton, May 12, 14, 15 (Match drawn)
```
b C.A.G.Russell         0   204        5    2   10   0                              198
b C.A.G.Russell         6   184        -    -    -   -                              7-0
```
5. Gloucestershire v Surrey, Kennington Oval, May 16, 17, 18 (Surrey won by eight wickets)
```
b H.A.Peach             0    64        -    -    -   -                              227
run out                 0   252      12.5   2   47   0                              90-2
```
6. Gloucestershire v Somerset, Taunton, May 19, 21, 22 (Somerset won by 343 runs)
```
not out                 0   106        3    0   17   0                              180
not out                 1    87       13    2   56   1   S.G.U.Considine b          356
```
7. Gloucestershire v Hampshire, Spa Ground, Gloucester, May 26, (28), (29) (Match drawn)
```
c H.A.W.Bowell b G.S.Boyes 5 113                                                    145
```
8. Gloucestershire v Leicestershire, Spa Ground, Gloucester, May 30, 31 (Gloucestershire won by five wickets)
```
st T.E.Sidwell b G.Geary 0    81                                                    88
did not bat               -  90-5                                                   82
```
9. Gloucestershire v Lancashire, Gloucester, June 2, 4, 5 (Lancashire won by 75 runs)
```
not out                 9   198       18    4   41   6   L.Green      b             173
                                                          J.Sharp c P.F.C.Williams
                                                          J.L.Hopwood  b
                                                          G.Duckworth  b
                                                          W.E.Hickmott lbw
                                                          C.H.Parkin   b
not out                 0   149       15    1   50   0                              249
```
10. Gloucestershire v Derbyshire, Bristol, June 6, 7, 8 (Gloucestershire won by an innings and 72 runs)
```
not out                 4   361       12    4   17   2   W.Carter     b             88
                                                          J.M.Hutchinson lbw
                                       6    2   20   0                              201
```
11. Gloucestershire v Warwickshire, Edgbaston, June 9, 11, 12 (Warwickshire won by eight wickets)
```
b H.Howell              0   262      25.2   7   76   4   L.T.A.Bates c B.H.Lyon    446   1
                                                          F.S.G.Calthorpe c E.G.Dennett
                                                          F.R.Santall  c and b
                                                          H.Howell c H.Smith
b R.E.S.Wyatt          15   257        6    2   12   0                              74-2
```
12. Gloucestershire v Warwickshire, Bristol, June 16, 18, 19 (Warwickshire won by two wickets)
```
not out                 0   215       19    2   44   1   G.W.Stephens
                                                              c C.W.L.Parker        238
b H.Howell              0   192       18    1   39   0                              171-8
```
13. Gloucestershire v Sussex, Hove, June 20, 21 (Sussex won by an innings and 213 runs)
```
not out                 0   102       13    1   66   0                              420   1
b A.H.H.Gilligan        0   105
```
14. Gloucestershire v Essex, Cheltenham, August 11, 13, 14 (Essex won by six wickets)
```
b C.A.G.Russell         0   324       34    9   77   1   C.A.G.Russell
                                                              c C.W.L.Parker        383   1
not out                 0   173        4    1   10   0                              118-4
```
15. Gloucestershire v Kent, Cheltenham, August 15, 16, 17 (Kent won by ten wickets)
```
st J.C.Hubble b F.E.Woolley 0  139    16    6   47   0                              356   2
not out                 0   286        -    -    -   -                              70-0
```
16. Gloucestershire v Middlesex, Cheltenham, August 18, 20, 21 (Middlesex won by eight wickets)
```
b H.W.Lee               0   154        4    1    8   1   H.L.Dales c A.E.Dipper     194
b F.J.Durston           4   144        2    1    4   0                              105-2
```
17. Gloucestershire v Hampshire, Southampton, August 22, 23, (24) (Match drawn)
```
b W.R.de la C.Shirley   0   212       11    3   22   2   J.A.Newman
                                                              c B.S.Bloodworth      147
                                                          R.Aird c B.S.Bloodworth
did not bat               -  95-3
```

18. Gloucestershire v Lancashire, Old Trafford, August (29), 30, 31 (Match drawn)
    not out   0   89   150   1
    did not bat   -   73-6

SEASON'S AVERAGES

Batting and Fielding	M	I	NO	Runs	HS	Ave	50	Ct
Championship	16	26	10	44	15	2.75	-	6
Career	18	29	13	72	20*	4.50	-	6

Bowling	O	M	R	W	BB	Ave	5i	10m	Strike	RunR
Championship	262.1	56	728	25	6-41	29.12	2	-	62.92	46.28
Career (6b)	280.1	61	776	26	6-41	29.84	2	-	64.65	46.16

1924

Goddard appeared in only eight of Gloucestershire's Championship matches in 1924. He took 19 wickets at an average of 18.47 which put him in second place in the County's bowling averages but he bowled only 141.5 overs compared to the 1139.1 sent down by Charlie Parker who took 184 wickets. There were some highlights, though, including his first hat-trick, against Sussex at Eastbourne. He took the wickets of A.H.H.Gilligan (bowled), W.L.Cornford (c H.Smith) and T.E.R.Cook (c E.G.Dennett) in the first innings. Against Glamorgan at Cheltenham (Victoria Park) he took 6-23 bowling unchanged with Hammond to dismiss Glamorgan for 54 in 70 minutes. His other first-class appearance was against Oxford University at Bristol. As a batsman he scored 15 runs in 11 innings. He held six catches.

	Own Team Total	O	M	R	W		Opp Total	Ct

19. Gloucestershire v Yorkshire, Gloucester, May (10), 12, 13 (Yorkshire won by eight wickets)
    c A.Dolphin b G.G.Macaulay   0   68   98
    not out   2   42   14-2

20. Gloucestershire v Leicestershire, Aylestone Road, Leicester, June 25, 26, 27 (Leicestershire won by 1 run)
    c G.Geary b W.E.Astill   3   276   15   3   29   1   S.S.Coulson b   178   3
    b G.Geary   1   124   10   2   28   1   J.H.King c F.G.Rogers 223

21. Gloucestershire v Oxford University, Bristol, June 28, 30 (Gloucestershire won by an innings and 57 runs)
    did not bat   -   504-5d 5   0   22   0   236
                                       16   3   42   3   J.E.Frazer b   211
                                                         J.L.Guise b
                                                         F.H.Barnard b

22. Gloucestershire v Hampshire, Bristol, July 2, 3, 4 (Match drawn)
    not out   0   191   4   0   12   0   71
    did not bat   -   97-5

23. Gloucestershire v Derbyshire, Gloucester, July 5, 7, 8 (Match drawn)
    not out   5   317   4   1   16   0   281
    did not bat   -   187-7d 7   1   16   1   H Storer b   49-3   1

24. Gloucestershire v Sussex, Eastbourne, July 12, 14, 15 (Gloucestershire won by nine wickets)
    did not bat   -   410-6d 16 2   58   5   A.H.H.Gilligan b   201
                                                              W.L.Cornford c H.Smith
                                                              T.E.R.Cook c E.G.Dennett
                                                              J.E.Frazer b
                                                              F.B.R.Browne c C.W.L.Parker
    did not bat   -   17-1   24 6   80   2   H.L.Wilson b   225
                                                              K.A.Higgs c H.Smith

25. Gloucestershire v Kent, Maidstone, July 16, 17, 18 (Kent won by eight wickets)
    not out   0   213   24 5   64   3   W.H.Ashdown c H.Smith 295   1
                                                              S.G.Hearn c A.E.Dipper
                                                              R.T.Bryan c P.T.Mills
    not out   1   92   -   -   -   -   13-2

26. Gloucestershire v Glamorgan, Victoria Park, Cheltenham, July 19, (21), 22 (Gloucestershire won by 202 runs)
c and b J.Mercer   1   224   10.5   3   23   6   G.B.Harrison b   54
                                                        W.E.Bates c H.Smith
                                                        D.Davies b
                                                        C.F.Walters c H.Smith
                                                        F.P.Ryan c H.Smith
                                                        D.Sullivan b
did not bat   -   130-3d   3   0   12   0   98   1

27. Gloucestershire v Worcestershire, Cheltenham, August 9, 11 (Gloucestershire won by 91 runs)
b C.F.Root   0   114   3   0   13   0   114
b G.C.Wilson   2   159   -   -   -   -   68

SEASON'S AVERAGES

Batting and Fielding	M	I	NO	Runs	HS	Ave	50	Ct
Championship	8	11	5	15	5*	2.50	-	6
Other Glos match	1	-	-	-	-	-	-	-
Season	9	11	5	15	5*	2.50	-	6
Career	27	40	18	87	20*	3.95	-	12

Bowling	O	M	R	W	BB	Ave	5i	10m	Strike	RunR
Championship	120.5	23	351	19	6-23	18.47	2	-	38.15	48.41
Other Glos match	21	3	64	3	3-42	21.33	-	-	42.00	50.79
Season	141.5	26	415	22	6-23	18.86	2	-	38.68	48.76
Career (6b)	422	87	1191	48	6-23	24.81	4	-	52.75	47.03

1925

Goddard played in only 11 of Gloucestershire's matches in 1925, bowling only 122 overs taking a mere eight wickets. His opportunities were strictly limited. In one match, against Essex at Gloucester, he did not bowl at all and in five other games he bowled less than ten overs. With Parker taking 200 wickets that season in Championship games alone, there was little need for Goddard's support. He contributed 78 runs at an average of 7.80 including his highest first-class innings to date when he hit 30 out of the 31 added for the tenth wicket against Leicestershire at Gloucester. He held five catches but really it was a most disappointing season for him.

                         Own Team   O   M   R   W   Opp   Ct
                         Total   Total

28. Gloucestershire v Derbyshire, Chesterfield, June 6, 8, 9 (Gloucestershire won by three wickets)
not out   1   278   14   2   40   2   L.F.Townsend c H.Smith   197
                                                        G.R.Jackson b
did not bat   -   98-7   4   1   13   0   178

29. Gloucestershire v Leicestershire, Aylestone Road, Leicester, June 13, 15, 16 (Leicestershire won by five wickets)
b W.E.Astill   0   124   5   0   14   0   258
b A.Skelding   0   252   -   -   -   -   119-5

30. Gloucestershire v Worcestershire, Victoria Park, Cheltenham, July 4, 6 (Gloucestershire won by four wickets)
c G.G.F.Greig b G.C.Wilson 12 135   -   -   -   -   91
did not bat   -   113-6   10   3   18   1   C.V.Tarbox b   155

31. Gloucestershire v Kent, Maidstone, July 15, 16, 17 (Kent won by 24 runs)
c A.C.Wright b H.L.Hever 10   351   9   0   24   1   H.T.W.Hardinge b   115
not out   0   129   13   2   48   0   389

32. Gloucestershire v Essex, Gloucester, July 25, 27, 28 (Gloucestershire won by an innings and 109 runs)
did not bat   -   287-6d   115
                                                                                  63

33. Gloucestershire v Hampshire, Cheltenham, August 8, 10, 11 (Match drawn)
not out   7   181   12   3   35   0   244
did not bat   -   20-0   6   0   25   0   244-6d

8

34. Gloucestershire v Nottinghamshire, Cheltenham, August (12), 13, 14 (Nottinghamshire won by seven wickets)
   b T.L.Richmond   3   66   -   -   -   -   122   2
   not out   0   89   3   1   3   0   36-3
35. Gloucestershire v Kent, Cheltenham, August 15, 17 (Kent won by an innings and 47 runs)
   b A.P.Freeman   0   71   1   0   11 0   418   1
   c W.H.Ashdown
      b A.P.Freeman   3   300
36. Gloucestershire v Lancashire, Old Trafford, August 19, 20, 21 (Match drawn)
   c G.Duckworth
      b E.A.Macdonald 0   456   5   1   18 0   323
   did not bat   -   53-1
37. Gloucestershire v Nottinghamshire, Trent Bridge, August 22, 24, 25 (Nottinghamshire won by six wickets)
   not out   6   168   22 4   73 3   W.R.D.Payton
                                                 c W.R.Hammond   292   1
                                                 B.Lilley c C.W.L.Parker
                                                 H.Larwood b
   not out   6   242   13 0   41 1   W.W.Whysall
                                                 c J.G.W.T.Bessant   122-4
38. Gloucestershire v Leicestershire, Gloucester, August 26, 27, 28 (Leicestershire won by an innings and 101 runs)
   b W.E.Astill   30 176   5   1   15 0   334   1
   b G.Geary   0   57

SEASON'S AVERAGES

Batting and Fielding	M	I	NO	Runs	HS	Ave	50	Ct	
Championship	11	16	6	78	30	7.80	-	5	
Career	38	56	24	165	30	5.15	-	17	

Bowling	O	M	R	W	BB	Ave	5i	10m	Strike	RunR
Championship	122	18	378	8	3-73	47.25	-	-	91.50	51.63
Career (6b)	544	105	1569	56	6-23	28.01	4	-	58.28	48.06

1926

Goddard was given more opportunities in 1926 and responded with his best season to date taking 68 wickets in the Championship at an average of 30.25. Spin-bowling was still the County's main attacking weapon with Parker taking 198 wickets and Mills 101. Goddard had two five wicket hauls, against Hampshire at Gloucester and Essex at Bristol. He was regularly given the new ball this season and often bowled lengthy spells. The season also brought his first encounter with the Australians. Playing at the Cheltenham College ground he took the wickets of J.M.Taylor, T.J.E.Andrews and A.J.Richardson for 58 runs. As a batsman he made 317 runs in 48 innings the highlight being an innings of 47 against Essex at Gloucester when he helped P.T.Mills to add 98 for the tenth Gloucestershire wicket. This is still the record tenth wicket stand for Gloucestershire against Essex. He held 26 catches.

                        Own Team   O   M   R   W   Opp   Ct
                        Total   Total
39. Gloucestershire v Lancashire, Gloucester, May 8, (10), (11) (Match drawn)
   did not bat   -   79-1   2   0   10 1   C.Hallows lbw   145   1
40. Gloucestershire v Surrey, Kennington Oval, May 12, 14 (Surrey won by an innings and 53 runs)
   not out   7   135   20   3   103 2   T.F.Shepherd c H.Smith 426-8d
                                                         R.J.Gregory b
   b P.G.H.Fender   0   238
41. Gloucestershire v Kent, Gravesend, May 15, 17, 18 (Kent won by seven wickets)
   run out   2   204   29.1   2   80 4   W.H.Ashdown c H.Smith   320
                                                         G.C.Collins lbw
                                                         A.C.Wright b
                                                         W.S.Conwallis c G.A.Wedel
   c W.S.Cornwallis
      b A.P.Freeman   1   206   6   3   12   0   93-3   1

9

42. Gloucestershire v Northamptonshire, Northampton, May 19, 20 (Gloucestershire won by 69 runs)
    c and b A.E.Thomas   1   54   7   2   17   1   C.N.Woolley c G.A.Wedel   126
    c J.V.Murdin b E.W.Clark   6   210   7   1   15   1   J.M.Fitzroy b   69

43. Gloucestershire v Somerset, Taunton, May 22, 24, 25 (Gloucestershire won by ten wickets)
    not out   8   364   23   4   99   1   C.C.C.Case b   319
    did not bat   -   66-0   17   6   27   1   M.D.Lyon lbw   110

44. Gloucestershire v Worcestershire, Stourbridge, May 29, 31 (Gloucestershire won by ten wickets)
    not out   10   236   23.4   2   54   4   M.F.S.Jewell b   144   1
                                                                                                                                 C.V.Tarbox c A.E.Dipper
                                                                                                                                 G.C.Wilson b
                                                                                                                                F.T.Summers b
    did not bat   -   45-0   10   2   30   0   135

45. Gloucestershire v Sussex, Gloucester, June 2, 3, 4 (Sussex won by 160 runs)
    b M.W.Tate   8   58   3   0   11   0   128   1
    not out   10   132   8   2   17   0   222-9d

46. Gloucestershire v Hampshire, Gloucester, June 5, 7, 8 (Hampshire won by five wickets)
    not out   7   304   31.5 3   123 5   G.Brown b   392   1
                                                                                                                                H.A.W.Bowell lbw
                                                                                                                                 C.P.Mead lbw
                                                                                                                                  G.S.Boyes b
                                                                                                                                A.S.Kennedy c D.C.Robinson
    st W.H.Livsey b G.S.Boyes   0   175   -   -   -   -   90-5

47. Gloucestershire v Sussex, Horsham, June 9, 10, 11 (Match drawn)
    b G.R.Cox   0   144   163
    did not bat   -   146-5d   54-7   1

48. Gloucestershire v Glamorgan, Victoria Park, Cheltenham, June (12), 14, 15 (Glamorgan won by four wickets)
    not out   0   133   -   -   -   -   149   1
    b F.P.Ryan   2   134   5   1   18   1   T.Arnott b   120-6   1

49. Gloucestershire v Lancashire, Liverpool, June 16, 17, 18 (Lancashire won by 138 runs)
    c G.Duckworth
        b R.K.Tyldesley   19   145   -   -   -   -   178   1
    b R.K.Tyldesley   0   98   2   0   4   0   203   2

50. Gloucestershire v Derbyshire, Burton-on-Trent, June 19, 21, 22 (Match drawn)
    b J.M.Hutchinson   5   363   22   4   38   0   256   2
    did not bat   -   82-1   18   3   41   1   G.M.Lee c B.H.Lyon   279   1

51. Gloucestershire v Yorkshire, Hull, June 23, 24, 25 (Match drawn)
    c W.Rhodes b R.Kilner   4   157   33   10   76   2   P.Holmes lbw   198   1
                                                                                                   M.Leyland c B.S.Bloodworth
    did not bat   -   59-5

52. Gloucestershire v Middlesex, Greenbank, Bristol, June 26, 28, 29 (Middlesex won by 227 runs)
    b N.E.Haig   2   261   16   1   47   1   G.B.Cuthbertson lbw   360   1
    not out   3   157   9   0   47   1   S.L.Beton c B.S.Bloodworth 285-7d

53. Gloucestershire v Derbyshire, Greenbank, Bristol, June 30, July 1, 2 (Derbyshire won by six wickets)
    not out   1   287   38   12   67   3   W.F.Parrington b   248
                                                                                                    J.M.Hutchinson c P.T.Mills
                                                                                                    L.F.Townsend c B.H.Lyon
    not out   8   182   27   6   67   2   G.M.Lee c   223-4
                                                                                                    L.F.Townsend c B.H.Lyon

54. Gloucestershire v Leicestershire, Aylestone Road, Leicester, July 3, 5, (6) (Match drawn)
    b W.E.Astill   27   258   15.4   2   38   3   A.W.Shipman b   102   2
                                                                                                   G.L.Berry c H.Smith
                                                                                                    T.E.Sidwell b
    run out   19   196   7   1   14   0   22-0

55. Gloucestershire v Essex, Bristol, July 10, 12, 13 (Essex won by six wickets)
    c J.R.Freeman
        b M.S.Nichols   47   220   31.3   6   62   6   J.A.Cutmore c H.J.H.Alpass 217
                                                                                                    C.A.G.Russell c P.T.Mills
                                                                                                    H.M.Morris c H.Smith
                                                                                                    L.C.Eastman c P.T.Mills
                                                                                                    A.B.Hipkin c F.J.Seabrook
                                                                                                    M.S.Nichols b
    c C.A.G.Russell
        b J.O'Connor   7   205   23.3   6   56   2   J.R.Freeman b   210-4
                                                                                                    N.G.Wykes b

56. Gloucestershire v Kent, Bristol, July 14, 15, 16 (Kent won by four wickets)
    b A.P.Freeman   1   241   13   6   19   0   185
    b H.T.W.Hardinge   12   210   3   1   9   1   H.T.W.Hardinge
                                                            c J.G.W.T.Bessant   267-6   1

57. Gloucestershire v Nottinghamshire, Trent Bridge, July 17, 19, 20 (Match drawn)
    b T.L.Richmond   20   380   24   3   54   3   W.Walker c H.Smith   301
                                                            W.R.D.Payton c H.Smith
                                                            A.Staples c R.A.Sinfield
    did not bat   -   163-3   34   6   109   2   W.Walker c sub   333-5d
                                                            W.R.D.Payton c F.J.Seabrook

58. Gloucestershire v Worcestershire, Victoria Park, Cheltenham, July 21, 22, 23 (Match drawn)
    c G.C.Wilson b C.F.Root 29   186   17   4   55   1   M.K.Foster c G.Wedel   271
    did not bat   -   278-8

59. Gloucestershire v Hampshire, Bournemouth, July 24, 26, 27 (Hampshire won by 75 runs)
    b J.A.Newman   5   107   36   10   59   4   G.Brown b   152   1
                                                            C.P.Mead c D.C.Robinson
                                                            C.P.Brutton b
                                                            A.S.Kennedy c R.A.Sinfield
    st W.H.Livsey b G.S.Boyes 24 174   14   2   54   2   C.P.Mead c G.Wedel   204-6d
                                                            A.S.Kennedy lbw

60. Gloucestershire v Yorkshire, Bristol, July 28, 29, 30 (Yorkshire won by an innings and 41 runs)
    b G.G.Macaulay   0   170   21   2   67   3   E.Oldroyd c H.Smith   279   1
                                                            W.Rhodes c D.C.Robinson
                                                            G.G.Macaulay b
    c W.Rhodes b G.G.Macaulay 2   68

61. Gloucestershire v Somerset, Bristol, July 31, August 2, 3 (Somerset won by 21 runs)
    b J.J.Bridges   3   175   21   6   53   1   J.Daniell b   193
    run out   0   190   14   5   33   1   A.Young c D.C.Robinson   193

62. Gloucestershire v Northamptonshire, Bristol, August 4, 5, 6 (Northamptonshire won by 41 runs)
    b E.W.Clark   0   190   7   2   14   1   J.E.Timms b   264
    not out   0   161   12   1   28   2   C.N.Woolley c H.Smith   128
                                                            B.W.Bellamy b

63. Gloucestershire v Australians, Cheltenham, August 7, 9 (Australians won by nine wickets)
    c T.J.E.Andrews
          b C.V.Grimmett   0   144   17   4   58   3   J.M.Taylor lbw   287
                                                            T.J.E.Andrews c H.Smith
                                                            A.J.Richardson lbw
    not out   9   178   -   -   -   -   39-1

64. Gloucestershire v Nottinghamshire, Cheltenham, August 11, 12, 13 (Nottinghamshire won by 224 runs)
    st B.Lilley b T.L.Richmond 0 128   2   1   8   0   155   1
    not out   1   102   7   0   22   0   299-6d 1

65. Gloucestershire v Essex, Leyton, August 21, 23, 24 (Match drawn)
    b L.C.Eastman   0   228   32   4   87   0   471
    did not bat   -   313-4

66. Gloucestershire v Middlesex, Lord's, August 25, 26, 27 (Middlesex won by 75 runs)
    not out   0   191   19   7   38   2   F.T.Mann lbw   111   2
                                                            N.E.Haig c H.Smith
    c F.T.Mann b J.A.Powell 4   245   42   11   108   2   H.J.Enthoven c E.G.Dennett 400-7d
                                                            S.L.Beton b

67. Gloucestershire v Leicestershire, Bristol, August 28, 30, 31 (Gloucestershire won by 54 runs)
    b G.Geary   0   306   27   5   67   1   W.E.Astill lbw   271
    not out   3   74   -   -   -   -   55   1

SEASON'S AVERAGES

Batting and Fielding	M	I	NO	Runs	HS	Ave	50	Ct
Championship	28	46	13	308	47	9.33	-	26
Other Glos match	1	2	1	9	9*	9.00	-	-
Season	29	48	14	317	47	9.32	-	26
Career	67	104	38	482	47	7.30	-	43

Bowling	O	M	R	W	BB	Ave	5i	10m	Strike	RunR
Championship	780.2	158	2057	68	6-62	30.25	2	-	68.85	43.93
Other Glos match	17	4	58	3	3-58	19.33	-	-	34.00	56.86
Season	797.2	162	2115	71	6-62	29.78	2	-	67.38	44.20
Career (6b)	1341.2	267	3684	127	6-23	29.00	6	-	63.37	45.77

1927

Goddard had a disappointing season in 1927, playing in only 18 of Gloucestershire's matches and taking 26 wickets at an expensive 58.80 apiece. He had one five wicket haul, against Leicestershire at Hinckley and he was often heavily punished, 0-116 against Surrey at Kennington Oval, 0-132 against Essex at Greenbank, Bristol, 0-81 off 20 overs against Lancashire at Old Trafford and 1-76 off 15 overs against the New Zealanders at Cheltenham. He was not making sufficient progress as a fast bowler and it was time to think seriously about the future. As a batsman he hit 147 runs in 24 innings and as a fielder he held eleven catches.

	Own Team Total	O	M	R	W		Opp Total	Ct
68. Gloucestershire v Surrey, Kennington Oval, May 11, 12, 13 (Match drawn)								
b T.F.Shepherd	2 406	26	4	116	0		557-7d	
st H.Strudwick b S.Fenley	1 363	5	0	27	0		31-1	
69. Gloucestershire v Yorkshire, Dewsbury, May 14, 16, 17 (Yorkshire won by an innings and 2 runs)								
st A.Dolphin b W.Rhodes	16 134	29	6	79	3	E.Oldroyd c R.A.Sinfield	318	
						G.G.Macaulay c A.E.Dipper		
						A.Waddington c G.Wedel		
c R.Kilner b W.Rhodes	1 182							
70. Gloucestershire v Lancashire, Old Trafford, May 18, 19, 20 (Match drawn)								
b E.A.Macdonald	1 235	20	2	81	0		336	1
not out	27 510							
71. Gloucestershire v Leicestershire, Hinckley, May 21, 23, 24 (Leicestershire won by 279 runs)								
not out	3 87	27.1	5	92	5	A.W.Shipman		
						c W.R.Hammond	243	
						J.C.Bradshaw b		
						G.Geary c W.R.Hammond		
						G.H.S.Fowke c E.G.Morrison		
						A.Skelding b		
b A.Skelding	0 148	23	3	88	0		271-5d	
72. Gloucestershire v Middlesex, Bristol, May 25, 26, 27 (Middlesex won by an innings and 158 runs)								
c H.W.Lee b N.E.Haig	2 225	49	4	179	3	H.W.Lee c W.R.Hammond	491-7d	
						N.E.Haig c W.R.Hammond		
						E.H.Hendren b		
b F.J.Durston	2 108							
73. Gloucestershire v Hampshire, Southampton, May 28, 30, 31 (Match drawn)								
not out	4 320	32	7	73	1	J.A.Newman		
						c W.R.Hammond	421	
did not bat	- 337-4d	-	-	-	-		135-4	
74. Gloucestershire v Lancashire, Bristol, June 1, 2, 3 (Lancashire won by an innings and 41 runs)								
b R.K.Tyldesley	13 180	43	3	118	4	C.Hallows c W.R.Hammond	469	1
						L.Green c C.W.L.Parker		
						F.M.Sibbles hit wkt		
						R.K.Tyldesley b		
not out	5 248							
75. Gloucestershire v Somerset, Taunton, June 4, 6, 7 (Match drawn)								
not out	3 331	18.4	5	48	3	J.Daniell c H.Smith	427	
						W.T.Greswell c B.H.Lyon		
						R.C.Robertson-Glasgow b		
did not bat	- 125-3	14	2	44	0		138	1
76. Gloucestershire v Nottinghamshire, Greenbank, Bristol, June 8, 9, 10 (Nottinghamshire won by four wickets)								
not out	15 289	26	8	63	2	G.Gunn b	327-9d	
						W.W.Whysall c B.S.Bloodwworth		
not out	29 342	6	0	40	0		305-6	

77. Gloucestershire v Cambridge University, Greenbank, Bristol, June 11, 13, 14 (Match drawn)
   not out   1   286   20   6   44   1   E.W.Dawson c and b   367   1
   did not bat   -   222-4   17   6   49   0   287-5d

78. Gloucestershire v Essex, Greenbank, Bristol, June 15, 16, 17 (Match drawn)
   did not bat   -   405-2   33   3   132 0   578-6d

79. Gloucestershire v Northamptonshire, Northampton, June 18, 20 (Gloucestershire won by seven wickets)
   not out   3   182   -   -   -   -   92
   did not bat   -   36-3   2   1   7   0   124

80. Gloucestershire v Derbyshire, Derby, June 22, 23, (24) (Match drawn)
   b L.F.Townsend 3   240   6   1   25   0   139-2

81. Gloucestershire v Nottinghamshire, Trent Bridge, June 25, 27, 28 (Match drawn)
   b S.J.Staples   0   149   264-6d   1
   did not bat   -   11-1

82. Gloucestershire v Derbyshire, Gloucester, June 29, 30, July (1) (Match drawn)
   did not bat   -   21-2   20   2   55   1   J.M.Hutchinson c W.L.Neale 353   1

83. Gloucestershire v Leicestershire, Victoria Park, Cheltenham, July 13, 14, 15 (Match drawn)
   b G.Geary   0   187   9   4   21   0   238   2
   did not bat   -   52-6   -   -   -   -   102-8d   1

84. Gloucestershire v Middlesex, Lord's, July 20, 21, 22 (Match drawn)
   b F.J.Durston   6   275   25   3   72   2   N.E.Haig c and b   280-9d   1
                                                   R.W.V.Robins b
   not out   8   301

85. Gloucestershire v New Zealanders, Cheltenham, August 10, 11, (12) (Match drawn)
   not out   2   148   15   0   76   1   M.L.Page c H.Smith   415-9d
   did not bat   -   130-3

SEASON'S AVERAGES

Batting and Fielding	M	I	NO	Runs	HS	Ave	50	Ct
Championship	16	22	9	144	29*	11.07	-	10
Other Glos matches	2	2	2	3	2*	-	-	1
Season	18	24	11	147	29*	11.30	-	11
Career	85	128	49	629	47	7.96	-	54

Bowling	O	M	R	W	BB	Ave	5i	10m	Strike	RunR
Championship	413.5	63	1360	24	5-92	56.66	1	-	103.45	54.77
Other Glos matches	52	12	169	2	1-44	84.50	-	-	156.00	54.16
Season	465.5	75	1529	26	5-92	58.80	1	-	107.50	54.70
Career (6b)	1807.1	342	5213	153	6-23	34.07	7	-	70.86	48.07

1928

Although Goddard played no first-class cricket in 1928 it was probably the most important season in his career to date. He developed his off-spin in the nets at Lord's and when the 1929 season started he was ready to show the cricket world what he could do in this new form of attack. Whereas he had taken only 153 wickets in six seasons at an average of 34.07 he was now to take a further 2826 wickets at 19.07 in the rest of his career, taking 100 wickets or more every season until 1950.

1929

In 1929 Goddard sprang to prominence with a total of 184 wickets in the season at an average of 16.38 which put him into sixth place in the national averages. Re-engaged by Gloucestershire to replace P.T.Mills who had gone to coach at Radley College, Goddard accepted his opportunity with both hands, forming a deadly spin partnership with Charlie Parker. The pair were to take 284 wickets in the Championship with Goddard capturing 154 at 15.97. He was the first bowler to obtain 100 wickets in the season, achieving this feat against Leicestershire at Bristol in June. Against Cambridge University at Victoria Ground, Cheltenham, he was practically unplayable taking 9 wickets for 21 in the first innings. He took five wickets in an innings 16 times and ten wickets in a match on six occasions. National recognition came in selection for the Players against the Gentlemen at Lord's, for the Rest v England in the Test Trial match at Lord's and for the Rest of England against the County Champions, Nottinghamshire at Kennington Oval. His career was well and truly launched. As a batsman he scored 203 runs in 37 innings. He held 22 catches.

	Own Team Total	O	M	R	W		Opp Total	Ct
86. Gloucestershire v Warwickshire, Edgbaston, May 4, 6, 7 (Match drawn)								
did not bat	- 493-8d	29	8	97	2	L.T.A.Bates c C.J.Barnett N.Kilner b	295	1
		-	-	-	-		76-0	
87. Gloucestershire v Essex, Leyton, May 8, 9, 10 (Gloucestershire won by 112 runs)								
b M.S.Nichols	4 201	9	5	13	3	L.C.Eastman c R.G.Ford A.G.Daer b G.F.Eastman lbw	144	
b L.C.Eastman	1 189	21	13	16	2	H.P.Waugh lbw M.S.Nichols b	134	
88. Gloucestershire v Sussex, Hove, May 11, 13, 14 (Sussex won by 374 runs)								
b J.H.Parks	5 134	34.1	10	73	2	T.E.R.Cook st H.Smith A.H.H.Gilligan c C.J.Barnett	280	
b E.H.Bowley	5 182	24	2	71	0		410-2d	
89. Gloucestershire v Middlesex, Lord's May 15, 16, 17 (Gloucestershire won by 196 runs)								
c W.F.F.Price b J.W.Hearne	7 190	19.3	9	25	7	H.W.Lee c and b J.W.Hearne c B.H.Lyon H.J.Enthoven c B.H.Lyon R.W.V.Robins c E.J.Stephens G.C.Newman c B.H.Lyon T.J.Durston b I.A.R.Peebles st H.Smith	70	1
did not bat	- 321-4d	40.3	14	95	6	J.W.Hearne lbw E.H.Hendren c H.Smith R.W.V.Robins b G.C.Newman c H.Smith F.J.Durston b I.A.R.Peebles lbw	245	
90. Gloucestershire v Kent, Bristol, May 18, 20, 21 (Kent won by eight wickets)								
c L.J.Todd b A.P.Freeman	4 119	33	7	97	2	W.H.Ashdown b L.J.Todd c C.W.L.Parker	334	
not out	0 367	15	3	38	0		153-2	
91. Gloucestershire v South Africans, Bristol, May 22, 23, 24 (Gloucestershire won by six wickets)								
b A.J.Bell	0 331	31.1	4	68	6	J.A.J.Christy st H.Smith E.L.Dalton b H.W.Taylor c and b H.B.Cameron c R.A.Sinfield Q.McMillan lbw A.L.Osche c W.R.Hammond	225	1
did not bat	- 129-4	20	6	62	3	J.A.J.Christy c C.C.R.Dacre E.L.Dalton c H.W.Taylor b	232	1
92. Gloucestershire v Hampshire, Southampton, May 25, 27, 28 (Gloucestershire won by an innings and 129 runs)								
not out	14 429	13.1	4	35	5	A.S.Kennedy c B.H.Lyon C.P.Brutton c B.H.Lyon W.H.Livesey c H.Smith A.E.Pothecary c W.R.Hammond O.W.Herman c W.R.Hammond	110	
		22	6	76	5	J.A.Newman b C.E.Dixon c B.H.Lyon C.P.Brutton c W.R.Hammond W.H.Livesey c W.R.Hammond A.E.Pothecary b	190	1

93. Gloucestershire v Worcestershire, Gloucester, June 1, 3 (Gloucestershire won by an innings and 2 runs)
    not out   0   242   42   12   117   8   J.B.Higgins   c and b   180   1
                                                             J.Fox   b
                                                             M.Nichol   lbw
                                                             H.H.I.H.Gibbons   c E.J.Stephens
                                                             W.V.Fox   c R.A.Sinfield
                                                             L.Wright   b
                                                             M.F.S.Jewell   b
                                                             C.F.Root   lbw
                                          12.4   3   37   5   H.H.I.H.Gibbons   c B.H.Lyon   60
                                                             W.V.Fox   c B.H.Lyon
                                                             M.F.S.Jewell   b
                                                             H.A.Gilbert   b
                                                             P.F.Jackson   b
94. Gloucestershire v Oxford University, The Parks, June 5, (6), 7 (Match drawn)
    did not bat   -   184-5d 32   7   88   3   A.M.Crawley   b   223-6
                                                             W.O'B.Lindsay   c R.A.Sinfield
                                                             K.R.M.Carlisle   b
95. The Rest v England (Test Trial), Lord's, June 8, 10, 11 (Match drawn)
    b J.C.White   15   370   25   7   57   1   M.W.Tate   c E.T.Killick   487-8d   1
    did not bat   -   84-4 20   5   36   3   W.R.Hammond   c W.Voce   169
                                                             G.E.Tyldesley   c P.G.H.Fender
                                                             M.W.Tate   c L.E.G.Ames
96. Gloucestershire v Cambridge University, Victoria Park, Cheltenham, June (12), 13, 14 (Match drawn)
    did not bat   -   220-3d 13.5 8   21   9   G.D.Kemp-Welch
                                                                        c B.H.Lyon   82
                                                             E.T.Killick   b
                                                             G.C.Grant   c G. Wedel
                                                             B.H.Valentine   b
                                                             M.J.L.Turnbull   c C.J.Barnett
                                                             W.K.Harbinson   b
                                                             J.T.Morgan   c L.P.Hedges
                                                             T.E.Drakes   b
                                                             E.D.Blundell   b
                                           9   1   23   0   135-3
97. Gloucestershire v Leicestershire, Aylestone Road, Leicester, June 15, 17, 18 (Leicestershire won by eight
    wickets)
    not out   0   201   53.3 16   95   5   A.W.Shipman   b   270
                                                             N.F.Armstrong   c H.Smith
                                                             W.E.Astill   c A.E.Dipper
                                                             W.H.Bradshaw   lbw
                                                             H.C.Snary   lbw
    c and b G.Geary   1   151   4   0   15   0   83-2
98. Gloucestershire v Lancashire, Bristol, June 19, 20, 21 (Gloucestershire won by an innings and 31 runs)
    c R.K.Tyldesley
         b F.M.Sibbles   0   395   44.2 20   89   5   C.Hallows   lbw   234
                                                             J.Iddon   c B.H.Lyon
                                                             G.Duckworth   c B.H.Lyon
                                                             P.T.Eckersley   lbw
                                                             E.A.Macdonald   lbw
                                          32.3   8   72   6   F.B.Watson   c B.H.Lyon   130
                                                             J.Iddon   c B.H.Lyon
                                                             J.L.Hopwood   c B.H.Lyon
                                                             P.T.Eckersley   c W.R.Hammond
                                                             F.M.Sibbles   c W.L.Neale
                                                             R.K.Tyldesley   c C.J.Barnett
99. Gloucestershire v Leicestershire, Bristol, June 22, 24, 25 (Gloucestershire won by 82 runs)
    not out   27   233   46   12   89   8   G.L.Berry   c and b   161   2
                                                             J.C.Bradshaw   lbw
                                                             W.H.Bradshaw   b
                                                             W.E.Astill   c H.Smith
                                                             T.E.Sidwell   c and b
                                                             C.A.R.Coleman   b
                                                             G.Geary   c B.H.Lyon
                                                             H.C.Snary   lbw

15

c G.L.Berry b W.E.Astill	3	156	25	6	46	4	J.C.Bradshaw c and b	146	2
							W.H.Bradshaw c A.E.Dipper		
							T.E.Sidwell b		
							H.C.Snary b		

100. Gloucestershire v Glamorgan, Swansea, June 26, 27, 28 (Gloucestershire won by seven wickets)

b J.Mercer	13	434	10	4	23	0		181
did not bat		52-3	44.3	25	65	7	W.E.Bates c B.H.Lyon	304
							D.Davies lbw	
							W.G.Morgan lbw	
							T.Arnott b	
							D.E.Davies b	
							J.Mercer b	
							F.P.Ryan c R.A.Sinfield	

101. Gloucestershire v Northamptonshire, Kettering, June 29, July 1 (Gloucestershire won by an innings and 17 runs)

b V.W.C.Jupp	0	358	20.2	6	39	2	A.L.Cox lbw	193	2
							E.W.Clark c and b		
			28	13	50	3	C.N.Woolley lbw	148	
							A.D.G.Matthews b		
							W.H.Hawtin b		

102. Gloucestershire v Essex, Gloucester, July 3, (4), (5) (Match drawn)

| did not bat | | - 432-3 |

103. Gloucestershire v Middlesex, Gloucester, July (6), 8, 9 (Gloucestershire won by eight wickets)

did not bat		- 185-6d	30.1	11	61	4	D.L.Russell b	184
							J.M.Sims lbw	
							J.H.A.Hulme st H.Smith	
							G.E.Hart c H.Smith	
did not bat		- 121-2	19.2	5	38	3	J.W.Hearne c H.Smith	121
							J.M.Sims b	
							G.E.Hart lbw	

104. Gloucestershire v Lancashire, Old Trafford, July 10, 11, 12 (Match drawn)

c F.B.Watson								
b R.K.Tyldesley	8	121	25.3	8	59	4	C.Hallows b	168
							T.M.Holliday c W.R.Hammond	
							G.Duckworth lbw	
							E.A.Macdonald b	
did not bat		- 200-8						

105. Players v Gentlemen, Lord's, July 17, 18, 19 (Players won by seven wickets)

not out	5	253	13	3	34	0		138
did not bat		- 196-3	19	2	58	2	E.T.Killick lbw	310
							A.W.Carr c E.H.Hendren	

106. Gloucestershire v Nottinghamshire, Bristol, July 20, 22, 23 (Nottinghamshire won by 6 runs)

b W.Voce	2	168	23	2	72	3	A.Staples b	219	
							G.V.Gunn lbw		
							S.J.Staples lbw		
c W.Walker b W.Voce	0	161	23	4	67	3	W.W.Whysall c H.Smith	116	1
							A.W.Carr lbw		
							F.Barratt c W.L.Neale		

107. Gloucestershire v Surrey, Kennington Oval, July 31, August (1), (2) (Match drawn)

| did not bat | | - 122-0 |

108. Gloucestershire v Kent, Canterbury, August 3, 5, (6) (Match drawn)

c A.C.Wright b C.S.Marriott	0	217	41	3	127	3	J.L.Bryan	339
							L.E.G.Ames lbw	
							G.B.Legge b	
did not bat		- 137-1						

109. Gloucestershire v Glamorgan, Clifton, August 7, 8, 9 (Gloucestershire won by an innings and 26 runs)

b J.C.Clay	6	315	25.5	4	66	5	W.E.Bates c A.E.Dipper	146	3
							J.J.Hills c A.E.Dipper		
							J.C.Clay c W.L.Neale		
							F.P.Ryan c and b		
							T.Arnott b		
			22	5	50	3	J.J.Hills c L.P.Hedges	143	
							W.G.Morgan lbw		
							J.C.Clay b		

110. Gloucestershire v Northamptonshire, Clifton, August 10, 12, 13 (Gloucestershire won by seven wickets)
not out   5   156   29   13   42   3 A.D.G.Matthews b   122
                                                             E.F.Towell   b
                                                             A.L.Cox   lbw
did not bat   -   88-3   31.4   11   35   4 J.E.Timms   lbw   118
                                                             V.W.C.Jupp   lbw
                                                             B.W.Bellamy   lbw
                                                             E.W.Clark   b

111. Gloucestershire v Sussex, Cheltenham, August 14, 15, 16 (Sussex won by 1 run)
c and b M.W.Tate   0   214   29.4   2   85   6 E.H.Bowley   b   263   1
                                                             J.Langridge   b
                                                             A.F.Wensley   c F.J.Seabrook
                                                             R.L.Holdsworth c B.H.Lyon
                                                             M.W.Tate   lbw
                                                             W.L.Cornford c B.H.Lyon
c W.L.Cornford
     b J.Langridge   1   164   17   7   33   3 E.H.Bowley   c B.H.Lyon   116
                                                             J.Langridge   b
                                                             M.W.Tate   c L.P.Hedges

112. Gloucestershire v Surrey, Cheltenham, August 17, 19, 20 (Match drawn)
not out   0   186   20   5   50   2 A.Sandham   lbw   286
                                                             H.S.Squires   b
not out   10   339

113. Gloucestershire v Nottinghamshire, Trent Bridge, August 21, 22, 23 (Nottinghamshire won by an innings and 27 runs)
not out   2   139   35   8 118   3 B.Lilley   b   396
                                                             W.A.Flint   b
                                                             F.Barratt   c B.H.Lyon
c F.W.Shipston
     b H.Larwood   23   230

114. Gloucestershire v Warwickshire, Victoria Park, Cheltenham, August 24, 26 (Gloucestershire won by 106 runs)
not out   0   173   12   1   29   4 E.J.Smith   c H.Smith   102   1
                                                             F.R.Santall   c H.Smith
                                                             R.E.S.Wyatt   b
                                                             N.Kilner   c C.J.Barnett
c N.Kilner b F.R.Santall   4   200   13   3   31   3 R.E.S.Wyatt   c F.J.Seabrook 165   2
                                                             L.T.A.Bates   b
                                                             G.A.E.Paine   lbw

115. Gloucestershire v Hampshire, Victoria Park, Cheltenham, August 28, 29, 30 (Gloucestershire won by 14 runs)
not out   4   212   25   8   78   4 G.Brown   b   167   1
                                                             L.H.Tennyson b
                                                             A.S.Kennedy   c B.H.Lyon
                                                             O.W.Herman   c L.P.Hedges
b A.S.Kennedy   8   117   21.3   5   46   7 G.Brown   b   148
                                                             L.Harfield   b
                                                             C.P.Mead   c C.J.Barnett
                                                             L.H.Tennyson lbw
                                                             W.C.L.Creese c H.Smith
                                                             G.C.A.Adams   c E.S.Hoare
                                                             W.H.Livsey   b

116. Rest of England v Champion County (Nottinghamshire), Kennington Oval, September 14, 16, 17, 18 (Rest of England won by 8 runs)
b H.Larwood   13   399   14   2   52   0   364
not out   13   282   23   5   56   3 W.W.Whysall   c J.O'Connor   309
                                                             A.W.Carr   b
                                                             B.Lilley   b

17

SEASON'S AVERAGES

Batting and Fielding	M	I	NO	Runs	HS	Ave	50	Ct
Players v Gentlemen	1	1	1	5	5*	-	-	-
Championship	25	32	11	157	27*	7.47	-	19
Other Glos matches	3	1	0	0	0	0.00	-	2
Other matches	2	3	1	41	15	20.50	-	1
Season	31	37	13	203	27*	8.45	-	22
Career	116	165	62	832	47	8.07	-	76

Bowling	O	M	R	W	BB	Ave	5i	10m	Strike	RunR
Players v Gentlemen	32	5	92	2	2-58	46.00	-	-	96.00	47.91
Championship	1066.5	311	2460	154	8-89	15.97	14	6	41.56	38.43
Other Glos matches	106	26	262	21	9-21	12.47	2	-	30.28	41.19
Other matches	82	19	201	7	3-36	28.71	-	-	70.28	40.85
Season	1286.5	361	3015	184	9-21	16.38	16	6	41.96	39.04
Career (6b)	3094	703	8228	337	9-21	24.41	23	6	55.08	44.32

1930

In 1930 Goddard's advance was rewarded by selection to play for England in the Test Match at Old Trafford, against Australia, the fourth Test of the series. The selectors were desperate to find a bowler to curb the run getting of Bradman who had hit scores of 131, 254, and 334 in the first three Tests. In the event Goddard did not bowl a ball at him but he performed tidily enough taking the wickets of Fairfax and Hornibrook for 49 runs in 32.1 overs. It was not enough to get him selected for the fifth Test and he was not to play for England again for seven years. In the Championship Goddard took 131 wickets at 18.92 and, with Parker (162 wickets at 11.90), nearly bowled Gloucestershire to the Championship. They won 15 matches as against only 10 won by the Champions, (Lancashire). Under the system then in vogue, eight points were awarded for a win and five for a lead on first innings and Lancashire had secured first innings lead on eight occasions to Gloucestershire's two and so finished up as Champions by just 3 points. As they had decisively won the encounter at Gloucester early in the season this was, perhaps, a fair result. Goddard took a hat-trick against Glamorgan at Swansea, W.E.Jones and F.P.Ryan caught and J.Mercer bowled. He took five wickets in an innings ten times including 5/52 in the first innings of the epic tied match against the Australians at Bristol. Twice he took ten wickets or more in a match. He scored 191 runs with the bat in 35 innings and held 13 catches. A fine season ended with his selection to tour South Africa with the MCC side in the winter of 1930/31.

	Own Team Total	O	M	R	W		Opp Total	Ct

117. Gloucestershire v Lancashire, Gloucester, May 7, 8, 9 (Lancashire won by ten wickets)
    c P.T.Eckersley
        b R.K.Tyldesley   0   54   52   21   66   4   C.Hallows c C.J.Barnett   218
                                                                       G.E.Tyldesley c W.L.Neale
                                                                     G.Duckworth c W.R.Hammond
                                                                     R.K.Tyldesley lbw
    c P.T.Eckersley
        b E.A.Macdonald   20   210   -   -   -   -   47-0

118. Gloucestershire v Lancashire, Old Trafford, May 10, 12, (13) (Match drawn)
    c C.Hallows b F.M.Sibbles   2   115   38.5   14   60   7   F.B.Watson b   118
                                                                            C.Hallows b
                                                                            J.L.Hopwood c R.A.Sinfield
                                                                            E.Paynter c C.C.R.Dacre
                                                                            P.T.Eckersley c W.L.Neale
                                                                            F.M.Sibbles b
                                                                            R.K.Tyldesley c B.H.Lyon
    did not bat   -   80-7

119. Gloucestershire v Oxford University, The Parks, May 17, 19, 20 (Gloucestershire won by an innings and 10 runs)
    did not bat   -   627-2d   28   10   80   1   C.K.H.Hill-Wood b   374

		23	5	58	2	W.E.Harbord b	243	
						W.H.Bradshaw lbw		

120. Gloucestershire v Essex, Bristol, May 21, 22, 23 (Match drawn)
    c J.O'Connor b M.S.Nichols 0   274   54   26   79   3   D.F.Pope c W.R.Hammond 286
                                                                                                    A.B.Hipkin c R.A.Sinfield
                                                                                                    M.S.Nichols c H.Smith
    did not bat   -   161-3   23   11   37   0   266-3d

121. Gloucestershire v Worcestershire, Bristol, May 24, 26, 27 (Gloucestershire won by an innings and 13 runs)
    b C.F.Root   18   280   23   7   42   1   H.H.I.H.Gibbons
                                                                                                                        c R.A.Sinfield 156
                                                                                 23.4 12   31   4   M.Nichol lbw   111
                                                                                                                             B.W.Quaife b
                                                                                                                             C.F.Root c C.J.Barnett
                                                                                                                             P.F.Jackson b

122. Gloucestershire v Surrey, Kennington Oval, May 28, 29, 30 (Match drawn)
    run out   5   150   44   15   67   5   A.Ducat c C.J.Barnett 194
                                                                                                            T.F.Shepherd b
                                                                                                            A.C.T.Geary c W.R.Hammond
                                                                                                             H.S.Squires b
                                                                                                            P.G.H.Fender c W.R.Hammond
    c J.B.Hobbs b A.C.T.Geary 0   366   33   16   45   2   E.F.Wilson c W.R.Hammond 149-7
                                                                                                              P.G.H.Fender lbw

123. Gloucestershire v Warwickshire, Edgbaston, May 31, June 2, 3 (Match drawn)
    not out   6   200   18   7   32   0   275
                                                                                    5   1   16   0   133-3

124. Gloucestershire v Somerset, Taunton, June 7, 9, 10 (Gloucestershire won by eight wickets)
    not out   6   441   39   3   142   2   M.D.Lyon c C.J.Barnett 372
                                                                                                                F.S.Lee c E.J.Stephens
    did not bat   -   79-2   20   7   39   3   M.D.Lyon c W.R.Hammond 144
                                                                                                                C.C.Case b
                                                                                                              F.S.Lee c E.J.Stephens

125. Gloucestershire v Kent, Bristol, June 11, 12, 13 (Gloucestershire won by 117 runs)
    c L.J.Todd b A.P.Freeman 8   198   34   13   61   4   H.T.W.Hardinge
                                                                                                                                c E.J.Stephens 170   1
                                                                                                              L.J.Todd c C.J.Barnett
                                                                                                              I.S.Akers-Douglas b
                                                                                                              G.B.Legge b
    b A.P.Freeman   8   245   28   8   61   3   L.J.Todd lbw   156   1
                                                                                                               T.A.Crawford c B.H.Lyon
                                                                                                              A.P.Freeman lbw

126. Gloucestershire v Hampshire, Southampton, June 14, 16, 17 (Hampshire won by 28 runs)
    b A.S.Kennedy   0   316   45.5 11   93   2   J.Arnold b   339
                                                                                                              O.W.Herman b
    c J.Arnold b J.A.Newman   0   188   32.3 14   43   5   A.S.Kennedy c B.H.Lyon 193
                                                                                                              C.P.Mead c H.Smith
                                                                                                              J.Arnold b
                                                                                                              A.L.Hosie lbw
                                                                                                              O.W.Herman c E.J.Stephens

127. Gloucestershire v Middlesex, Lord's, June (18), 19, 20 (Gloucestershire won by 50 runs)
    did not bat   -   204-5d   17   3   54   2   H.W.Lee b   185
                                                                                                              N.E.Haig b
    not out   0   151   15   3   37   4   J.W.Hearne c B.H.Lyon 120
                                                                                                              D.L.Russell c C.C.R.Dacre
                                                                                                              C.G.Howard lbw
                                                                                                              E.G.Canning c W.L.Neale

128. Gloucestershire v Middlesex, Victoria Park, Cheltenham, June 25, 26 (Gloucestershire won by eight wickets)
    b N.E.Haig   24   233   12   3   26   0   134   1
    did not bat   -   44-2   13   2   39   2   G.E.Hart c C.J.Barnett 142
                                                                                                              J.H.A.Hulme b

129. Gloucestershire v Essex, Chelmsford, June 28, 30 (Gloucestershire won by four wickets)
    not out   4   236   22   4   53   3   J.A.Cutmore c C.J.Barnett 195
                                                                                                              K.Farnes b
                                                                                                              H.M.Morris c C.J.Barnett

did not bat   -   146-6   27.1   2   66   5   D.F.Pope   c C.C.R.Dacre   186
                                                                 J.O'Connor c W.L.Neale
                                                                 C.H.Gosling b
                                                                 J.R.Sheffield c sub
                                                                 T.P.B.Smith c B.H.Lyon

130. Gloucestershire v Sussex, Gloucester, July 2, 3, 4 (Gloucestershire won by an innings and 9 runs)
    not out   4   358   15   3   40   2   J.Langridge c B.H.Lyon   142
                                                                 A.H.H.Gilligan lbw
                                            23   7   54   5   T.E.R.Cook c C.C.R.Dacre   207
                                                                 A.H.H.Gilligan lbw
                                                                 H.W.Parks lbw
                                                                 H.E.Hammond b
                                                                 W.L.Cornford b

131. Gloucestershire v Hampshire, Gloucester, July 5, 7, 8 (Gloucestershire won by 241 runs)
    b J.A.Newman   22   394   37   11   79   5   J.Arnold c W.L.Neale   231   2
                                                                 C.P.Mead c and b
                                                                 A.S.Kennedy b
                                                                 L.H.Tennyson c C.C.R.Dacre
                                                                 W.C.L.Creese c and b
    b J.A.Newman   6   207-8d   22   7   44   3   C.P.Mead b   129
                                                                 G.C.A.Adams b
                                                                 W.C.L.Creese lbw

132. Gloucestershire v Sussex, Hove, July 9, 10, 11 (Sussex won by eight wickets)
    c H.E.Hammond b J.H.Parks 0   130   4.2   1   9   1   H.W.Parks st H.Smith   234
    c H.W.Parks
         b H.E.Hammond   17   298   6   1   12   0   195-2

133. Gloucestershire v Worcestershire, Worcester, July 12, 14, (15) (Match drawn)
    c W.V.Fox b L.Wright   3   489   14.2   2   34   1   L.Wright c C.J.Barnett   70-1

134. Gloucestershire v Yorkshire, Bristol, July 16, 17, 18 (Yorkshire won by an innings and 187 runs)
    b H.Verity   0   125   51.3 13   153   4   E.Robinson b   462
                                                                 F.Dennis c E.J.Stephens
                                                                 A.Wood b
                                                                 W.Rhodes lbw
    c A.Mitchell b H.Verity   15   150

135. Gloucestershire v Kent, Maidstone, July 19, (21), 22 (Match drawn)
    c H.T.W.Hardinge
         b C.W.Peach   2   299   38   11   92   4   A.P.F.Chapman lbw   223
                                                                 F.E.Woolley c E.J.Stephens
                                                                 A.P.Freeman c B.H.Lyon
                                                                 A.C.Wright b
    did not bat   -   133-4

136. ENGLAND V AUSTRALIA, Old Trafford, July 25, 26, 28, (29) (Match drawn)
    did not bat   -   251-8   32.1 14   49   2   A.G.Fairfax lbw   345
                                                                 P.M.Hornibrook c K.S.Duleepsinhji

137. Gloucestershire v Yorkshire, Hull, July (30), 31, August 1 (Match drawn)
    c M.Leyland b G.G.Macaulay 4   108   14   2   55   0   207-9d
    did not bat   -   263-3

138. Gloucestershire v Somerset, Clifton, August 2, 4, 5 (Gloucestershire won by nine wickets)
    b J.W.Lee   0   181   32   14   38   1   R.A.Ingle c W.R.Hammond   123
    did not bat   -   25-1   4   2   6   0   82

139. Gloucestershire v Glamorgan, Clifton, August 6, 7 (Gloucestershire won by an innings and 39 runs)
    b J.Mercer   0   230   8   3   15   0   62
                                            8   1   17   3   M.J.L.Turnbull
                                                                   c W.R.Hammond   129
                                                                 D.Davies c W.L.Neale
                                                                 J.T.Bell c W.L.Neale

140. Gloucestershire v Warwickshire, Cheltenham, August 9, 11 (Gloucestershire won by ten wickets)
    c W.Sanders
         b F.S.G.Calthorpe   1   201   27   11   29   4   L.T.A.Bates c C.J.Barnett   120
                                                                 N.Kilner lbw
                                                                 G.D.Kemp-Welch lbw
                                                                 W.Sanders b
    did not bat   -   29-0   17   5   31   1   F.R.Santall c C.J.Barnett   107

141. Gloucestershire v Surrey, Cheltenham, August 13, 14 (Gloucestershire won by an innings and 115 runs)
    did not bat   -   349-8d   17   11   23   2   A.Ducat b   79
                                                                 T.F.Shepherd c E.J.Stephens

20

				29.3	7	68	3	A.Ducat c W.L.Neale	155	1
								S.A.Block lbw		
								A.R.Gover c and b		

142. Gloucestershire v Leicestershire, Cheltenham, August 16, 18, 19 (Gloucestershire won by eight wickets)

b G.Geary		4	335	33.1	14	42	3	A.W.Shipman lbw	144	1
								W.E.Astill c and b		
								J.A.F.M.P.de Lisle lbw		
did not bat		-	50-2	39	11	100	7	A.W.Shipman b	239	
								G.L.Berry c B.H.Lyon		
								J.C.Bradshaw c D.N.Moore		
								N.F.Armstrong c B.H.Lyon		
								H.Riley c B.H.Lyon		
								W.E.Astill lbw		
								J.A.F.M.P. de Lisle c B.H.Lyon		

143. Gloucestershire v Derbyshire, Chesterfield, August 20, 21, 22 (Match drawn)

c A.E.Alderman b A.G.Slater	3	171	35	6	71	5	G.R.Jackson c F.J.Seabrook	200	1
							L.F.Townsend c H.Smith		
							J.M.Hutchinson b		
							T.S.Worthington lbw		
							A.E.Alderman b		
did not bat	-	57-2	35	12	70	1	A.E.Alderman lbw	170	

144. Gloucestershire v Australians, Bristol, August 23, 25, 26 (Match tied)

c A.F.Kippax									
b P.M.Hornibrook	3	72	26	7	52	5	A.Jackson b	157	
							V.Y.Richardson lbw		
							E.L.a'Beckett c R.A.Sinfield		
							A.Hurwood b		
							P.M.Hornibrook b		
run out	0	202	34.1	10	54	2	A.Jackson lbw	117	
							P.M.Hornibrook lbw		

145. Gloucestershire v Glamorgan, Swansea, August 27, 28 (Gloucestershire won by nine wickets)

c D.Davies b F.P.Ryan	6	192	12.3	1	44	8	A.H.Dyson st H.Smith	106	
							M.J.L.Turnbull c R.A.Sinfield		
							J.T.Bell b		
							D.Davies lbw		
							D.E.Davies c W.L.Neale		
							W.E.Jones c F.J.Seabrook		
							J.Mercer b		
							F.P.Ryan c C.C.R.Dacre		
did not bat	-	90-1	36	13	53	4	W.E.Bates b	175	2
							J.T.Bell lbw		
							D.E.Davies b		
							W.E.Jones c H.Smith		

146. Gloucestershire v Derbyshire, Bristol, August 30, September 1, 2 (Gloucestershire won by eight wickets)

b T.B.Mitchell	0	176	21	3	45	2	L.F.Townsend c C.J.Barnett	172	1
							T.S.Worthington c C.C.R.Dacre		
did not bat	-	180-2	26	3	66	1	L.F.Townsend b	182	

147. MCC South African XI v Lord Hawke's XI, Scarborough, September 6, 8, (9) (Match drawn)

did not bat	-	341-4	34	11	47	1	H.Sutcliffe lbw	345-9d	1

SEASON'S AVERAGES

Batting and Fielding	M	I	NO	Runs	HS	Ave	50	Ct
Test Match	1	-	-	-	-	-	-	-
Championship	27	33	5	188	24	6.71	-	12
Other Glos matches	2	2	0	3	3	1.50	-	-
Other match	1	-	-	-	-	-	-	1
Season	31	35	5	191	24	6.36	-	13
Career	147	200	67	1023	47	7.69	-	89

Bowling	O	M	R	W	BB	Ave	5i	10m	Strike	RunR
Test Match	32.1	14	49	2	2-49	24.50	-	-	96.50	25.38
Championship	1225.2	378	2479	131	8-44	18.92	9	2	56.12	33.71
Other Glos matches	111.1	32	244	10	5-52	24.40	1	-	66.70	36.58
Other match	34	11	47	1	1-47	47.00	-	-	204.00	23.03
Season	1402.4	435	2819	144	8-44	19.57	10	2	58.44	33.49
Career (6b)	4496.4	1138	11047	481	9-21	22.96	33	8	56.09	40.94

1930/31 - MCC Tour of South Africa

It has to be said that Goddard's first tour with an official MCC side was disappointing. He played in only seven matches and took thirteen wickets at a rather expensive 29.23. The first choice spinners were Ian Peebles and J.C.White who performed far better than Goddard. He never appeared in any of the Test Matches and he bowled only 159.1 overs on the whole tour. For a bowler who thrived on long spells with Gloucestershire he was probably under-used. As a batsman he scored 53 runs in six innings and he held one catch.

		Own Team Total	O	M	R	W		Opp Total	Ct

148. MCC v Griqualand West, Kimberley, November 15, 17, 18 (Match drawn)
    c D.G.Helfrich
    b H.L.E.Promnitz   10   232   18.1   7   43   2   J.A.K.Cochran b   310   1
                                                              H.L.E.Promnitz b
                                            7   0   27   0   156-2d

149. MCC v Natal, Durban, November 21, 22, 24 (Match drawn)
    c H.F.Wade b C.Payne   25   402   18   6   42   0   288
                                                11   2   20   0   114-2

150. MCC v Transvaal, Johannesburg, December 16, (17), 18 (Match drawn)
    c E.S.Newson b C.L.Vincent 13   317   29   5   71   2   B.Mitchell lbw   279
                                                                            S.S.L.Steyn b

151. MCC v Natal, Pietermaritzburg, January 10, 12 (MCC won by an innings and 70 runs)
    lbw b A.P.Woods   4   384   11   4   28   0   107
                                                         -   -   -   107

152. MCC v Cape Province, East London, January 24, 26 (MCC won by an innings and 49 runs)
    did not bat   - 336-8d   16   6   29   3   L.E.Miles b   156
                                                                            G.E.Bond lbw
                                                                            J.F.J.Phillips b
                                                 20   5   43   4   F.Nicholson c W.Farrimond 131
                                                                            F.C.Martin b
                                                                            X.C.Balaskas c M.W.Tate
                                                                            G.E.Bond c I.A.R.Peebles

153. MCC v Eastern Province, Port Elizabeth, January 31, February 2, 3 (MCC won by 226 runs)
    c T.C.Whitlock b C.M.Maritz 0   272   15   1   31   1   C.M.Maritz c W.Voce   140
    did not bat   - 199-6d   -   -   -   -   105

154. MCC v Western Province, Cape Town, March 7, 9, 10 (Match drawn)
    b I.F.Goulden   1   254   11   4   33   0   316
    did not bat   - 335-6d   3   0   13   1   F.C.Martin c W.Farrimond   141-2

SEASON'S AVERAGES

Batting and Fielding	M	I	NO	Runs	HS	Ave	50	Ct
Other matches	7	6	0	53	25	8.83	-	1
Career	154	206	67	1076	47	7.74	-	90

Bowling	O	M	R	W	BB	Ave	5i	10m	Strike	RunR
Other matches	159.1	40	380	13	4-43	29.23	-	-	73.46	39.79
Career (6b)	4655.5	1178	11427	494	9-21	23.13	33	8	56.54	40.90

1931

Goddard started the 1931 season in indifferent form taking only 21 wickets in the first nine matches but he then struck form again and finished the season with 141 wickets at an average of 18.69. He took five wickets in an innings eight times and twice took ten wickets in a match. Gloucestershire finished as runners-up in the Championship, again, thanks to Goddard and Parker who took 327 wickets between them in the Championship, Parker taking 205. The other bowlers took 91 wickets between them. With 15 points being awarded for a win this year the County were involved in a unique match at Sheffield against Yorkshire. The first two days were washed out and the two captains agreed that both first innings should be declared closed after just one ball at 4-0, leaving the teams to play for 15 points on the second innings. Goddard ensured that Gloucestershire took the honours taking 5-21 in thirteen overs. It was Yorkshire's only defeat of the season. Ironically, Gloucestershire would have won the 1930 Championship under this points system. As a batsman Goddard scored only 93 runs in 33 innings and he took 17 catches. He played in two representative games, both at Folkestone, for Players against Gentlemen and for MCC South African Team against the Rest of England when his second innings figures of 6-72 set up victory for his side.

	Own Team Total	O	M	R	W		Opp Total	Ct
155. Gloucestershire v Surrey, Kennington Oval, May 2, 4, 5 (Gloucestershire won by three wickets)								
did not bat	- 175-7d	55	27	75	1	H.T.Barling c B.H.Lyon	258	
did not bat	- 145-7	10	2	34	1	A.Sandham c H.Smith	60-6d	
156. Gloucestershire v Derbyshire, Victoria Park, Cheltenham, May 6, 7 (Gloucestershire won by four wickets)								
b T.S.Worthington	14 112	16	7	26	1	D.Smith b	100	1
did not bat	- 111-6	33	18	30	1	A.W.Richardson lbw	120	
157. Gloucestershire v Nottinghamshire, Bristol, May 9, 11 (Gloucestershire won by an innings and 131 runs)								
b S.J.Staples	3 376	16	5	55	2	B.Lilley b A.W.Carr c H.Smith	114	
		20	7	50	3	W.Walker b H.Larwood b A.W.Carr c C.J.Barnett	131	
158. Gloucestershire v Middlesex, Lord's, May 13, 14, 15 (Match drawn)								
c H.W.Lee b I.A.R.Peebles	12 200	18.5	2	26	4	E.H.Hendren c H.Smith N.McCaskie b F.J.Durston st H.Smith R.Beveridge b	258	
did not bat	- 46-1	9	0	37	0		254	2
159. Gloucestershire v Sussex, Hove, May (16), 18, 19 (Match drawn)								
did not bat	- 289-5d	16	7	25	2	E.H.Bowley c R.A.Sinfield K.S.Duleepsinhji b	107	1
		32	13	48	0		278-3	
160. Gloucestershire v Oxford University, The Parks, May 20, 21, (22) (Match drawn)								
c B.W.Hone b D.L.Russell	5 374	35	7	92	0		398-8	
161. Gloucestershire v Hampshire, Bristol, May 23, 25, 26 (Hampshire won by 66 runs)								
b G.S.Boyes	0 195	38	12	81	1	C.P.Mead b	267	
not out	1 122	8	1	18	0		116-9d	
162. Gloucestershire v Somerset, Bristol, May 27, (28), 29 (Match drawn)								
c G.F.Earle b J.W.Lee	0 214	-	-	-	-		31	1
		6	3	6	0		36-2	
163. Gloucestershire v Worcestershire, Stourbridge, May 30, June 1, 2 (Worcestershire won by 101 runs)								
b R.T.D.Perks	0 207	24	12	37	1	F.D.Ahl b	178	
c C.F.Walters b G.W.Brook	4 118	12.1	4	26	4	T.L.Winwood b F.D.Ahl b C.F.Root c C.J.Barnett R.T.D.Perks b	248	
164. Gloucestershire v Yorkshire, Bramall Lane, June (3), (4), 5 (Gloucestershire won by 47 runs)								
did not bat	- 4-0d	-	-	-	-		4-0d	

```
              c F.E.Greenwood
                b M.Leyland        13   171      13    4   21   5   H.Sutcliffe    lbw              124
                                                                    M.Leyland    c C.C.R.Dacre
                                                                    E.Oldroyd    b
                                                                    A.Mitchell   lbw
                                                                    E.Robinson   lbw
```

165. Gloucestershire v Worcestershire, Gloucester, June 6, 8 (Gloucestershire won by an innings and 71 runs)
```
              did not bat              - 253-5d    20    8   28   2   M.Nichol    c and b          103       2
                                                                     H.H.I.H.Gibbons   b
                                                  16.2   5   29   4   B.W.Quaife   b                79
                                                                     C.F.Walters   b
                                                                     L.Wright    b
                                                                     P.F.Jackson   c J.A.Rogers
```

166. Gloucestershire v New Zealanders, Gloucester, June (10), 11, 12 (Match drawn)
```
              c C.S.Dempster
                b W.E.Merritt      4   132       13   4   36   4   R.C.Blunt    lbw               89
                                                                   T.C.Lowry    b
                                                                   H.G.Vivian   st H.Smith
                                                                   K.C.James    lbw
              did not bat              - 86-4d   14   5   21   4   J.E.Mills    b                 65-6
                                                                   R.C.Blunt    lbw
                                                                   M.L.Page     lbw
                                                                   G.L.Weir     lbw
```

167. Gloucestershire v Warwickshire, Nuneaton, June 13, 15, 16 (Match drawn)
```
              hit wkt b J.H.Mayer    0   383      30   4  101   4   J.H.Parsons   lbw             188       1
                                                                    F.R.Santall   c C.C.R.Dacre
                                                                    J.A.Smart    c C.J.Barnett
                                                                    D.G.Foster   c and b
                                                  31   5  110   4   A.J.W.Croom   b               302-5
                                                                    N.Kilner    c R.A.Sinfield
                                                                    L.T.A.Bates   lbw
                                                                    F.R.Santall   b
```

168. Gloucestershire v Leicestershire, Aylestone Road, Leicester, June 27, 29, 30 (Match drawn)
```
              c E.W.Dawson b G.Geary   6   439    35  11   54   3   E.W.Dawson    b               271
                                                                    H.Riley      c E.J.Stephens
                                                                    C.A.R.Coleman  lbw
                                                  30   5   85   3   G.L.Berry    b                250       1
                                                                    H.Riley      b
                                                                    W.E.Astill   lbw
```

169. Gloucestershire v Lancashire, Bristol, July 1, 2, 3 (Gloucestershire won by eight wickets)
```
              not out                 0   330    49.2 14   92   5   G.E.Tyldesley
                                                                                c W.R.Hammond    239
                                                                    M.L.Taylor   lbw
                                                                    E.Paynter    b
                                                                    P.T.Eckersley  c E.J.Stephens
                                                                    E.A.Macdonald  b
              did not bat              - 25-2    25.5  7   46   4   J.L.Hopwood  c E.J.Stephens 111
                                                                    M.L.Taylor   c R.A.Sinfield
                                                                    P.T.Eckersley  b
                                                                    E.A.Macdonald  c W.L.Neale
```

170. Gloucestershire v Northamptonshire, Kettering, July 4, 6, 7 (Match drawn)
```
              did not bat             - 453-9d    24   10   33   1   C.N.Woolley   lbw            150
                                                  20   9   28   0                                 229-4
```

171. Gloucestershire v Middlesex, Victoria Park, Cheltenham, July 11, 13 (Gloucestershire won by four wickets)
```
              c E.H.Hendren b J.W.Hearne 6  273   28   5  118   3   J.W.Hearne    b               293
                                                                    N.E.Haig     st H.Smith
                                                                    J.M.Sims     c A.E.Dipper
              did not bat              - 165-6   15.5  2   55   6   J.W.Hearne    lbw             144
                                                                    H.W.Lee      c W.R.Hammond
                                                                    N.E.Haig     c R.A.Sinfield
                                                                    J.M.Sims     lbw
                                                                    C.W.H.Howard  c R.A.Sinfield
                                                                    W.F.F.Price   b
```

172. Gloucestershire v Nottinghamshire, Trent Bridge, July (15), 16, 17 (Match drawn)
    b W.Voce   0   117   20   8   39   3   G.Gunn lbw   125
                                                              G.F.H.Heane b
                                                              F.Barratt c C.C.R.Dacre
    not out   1   267-9
173. Gloucestershire v Derbyshire, Chesterfield, July 18, 20, 21 (Gloucestershire won by 18 runs)
    b T.B.Mitchell   0   217   40.5 15   79   8   A.E.Alderman c and b   210   1
                                                              G.R.Jackson b
                                                              G.M.Lee c R.A.Sinfield
                                                              L.F.Townsend lbw
                                                              A.G.Slater b
                                                              A.W.Richardson lbw
                                                              T.S.Worthington c C.J.Barnett
                                                              H.Elliott b
    st H.Elliott b T.B.Mitchell 0 191   30   10   53   3 H.Storer c W.R.Hammond   180
                                                              A.E.Alderman lbw
                                                              A.G.Slater c W.L.Neale
174. Gloucestershire v Yorkshire, Bristol, July 25, 27, 28 (Yorkshire won by nine wickets)
    did not bat   -   182-9d   21   7   46   4   H.Sutcliffe c C.J.Barnett 118-9d
                                                              W.Barber b
                                                              F.E.Greenwood lbw
                                                              E.Robinson lbw
    c M.Leyland b G.G.Macaulay 0 70   14   3   28   0   137-1
175. Gloucestershire v Leicestershire, Bristol, July 29, 30, 31 (Gloucestershire won by 126 runs)
    st T.E.Sidwell b W.E.Astill 2 151   16   7   24   4 E.W.Dawson c R.G.Ford   77   2
                                                              G.L.Berry c W.L.Parker
                                                              N.F.Armstrong lbw
                                                              W.E.Astill c R.G.Ford
    b G.Geary   2   203   23   5   59   2   W.E.Astill lbw   151
                                                              C.A.R.Coleman b
176. Gloucestershire v Hampshire, Southampton, August 1, 3, 4 (Gloucestershire won by 256 runs)
    c O.W.Herman b J.Bailey 0 253   30.5   7   75   4 E.J.Drake c R.A.Sinfield   172
                                                              A.S.Kennedy c C.J.Barnett
                                                              G.S.Boyes b
                                                              A.E.G.Baring b
    did not bat   -   280-9d   13   1   58   5   J.Arnold c E.J.Stephens   105
                                                              G.Brown c J.A.Rogers
                                                              C.P.Mead c C.C.R.Dacre
                                                              A.S.Kennedy lbw
                                                              A.E.Pothecary c W.L.Neale
177. Gloucestershire v Somerset, Weston-super-Mare, August (5), (6), 7 (Match drawn)
    did not bat   -   128-7d   23.4 12   57   3   E.F.Longrigg b   129-7   1
                                                              J.W.Lee lbw
                                                              A.W.Wellard b
178. Gloucestershire v New Zealanders, Clifton, August 8, 10, 11 (New Zealanders won by an innings and 25 runs)
    c M.L.Page b A.M.Matheson 0 123   23   3   77   2   G.L.Weir lbw   257-9d   1
                                                              M.L.Page c and b
    b R.C.Blunt   0   109
179. Gloucestershire v Sussex, Cheltenham, August 12, 13, (14) (Match drawn)
    b A.F.Wensley   0   104   18   6   45   2   T.E.R.Cook b   173
                                                              G.A.K.Collins c W.R.Hammond
    not out   1   3-1
180. Gloucestershire v Surrey, Cheltenham, August 15, (17), 18 (Match drawn)
    not out   1   135   13   4   36   0   98-8
181. Gloucestershire v Glamorgan, Cheltenham, August 19, (20), 21 (Match drawn)
    not out   9   175-8d   6   2   10   0   111   2
                                         3   0   10   0   76-3
182. Gloucestershire v Warwickshire, Gloucester, August 22, 24, 25 (Gloucestershire won by eight wickets)
    b J.H.Mayer   4   224   26   10   46   6   R.E.S.Wyatt b   167
                                                              N.Kilner b
                                                              F.R.Santall b
                                                              J.A.Smart lbw
                                                              D.G.Foster c C.C.R.Dacre
                                                              J.H.Mayer lbw

25

did not bat   - 104-2   29   9   51   5   G.D.Kemp-Welch
                                                              c W.L.Neale   157
                                                       N.Kilner c E.J.Stephens
                                                       J.A.Smart c C.J.Barnett
                                                       W.Sanders c H.Smith
                                                       J.H.Mayer b

183. Gloucestershire v Glamorgan, Cardiff, August 26, 27, 28 (Match drawn)
     not out   4   541   20   5   41   1   G.Lavis b   356
     did not bat   - 132-6d   21   7   49   2   A.H.Dyson c C.W.L.Parker 164-8
                                                              G.Lavis b

184. Gloucestershire v Northamptonshire, Bristol, August 29, 31, September 1 (Match drawn)
     b V.W.C.Jupp   0   194   22   11   25   2   V.W.C.Jupp b   224
                                                              T.B.G.Welch c C.C.R.Dacre
     did not bat   - 65-2   13.1 5   18   3   J.E.Timms c W.R.Hammond   91
                                                              V.W.C.Jupp lbw
                                                              W.C.Brown c W.R.Hammond

185. Players v Gentlemen, Folkestone, September (2), 3, 4 (Match drawn)
     did not bat   - 357-6d   4   2   20   1   Nawab of Pataudi
                                                              c L.E.G.Ames   196   1

186. MCC South African Team v Rest of England, Folkestone, September 9, 10, 11 (MCC South African Team
     won by six wickets)
     c F.S.G.Calthorpe
             b A.P.Freeman 1   210   26   5   95   2   B.W.Hone b   295
                                                              F.S.G.Calthorpe c W.Voce
     did not bat   - 307-4   22.2 5   72   6   G.D.Kemp-Welch
                                                              c W.R.Hammond   220
                                                              H.G.O.Owen-Smith c A.Sandham
                                                              R.S.G.Scott b
                                                              F.S.G.Calthorpe b
                                                              A.P.Freeman b
                                                              R.T.D.Perks c E.H.Hendren

SEASON'S AVERAGES

Batting and Fielding	M	I	NO	Runs	HS	Ave	50	Ct
Players v Gentlemen	1	-	-	-	-	-	-	1
Championship	27	28	7	83	14	3.95	-	15
Other Glos matches	3	4	0	9	5	2.25	-	1
Other match	1	1	0	1	1	1.00	-	-
Season	32	33	7	93	14	3.57	-	17
Career	186	239	74	1169	47	7.08	-	107

Bowling	O	M	R	W	BB	Ave	5i	10m	Strike	RunR
Players v Gentlemen	4	2	20	1	1-20	20.00	-	-	24.00	83.33
Championship	1055.5	343	2223	122	8-79	18.22	7	2	51.92	35.09
Other Glos matches	85	19	226	10	4-21	22.60	-	-	51.00	44.31
Other match	48.2	10	167	8	6-72	20.87	1	-	36.25	57.58
Season	1193.1	374	2636	141	8-79	18.69	8	2	50.77	36.82
Career (6b)	5849	1552	14063	635	9-21	22.14	41	10	55.26	40.07

1932

Goddard had another fine season in 1932 taking 170 wickets in all matches at an average of 19.16. He topped the Gloucestershire averages taking 159 wickets in Championship matches alone. He was often called upon to do a lot of bowling, 58 overs against Yorkshire, 61 against Nottinghamshire, 59 against Warwickshire and 60.5 against Lancashire. Only three bowlers bowled more overs than the 1316 he sent down that summer. He frequently carried the Gloucestershire attack as Charlie Parker was not quite as effective as normal. He took five wickets in an innings fourteen times and ten wickets in a match on six occasions. But, perhaps, he got more pleasure out of making his highest first-class score and maiden fifty in the match against Essex at Southend-on-Sea. He hit 71 in eighty minutes out of a total of 149 all out. Altogether he hit 373 runs in forty innings and he held twenty catches.

	Own Team Total	O	M	R	W		Opp Total	Ct
187. Gloucestershire v Worcestershire, Victoria Park, Cheltenham, May 7, 9, 10 (Gloucestershire won by 143 runs)								
not out	0 176	24	3	57	3	S.H.Martin lbw	155	
						M.E.White c R.G.Ford		
						G.W.Brook c R.A.Sinfield		
did not bat	- 254-8d	23.4	5	64	3	C.F.Walters		
						c W.R.Hammond	132	1
						H.H.I.H.Gibbons c W.R.Hammond		
						G.W.Brook lbw		
188. Gloucestershire v Kent, Bristol, May 14, (16), 17 (Kent won by 150 runs)								
c and b A.P.Freeman	0 94	23	6	62	4	H.T.W.Hardinge		
						c C.J.Barnett	167	
						L.E.G.Ames c C.J.Barnett		
						A.P.F.Chapman c E.J.Stephens		
						A.P.Freeman b		
not out	0 131	18	4	65	1	H.T.W.Hardinge		
						c W.L.Neale	208-2d	
189. Gloucestershire v Somerset, Bristol, May 18, 19, 20 (Match drawn)								
did not bat	- 153-3d	15.2	4	53	4	J.W.Lee c W.R.Hammond	103	
						E.F.Longrigg b		
						A.W.Wellard c W.L.Neale		
						G.M.Bennett c C.C.R.Dacre		
		15	9	13	0		23-1	
190. Gloucestershire v Northamptonshire, Bristol, May (21), 23, (24) (Match drawn)								
did not bat	- -	4	2	7	1	J.E.Timms b	16-3	
191. Gloucestershire v Oxford University, The Parks, May 25, 26, (27) (Match drawn)								
not out	1 196	6.5	0	28	1	E.A.Barlow b	139	
not out	11 280	-	-	-	-		28-0	
192. Gloucestershire v Middlesex, Lord's, June 1, 2, 3 (Middlesex won by 106 runs)								
b I.A.R.Peebles	1 133	25	6	44	5	J.W.Hearne		
						c W.R.Hammond	131	
						N.E.Haig b		
						J.H.A.Hulme c B.H.Lyon		
						J.C.Atkinson-Clark lbw		
						W.F.F.Price b		
not out	0 259	35.3	8	74	1	W.F.F.Price c and b	367	1
193. Gloucestershire v Sussex, Horsham, June 4, 6, 7 (Sussex won by two wickets)								
c E.H.Bowley b A.F.Wensley	2 229	23	6	59	3	J.Langridge		
						st B.S.Bloodworth	335	1
						H.W.Parks c C.J.Barnett		
						A.F.Wensley b		
not out	0 191	16.4	1	45	1	T.E.R.Cook c E.J.Stephens	86-8	
194. Gloucestershire v Yorkshire, Bristol, June 8, 9, 10 (Yorkshire won by an innings and 95 runs)								
not out	3 173	58	18	107	3	H.Sutcliffe b	418	1
						A.Mitchell c and b		
						M.Leyland lbw		
not out	0 150							
195. Gloucestershire v Nottinghamshire, Bristol, June 18, 20, 21 (Match drawn)								
not out	0 257	61	20	130	6	G.Gunn c W.L.Neale	387	
						F.W.Shipston b		
						W.Walker c E.J.Stephens		
						J.Hardstaff b		
						S.J.Staples b		
						A.Staples b		
did not bat	- 161-2	19	2	60	1	C.B.Harris c C.J.Barnett	183-1d	
196. Gloucestershire v Glamorgan, Swansea, June 22, 23, 24 (Glamorgan won by two wickets)								
c D.E.Davies b J.Mercer	2 245	24	10	48	3	D.E.Davies lbw	273	1
						M.J.L.Turnbull b		
						G.Lavis c and b		
did not bat	- 337-5d	27	3	88	3	D.Davies c C.C.R.Dacre	311-8	
						W.D.E.Davies b		
						J.Mercer c E.J.Stephens		

197. Gloucestershire v Worcestershire, Worcester, June 25, 27, 28 (Worcestershire won by ten wickets)
    not out   14   201   44.3 16 121   7   C.F.Walters   b   367
                                                        L.Wright   b
                                                        S.H.Martin b
                                                        J.Fox   c C.W.L.Parker
                                                        C.J.Lyttelton c W.L.Neale
                                                        C.F.Root   b
    b P.F.Jackson   34   257   8   0   38   0   P.F.Jackson b   92-0

198. Gloucestershire v Nottinghamshire, Trent Bridge, June 29, 30, July 1 (Nottinghamshire won by six wickets)
    not out   15   262   20   7   46   1   F.W.Shipston
                                                                    c C.W.L.Parker   262
    c C.B.Harris b W.Voce 6   94   16.3 3   37   0   95-4

199. Gloucestershire v Glamorgan, Bristol, July 2, 4, 5 (Match drawn)
    b J.Mercer   7   361   36   8   71   4   A.H.Dyson c R.A.Sinfield   279   2
                                                        D.Davies   c J.A.Rogers
                                                        J.C.Clay   c and b
                                                        G.Lavis   b
                                 20   5   56   0   303-6

200. Gloucestershire v Yorkshire, Bradford, July 6, 7, 8 (Yorkshire won by 133 runs)
    run out   7   404   50   14 121   1   M.Leyland c W.R.Hammond   472-7d
    b W.E.Bowes   0   175   11   1   58   2   A.Mitchell lbw   240-6d
                                                        M.Leyland c R.A.Sinfield

201. Gloucestershire v Northamptonshire, Northampton, July 9, 11 (Gloucestershire won by 262 runs)
    c B.W.Bellamy b M.H.D.Cox 0 228 4.4 1 6   3   J.E.Timms   b   105   2
                                                        V.W.C.Jupp c C.C.R.Dacre
                                                        A.D.G.Matthews c and b
    did not bat   -   245-3d   9.2   3   34   4   J.E.Timms   c R.A.Sinfield   106
                                                        M.H.D.Cox lbw
                                                        W.C.Brown c B.O.Allen
                                                        A.D.G.Matthews c C.J.Barnett

202. Gloucestershire v Somerset, Bath, July (13), 14, 15 (Match drawn)
    not out   0   130   27   8   57   2   A.W.Wellard b   108   1
                                                        H.D.Burrough c B.T.L.Watkins
    not out   37   158   17   4   37   1   J.W.Lee   lbw   122-6

203. Gloucestershire v Warwickshire, Gloucester, July 16, 18, 19 (Warwickshire won by four wickets)
    b J.H.Mayer   11   385   59   10 182   6   G.D.Kemp-Welch lbw   478   1
                                                        N.Kilner   c C.J.Barnett
                                                        F.R.Santall c W.L.Neale
                                                        J.A.Smart b
                                                        G.A.E.Paine c W.L.Neale
                                                        E.Brown   b
    c F.R.Santall b G.A.E.Paine 2 227 13.3 4 72 4   A.J.W.Croom c C.J.Barnett   135-6
                                                        G.D.Kemp-Welch lbw
                                                        N.Kilner c W.R.Hammond
                                                        J.A.Smart c C.J.Barnett

204. Gloucestershire v Surrey, Gloucester, July 20, 21 (Surrey won by 49 runs)
    c E.W.J.Brooks b F.R.Brown 2 114 20 6 39 6   H.S.Squires lbw   156
                                                        D.R.Jardine lbw
                                                        F.R.Brown   b
                                                        H.T.Barling b
                                                        P.G.H.Fender b
                                                        E.W.J.Brooks b
    run out   2   195   37   15   70   5   H.S.Squires lbw   202   1
                                                        G.S.Mobey   lbw
                                                        F.R.Brown   b
                                                        H.T.Barling c B.T.L.Watkins
                                                        J.F.Parker   b

205. Gloucestershire v Hampshire, Bournemouth, July 23, (25), (26) (Match drawn)
    did not bat   -   232-4   26.5   7   59   7   G.Brown   lbw   141
                                                        J.Bailey   c C.C.R.Dacre
                                                        C.P.Mead   c C.J.Barnett
                                                        L.H.Tennyson c R.A.Sinfield
                                                        A.E.Pothecary lbw
                                                        W.C.L.Creese b
                                                        G.S.Boyes   b

206. Gloucestershire v Surrey, Kennington Oval, July 27, (28), (29) (Match drawn)
did not bat   -   99-2
207. Gloucestershire v Kent, Canterbury, July 30, August 1 (Gloucestershire won by nine wickets)
not out   2   325   27   6   72   4   H.T.W.Hardinge lbw   163   1
                                                  F.E.Woolley c B.H.Lyon
                                                  A.P.F.Chapman c W.R.Hammond
                                                  T.A.Pearce lbw
did not bat   -   38-1   12   2   23   2   W.H.Ashdown b   197
                                                  F.E.Woolley b
208. Gloucestershire v Middlesex, Clifton, August 3, 4 (Gloucestershire won by an innings and 94 runs)
c and b J.L.Guise   0   334   22   5   102   5   J.M.Sims c W.R.Hammond   177   1
                                                        J.W.Hearne b
                                                        E.H.Hendren c and b
                                                        E.T.Killick c W.L.Neale
                                                        G.E.Hart c W.R.Hammond
                              14.2   4   19   7   J.L.Guise c W.L.Neale   63   1
                                                        J.W.Hearne lbw
                                                        E.H.Hendren b
                                                        J.H.A.Hulme b
                                                        E.T.Killick c and b
                                                        G.E.Hart c W.R.Hammond
                                                        W.F.F.Price b
209. Gloucestershire v All India, Bristol, August 6, 8, 9 (All India won by 55 runs)
c Naoomal Jaoomal
         b M.J.Khan   5   230   29   6   58   4   Naoomal Jaoomal b   236   1
                                                        S.H.M.Colah c and b
                                                        C.K.Nayudu c W.L.Neale
                                                        L.Amar Singh c B.H.Lyon
c sub b C.K.Nayudu   14   341   33.5   8   115   6   C.K.Nayudu lbw   390
                                                        Lall Singh b
                                                        Joginder Singh b
                                                        K.S.G.Limbdi b
                                                        Ghulam Mahomed b
                                                        B.E.Kapadia b
210. Gloucestershire v Lancashire, Cheltenham, August 10, 11, 12 (Gloucestershire won by 44 runs)
b E.A.Barlow   24   378   30   11   54   0   276
c E.Paynter
      b L.W.Parkinson 20   165   34   5   87   3   E.Paynter c W.R.Hammond   223   1
                                                       J.Iddon c W.R.Hammond
                                                       E.A.Barlow st B.T.L.Watkins
211. Gloucestershire v Essex, Cheltenham, August 13, 15 (Gloucestershire won by an innings and 12 runs)
not out   25   267   12   2   35   4   D.F.Pope lbw   115
                                                       R.M.Taylor c J.A.Rogers
                                                       K.Farnes c W.R.Hammond
                                                       T.P.B.Smith c C.C.R.Dacre
                                   17   4   35   3   R.M.Taylor b   140
                                                        J.R.Sheffield b
                                                        K.Farnes c D.N.Moore
212. Gloucestershire v Sussex, Cheltenham, August 17, 18 (Sussex won by 56 runs)
lbw b A.F.Wensley   0   86   13   3   26   6   J.G.Langridge c D.N.Moore 133
                                                       H.W.Parks c C.J.Barnett
                                                       A.Melville c C.J.Barnett
                                                       A.F.Wensley b
                                                       R.S.G.Scott b
                                                       W.L.Cornford b
not out   7   132   17   1   55   3   T.E.R.Cook
                                                           c W.R.Hammond   141
                                                       A.Melville b
                                                       R.S.G.Scott lbw
213. Gloucestershire v Essex, Southend-on-Sea, August 20, 22 (Essex won by an innings and 119 runs)
b K.Farnes   71   149   44   11   111   3   M.S.Nichols c D.C.G.Raikes 377   1
                                                       D.R.Wilcox b
                                                       J.R.Sheffield b
b M.S.Nichols   16   109

214. Gloucestershire v Lancashire, Liverpool, August 24, 25, 26 (Match drawn)
b J.Iddon   19   514   60.5   22   101   7   F.B.Watson b   248   1
                                                          E.Paynter b
                                                          J.Iddon st D.C.G.Raikes
                                                          L.W.Parkinson c C.C.R.Dacre
                                                          H.R.W.Butterworth b
                                                          L.Green b
                                                          G.Duckworth c and b
                                 38   18   59   3   F.B.Watson lbw   157-7
                                                          L.W.Parkinson c C.J.Barnett
                                                          F.M.Sibbles b
215. Gloucestershire v Hampshire, Gloucester, August 27, 29, 30 (Match drawn)
c sub b O.W.Herman   13   345   39.4   10   92   7   G.Brown c J.A.Rogers   305
                                                                 A.E.Pothecary c D.C.G.Raikes
                                                                 C.P.Mead c B.O.Allen
                                                                 L.H.Tennyson c B.O.Allen
                                                                 W.C.L.Creese b
                                                                 G.S.Boyes b
                                                                 N.T.McCorkell b
did not bat   -   95-5   33   6   106   7   J.Arnold c W.R.Hammond   220-9d   1
                                                                 A.E.Pothecary lbw
                                                                 C.P.Mead c W.R.Hammond
                                                                 J.Bailey c W.R.Hammond
                                                                 A.S.Kennedy b
                                                                 G.S.Boyes c R.A.Sinfield
                                                                 N.T.McCorkell c and b

SEASON'S AVERAGES

Batting and Fielding	M	I	NO	Runs	HS	Ave	50	Ct
Championship	27	36	14	342	71	15.54	1	19
Other Glos matches	2	4	2	31	14	15.50	-	1
Season	29	40	16	373	71	15.54	1	20
Career	215	279	90	1542	71	8.15	1	127

Bowling	O	M	R	W	BB	Ave	5i	10m	Strike	RunR
Championship	1246.2	329	3057	159	7-19	19.22	13	5	47.03	40.87
Other Glos matches	69.4	14	201	11	6-115	18.27	1	1	38.00	48.08
Season	1316	343	3258	170	7-19	19.16	14	6	46.44	41.26
Career (6b)	7165	1895	17321	805	9-21	21.51	55	16	53.40	40.29

1933

Goddard topped the Gloucestershire averages in 1933 taking 170 wickets in Championship matches alone at an average of 17.74 and 183 wickets overall in the season at 17.41. Only two other bowlers, Freeman of Kent and Verity of Yorkshire took more wickets in the season. Eighteen times he took five wickets in an innings and seven times did he take ten wickets in a match. *Wisden* remarks on his increased consistency. Among outstanding performances were 11-101 against Derbyshire at Chesterfield, 12-140 against Worcestershire at Cheltenham, 11-105 against Warwickshire at Edgbaston , 8-77 against Yorkshire at Gloucester and 10-64 against Hampshire at Bournemouth, including 4-8 off 14.1 overs in the second innings. As a batsman he scored 470 runs in 46 innings. He held nineteen catches.

                              Own Team   O   M   R   W   Opp   Ct
                               Total   Total
216. Gloucestershire v Oxford University, The Parks, May 6, 8, 9 (Gloucestershire won by 124 runs)
c B.W.Hone b C.Middleton 45   379   28.5   7   78   5   F.G.H.Chalk lbw   236
                                                                R.G.Stainton b
                                                                D.C.H.Townsend c P.I.van der Gucht
                                                                R.G.Tindall lbw
                                                                A.R.Legard b

did not bat	-	113-2d	17	6	55	6	F.G.H.Chalk c W.L.Neale 132
							R.G.Stainton lbw
							D.C.H.Townsend lbw
							V.G.J.Jenkins st P.I.van der Gucht
							R.G.Tindall lbw
							C.Middleton c B.H.Lyon

217. Gloucestershire v Kent, Bristol, May 10, 11, 12 (Gloucestershire won by 8 runs)

b A.P.Freeman	8	168	36	3	114	5	L.J.Todd b 223
							H.T.W.Hardinge c D.A.C.Page
							A.P.F.Chapman c C.J.Barnett
							E.J.Sheffield b
							D.V.P.Wright b
b E.J.Sheffield	0	291	35	9	71	6	C.Fairservice b 228
							L.E.G.Ames b
							L.J.Todd b
							H.T.W.Hardinge c C.J.Barnett
							E.J.Sheffield c C.J.Barnett
							A.P.Freeman b

218. Gloucestershire v Surrey, Kennington Oval, May 13, 15, 16 (Surrey won by three wickets)

c R.J.Gregory b A.R.Gover	6	180	30.2	13	56	3	G.S.Mobey lbw 228
							F.R.Brown c C.J.Barnett
							A.R.Gover b
not out	10	172	26	15	32	3	H.S.Squires
							c W.R.Hammond 125-7
							E.W.Whitfield b
							F.R.Brown b

219. Gloucestershire v Middlesex, Lord's, May 17, 18, 19 (Middlesex won by 39 runs)

c I.A.R.Peebles							
b H.J.Enthoven	1	229	12	1	40	1	R.W.V.Robins
							c W.R.Hammond 376
c H.J.Enthoven b F.J.Durston	6	351	8	2	24	1	H.W.Lee b 243-8d

220. Gloucestershire v Sussex, Hove, May 20, 22, 23 (Sussex won by an innings and 35 runs)

b E.H.Bowley	17	297	39	13	81	1	E.H.Bowley c E.J.Stephens 546
c H.W.Parks b A.F.Wensley	7	214					

221. Gloucestershire v Essex, Victoria Park, Cheltenham, May 24, 25 (Essex won by four wickets)

b M.S.Nichols	11	139	11	1	39	1	J.O'Connor c W.L.Neale 187	
c L.C.Eastman b A.G.Daer	4	162	15	4	41	3	D.F.Pope c W.R.Hammond 116-6	1
							J.O'Connor c D.A.C.Page	
							R.M.Taylor c W.R.Hammond	

222. Gloucestershire v Leicestershire, Aylestone Road, Leicester, May 27, 29, 30 (Gloucestershire won by nine wickets)

b A.W.Shipman	18	518-9d	25.5	6	42	3	E.W.Dawson c C.J.Barnett 234	1
							E.A.Broughton b	
							P.Corrall c and b	
did not bat	-	24-1	25	7	50	1	H.C.Snary	
							c P.I.van der Gucht 304	

223. Gloucestershire v Yorkshire, Bramall Lane, May 31, June 1, 2 (Yorkshire won by ten wickets)

b G.G.Macaulay	5	245	38	13	82	2	H.Sutcliffe
							c P.I.van der Gucht 369
							H.Verity b
not out	1	148	-	-	-	-	25-0

224. Gloucestershire v Somerset, Taunton, June 3, 5, 6 (Somerset won by an innings and 110 runs)

run out	4	132	38	15	88	2	E.F.Longrigg c and b 443	1
							W.T.Luckes b	
b A.Young	13	201						

225. Gloucestershire v Glamorgan, Pontypridd, June 7, 8 (Gloucestershire won by an innings and 89 runs)

b J.Mercer	2	332	19.2	5	48	7	A.H.Dyson b 129	2
							D.E.Davies c C.C.R.Dacre	
							D.Davies c B.H.Lyon	
							T.Every c B.H.Lyon	
							T.L.Brierley lbw	
							G.Lavis c C.C.R.Dacre	
							W.E.Jones b	

| | | | | | 15 | 5 | 42 | 5 | A.H.Dyson b
D.E.Davies lbw
M.J.L.Turnbull b
T.Every c B.H.Lyon
G.Lavis lbw | 114 | |

226. Gloucestershire v Glamorgan, Gloucester, June 14, 15, 16 (Match drawn)
```
       not out                2    529      53   12   142  5   D.E.Davies c and b          454    2
                                                               D.Davies c and b
                                                               H.W.Vaughan-Thomas b
                                                               G.Lavis c B.H.Lyon
                                                               E.R.K.Glover b
       did not bat            -    104-1d   11    5    24  0                                63-3
```
227. Gloucestershire v Yorkshire, Gloucester, June 17, 19, 20 (Yorkshire won by 101 runs)
```
       not out               12    144      25    4    55  1   W.Barber c B.H.Lyon         227
       not out               27    135      19    2    77  8   P.Holmes c G.W.Parker       153    1
                                                               W.Barber c C.C.R.Dacre
                                                               H.Sutcliffe c W.L.Neale
                                                               M.Leyland c W.R.Hammond
                                                               A.B.Sellers lbw
                                                               F.Dennis b
                                                               H.Verity b
                                                               A.Wood c B.H.Lyon
```
228. Gloucestershire v Derbyshire, Chesterfield, June 21, 22, 23 (Derbyshire won by 71 runs)
```
       c T.S.Worthington
               b L.F.Townsend  3   200      34   14    49  5   L.F.Townsend c and b        260    2
                                                               D.Smith b
                                                               T.S.Worthington c E.J.Stephens
                                                               A.E.Alderman b
                                                               A.V.Pope c and b
       c H.Elliott b G.M.Lee   9   112      19    5    52  6   H.Storer b                  123    1
                                                               L.F.Townsend lbw
                                                               D.Smith c and b
                                                               G.M.Lee b
                                                               A.V.Pope b
                                                               W.H.Copson c E.J.Stephens
```
229. Gloucestershire v Middlesex, Bristol, June 24, 26 (Middlesex won by eight wickets)
```
       b I.A.R.Peebles         9   128      31.1  8    54  7   J.W.Hearne
                                                                  c P.I.van der Gucht      183
                                                               J.H.A.Hulme c E.J.Stephens
                                                               N.E.Haig c D.A.C.Page
                                                               J.M.Sims b
                                                               F.J.Durston c B.H.Lyon
                                                               A.E.Wilson st P.I.van der Gucht
                                                               I.A.R.Peebles c W.L.Neale
       not out                12    84      4.4   0    17  1   G.E.Hart c R.A.Sinfield      30-2
```
230. Gloucestershire v Nottinghamshire, Trent Bridge, June 28, 29, 30 (Match drawn)
```
       not out                35   347      46   13   113  4   W.Walker b                  301-9d
                                                               A.Staples c W.L.Neale
                                                               H.Larwood c R.A.Sinfield
                                                               S.J.Staples lbw
       did not bat             -    55-0    32.2  9    77  4   W.Walker c G.W.Parker       196-9d
                                                               A.Staples c W.R.Hammond
                                                               G.V.Gunn lbw
                                                               S.J.Staples c E.J.Stephens
```
231. Gloucestershire v Worcestershire, Worcester, July 1, 3, 4 (Match drawn)
```
       c P.F.Jackson b S.H.Martin 16 541    46   14   114  3   L.Wright b                  448    1
                                                               F.D.Ahl b
                                                               M.E.White b
       did not bat             -   270-1d    9    5    10  1   L.Wright c B.H.Lyon          71-4
```
232. Gloucestershire v Kent, Folkestone, July 5, 6 (Kent won by an innings and 294 runs)
```
       c W.H.Ashdown b A.E.Watt 4  125      29    4   107  1   A.E.Fagg lbw                592-5d
       st A.E.Fagg b A.P.Freeman 0 173
```
233. Gloucestershire v Surrey, Bristol, July 8, 10, 11 (Gloucestershire won by an innings and 102 runs)
```
       did not bat             -   464-5d   13.3  6    17  4   H.T.Barling c B.H.Lyon       44
                                                               P.G.H.Fender b
                                                               F.C.Gamble c E.J.Stephens
                                                               E.W.J.Brooks c C.W.L.Parker
```

| | | | | | | | 33.3 | 13 | 67 | 5 | R.J.Gregory c B.H.Lyon | 318 | 1 |

...

```
                                        33.3  13  67  5   R.J.Gregory   c B.H.Lyon        318      1
                                                              H.T.Barling   c W.R.Hammond
                                                              E.W.Whitfield  b
                                                              J.F.Parker  b
                                                              F.C.Gamble   c C.C.R.Dacre
```

234. Gloucestershire v Nottinghamshire, Bristol, July 12, 13, 14 (Match drawn)
     not out   21   368   9   5   31   0   108   1
                                             20   9   28   0   141-4

235. Gloucestershire v Warwickshire, Edgbaston, July 15, 17, 18 (Gloucestershire won by seven wickets)
     c L.T.A.Bates b W.E.Hollies   4   187   16.4   2   42   4   L.T.A.Bates lbw   139   1
                                                                    J.H.Mayer b
                                                                    J.A.Smart   c R.G.W.Melsome
                                                                    E.Brown   c and b
     did not bat   -   89-3   27   9   63   7   N.Kilner b   134
                                                                    L.T.A.Bates lbw
                                                                    R.E.S.Wyatt c C.W.L.Parker
                                                                    F.R.Santall c R.G.W.Melsome
                                                                    G.A.E.Paine b
                                                                    J.A.Smart b
                                                                    J.H.Mayer c W.R.Hammond

236. Gloucestershire v Hampshire, Gloucester, July 19, 20, 21 (Match drawn)
     not out   10   370   25   7   73   3   A.E.Pothecary lbw   238
                                                                A.S.Kennedy c P.I.van der Gucht
                                                                N.T.McCorkell b
                                            44   16   92   2   J.Arnold b   333-6
                                                                A.E.Pothecary c E.J.Stephens

237. Gloucestershire v Sussex, Gloucester, July 22, 24 (Sussex won by an innings and 19 runs)
     c J.H.Parks b E.H.Bowley   19   171   38.2   15   82   5   F.H.Bowley c C.W.L.Parker   346   1
                                                                   A.Melville b
                                                                   R.S.G.Scott b
                                                                   A.F.Wensley b
                                                                   J.H.Cornford   c and b
     c M.W.Tate b A.F.Wensley   5   156

238. Gloucestershire v Essex, Clacton-on-Sea, July 26, 27 (Essex won by an innings and 48 runs)
     c J.R.Sheffield
       b M.S.Nichols   17   145   31.2   6   109   4   J.O'Connor lbw   404   1
                                                                 M.S.Nichols c P.I.van der Gucht
                                                                 T.P.B.Smith c R.A.Sinfield
                                                                 K.Farnes c B.H.Lyon
     c J.R.Sheffield b K.Farnes   1   211

239. Gloucestershire v Lancashire, Bristol, July 29, 31, August 1 (Match drawn)
     c J.Iddon b F.M.Sibbles   45   228   48   17   93   2   F.B.Watson b   466-6d
                                                                 J.L.Hopwood b
     not out   11   319-3

240. Gloucestershire v Lancashire, Old Trafford, August (2), 3, 4 (Match drawn)
     b W.E.Phillipson   4   234   47.3   18   73   4   F.B.Watson c C.J.Barnett   262
                                                                 J.L.Hopwood b
                                                                 W.H.L.Lister b
                                                                 G.Duckworth hit wkt

241. Gloucestershire v Somerset, Bristol, August 5, 7, 8 (Gloucestershire won by 106 runs)
     c A.W.Wellard b A.Young   1   367   36   11   89   4   E.F.Longrigg c R.A.Sinfield   325
                                                                  J.W.Lee lbw
                                                                  C.C.C.Case b
                                                                  A.W.Wellard b
     b H.L.Hazell   0   178-8d   15   5   36   3   F.S.Lee lbw   114
                                                                  A.W.Wellard c W.R.Hammond
                                                                  J.W.Seamer b

242. Gloucestershire v Worcestershire, Cheltenham, August 9, 10 (Gloucestershire won by nine wickets)
     b M.E.White   14   253   26.4   8   67   6   H.H.I.H.Gibbons b   193   1
                                                                M.Nichol lbw
                                                                C.A.F.Fiddian-Green c B.H.Lyon
                                                                E.H.Perry c G.W.Parker
                                                                M.E.White c W.R.Hammond
                                                                E.S.Baker b

did not bat - 146-1 23.1 3 73 6 C.F.Walters lbw 205
M.Nichol b
C.A.F.Fiddian-Green c W.R.Hammond
B.W.Quaife c W.L.Neale
G.W.Brook lbw
P.F.Jackson b

243. Gloucestershire v Leicestershire, Cheltenham, August 12, 14, 15 (Gloucestershire won by 46 runs)
b H.A.Smith 14 278 40 10 94 2 N.F.Armstrong b 437
H.B.Bowley c P.I.van der Gucht
not out 3 340-8d 18 7 41 6 A.W.Shipman c B.H.Lyon 135
N.F.Armstrong c B.H.Lyon
A.Riddington c P.I.van der Gucht
H.B.Bowley b
G.Geary c B.H.Lyon
T.E.Sidwell b

244. Gloucestershire v Derbyshire, Cheltenham, August 16, 17, 18 (Gloucestershire won by an innings and 85 runs)
b W.H.Copson 0 431 19 7 24 1 L.F.Townsend c C.C.R.Dacre 196
10 4 17 2 D.Smith c P.I van der Gucht 150 1
L.B.Blaxland c and b

245. Gloucestershire v West Indies, Bristol, August 19, 21, 22 (Gloucestershire won by seven wickets)
c V.A.Valentine
b E.E.Achong 13 570 10 0 38 2 B.J.Sealey lbw 271
E.E.Achong b
did not bat - 73-3 - - - - 371

246. Gloucestershire v Hampshire, Bournemouth, August 26, 28 (Gloucestershire won by an innings and 89 runs)
c W.C.L.Creese
b O.W.Herman 1 403 27.3 6 56 6 C.P.Mead
c P.I.van der Gucht 221
A.E.Pothecary lbw
W.C.L.Creese b
G.S.Boyes b
O.W.Herman c B.O.Allen
G.Hill b
14.1 10 8 4 G.Brown c W.R.Hammond 93
J.Arnold c W.R.Hammond
W.C.L.Creese c B.H.Lyon
A.S.Kennedy lbw

SEASON'S AVERAGES

Batting and Fielding	M	I	NO	Runs	HS	Ave	50	Ct
Championship	29	44	11	412	45	12.48	-	19
Other Glos matches	2	2	0	58	45	29.00	-	-
Season	31	46	11	470	45	13.42	-	19
Career	246	325	101	2012	71	8.98	1	146

Bowling	O	M	R	W	BB	Ave	5i	10m	Strike	RunR
Championship	1316	401	3016	170	8-77	17.74	16	6	46.44	38.19
Other Glos matches	55.3	13	171	13	6-55	13.15	2	1	25.76	51.04
Season	1371.5	414	3187	183	8-77	17.41	18	7	44.97	38.71
Career (6b)	8536.5	2309	20508	988	9-21	20.75	73	23	51.84	40.03

1934

Goddard missed seven matches this season after injuring his hand playing against Essex at Westcliff-on-Sea in June. Returning to the side against Leicestershire at Bristol on 14th July he took 9 for 37, his best figures of the season. Overall he was less effective than in 1933 taking 119 wickets in the Championship at an average of 23.71, nearly six runs a wicket higher than the previous year. He was again called upon to bowl many long spells and he was deadly again on occasions such as his 11 for 154 against Sussex at Cheltenham and 11 for 125 against Somerset at Bristol. He took ten wickets in a match on two other occasions and nine times took five wickets in an innings. As a batsman he scored 241 runs in 36 innings and he held nineteen catches. A notable landmark came when he took his 1000th wicket at Lord's against Middlesex.

	Own Team Total	O	M	R	W		Opp Total	Ct
247. Gloucestershire v Oxford University, The Parks, May 2, 3, 4 (Match drawn)								
c T.M.Watson								
b K.L.T.Jackson	3 276	29.2	4	96	4	D.F.Walker b	397	
						F.C.de Saram c D.A.C.Page		
						K.L.T.Jackson b		
						N.S.Knight c C.C.R.Dacre		
b A.P.Singleton	4 267-9	7.4	2	20	3	T.M.Watson st V.Hopkins	227-9d	
						A.P.Singleton b		
						J.K.Dyson b		
248. Gloucestershire v Middlesex, Lord's, May 9, 10, 11 (Gloucestershire won by 60 runs)								
c E.H.Hendren								
b I.A.R.Peebles	2 351	19.1	3	132	8	G.E.Hart c and b	213	1
						R.Beveridge b		
						E.H.Hendren c R.A.Sinfield		
						J.H.A.Hulme c C.W.L.Parker		
						H.J.Enthoven c B.O.Allen		
						N.E.Haig c B.O.Allen		
						C.I.J.Smith b		
						I.A.R.Peebles c C.J.Barnett		
lbw b I.A.R.Peebles	5 119	13	0	44	2	H.J.Enthoven c C.J.Barnett	197	
						R.W.V.Robins b		
249. Gloucestershire v Surrey, Kennington Oval, May 12, 14, 15 (Surrey won by an innings and 75 runs)								
not out	10 140	30	9	70	1	A.Sandham b	482-7d	
c R.J.Gregory b A.R.Gover	6 267							
250. Gloucestershire v Sussex, Hove, May 16, 17, 18 (Sussex won by an innings and 138 runs)								
not out	0 101	36	7	104	4	T.E.R.Cook c R.A.Sinfield	406-8d	
						J.Langridge lbw		
						G.Cox b		
						G.S.Pearce c A.I.Matthews		
c J.G.Langridge								
b J.Langridge	0 167							
251. Gloucestershire v Hampshire, Southampton, May 19, 21, 22 (Match drawn)								
b A.E.G.Baring	0 223	31	8	58	0		263	
not out	16 342-9d	20	7	41	1	R.H.Moore c V.Hopkins	191-2	
252. Gloucestershire v Kent, Bristol, May 23, 24, 25 (Kent won by 235 runs)								
not out	2 173	27.3	6	96	4	L.E.G.Ames c A.I.Matthews	333	
						L.J.Todd c V.Hopkins		
						I.S.Akers-Douglas c B.O.Allen		
						A.P.Freeman lbw		
c W.H.Ashdown								
b A.P.Freeman	22 136	15	5	51	3	L.E.G.Ames c B.O.Allen	211	1
						L.J.Todd c B.O.Allen		
						A.P.F.Chapman c C.C.R.Dacre		
253. Gloucestershire v Somerset, Bristol, May 26, 28, 29 (Somerset won by 39 runs)								
not out	6 275	26.4	10	54	4	F.S.Lee c V.Hopkins	225	2
						C.C.C.Case b		
						J.C.White c C.C.R.Dacre		
						G.M.Bennett b		
c F.S.Lee b J.C.White	4 103	30	6	71	7	J.W.Lee c C.C.R.Dacre	192	1
						F.S.Lee b		
						E.F.Longrigg c L.M.Cranfield		
						L.C.Hawkins b		
						G.M.Bennett c L.M.Cranfield		
						W.T.Luckes b		
						H.F.T.Buse c B.O.Allen		
254. Gloucestershire v Leicestershire, Aylestone Road, Leicester, May 30, 31, June 1 (Leicestershire won by nine wickets)								
b H.A.Smith	1 161	48	17	90	2	G.L.Berry c D.A.C.Page	326	2
						A.Riddington c and b		
b G.Geary	1 293	15	3	32	0		129-1	

255. Gloucestershire v Lancashire, Bristol, June 6, 7, 8 (Lancashire won by an innings and 145 runs)
b J.L.Hopwood   14   206   50   8   138   3   F.B.Watson b   454-5d
                                                              J.L.Hopwood b
                                                              F.S.Booth   c C.J.Barnett
st G.Duckworth
   b F.B.Watson   7   103
256. Gloucestershire v Somerset, Bath, June 9, 11, 12 (Gloucestershire won by ten wickets)
c W.T.Luckes b A.W.Wellard 0 407   22.3   8   66   2   R.A.Ingle c A.I.Matthews   213
                                                              H.L.Hazell c E.J.Stephens
did not bat   -   32-0   35.1   13 75   5   G.M.Bennett c and b   225   1
                                                              E.F.Longrigg b
                                                              A.W.Wellard c C.C.R.Dacre
                                                              R.A.Ingle b
                                                              H.L.Hazell c C.C.R.Dacre
257. Gloucestershire v Derbyshire, Derby, June 13, 14, 15 (Match drawn)
b L.F.Townsend   10   299   42.3   16 99   4   L.F.Townsend b   336
                                                              E.Carrington st V.Hopkins
                                                              H.Elliott c L.M.Cranfield
                                                              G.H.Pope lbw
st H.Elliott b T.B.Mitchell 13 307   -   -   -   -   93-0
258. Gloucestershire v Essex, Westcliff-on-Sea, June 16, 18, 19 (Gloucestershire won by 8 runs)
c M.S.Nichols
   b J.W.A.Stephenson   26   306   42.3   15 104   3   J.A.Cutmore c A.I.Matthews   360
                                                              T.P.B.Smith c B.O.Allen
                                                              R.Smith b
b M.S.Nichols   1   252   -   -   -   -   190
259. Gloucestershire v Leicestershire, Bristol, July 14, 16 (Gloucestershire won by an innings and 221 runs)
c G.A.Ball b H.A.Smith   2   464-9d   12   3   40   1   N.F.Armstrong b   137   1
                                        14.2   2   37   9   A.W.Shipman b   106
                                                              G.L.Berry b
                                                              S.H.Wigginton c B.H.Lyon
                                                              G.A.Ball c C.C.R.Dacre
                                                              A.Riddington c V.Hopkins
                                                              W.E.Astill c B.O.Allen
                                                              P.Corrall b
                                                              W.H.Marlow lbw
                                                              H.A.Smith b
260. Gloucestershire v Derbyshire, Gloucester, July 18, 19, 20 (Match drawn)
c H.Elliott b W.H.Copson 30   337   39.4   11 90   5   A.E.Alderman lbw   224   2
                                                              D.Smith c and b
                                                              A.F.Skinner lbw
                                                              A.V.Pope c B.O.Allen
                                                              W.H.Copson c E.J.Stephens
did not bat   -   54-0   49.1   6   146   3   L.F.Townsend c and b   333   1
                                                              T.S.Worthington c C.C.R.Dacre
                                                              W.H.Copson c D.A.C.Page
261. Gloucestershire v Warwickshire, Edgbaston, July 21, 23, 24 (Warwickshire won by ten wickets)
b W.E.Hollies   0   165   32.5   3   109   3   J.Buckingham c V.Hopkins   336
                                                              G.A.E.Paine c C.W.L.Parker
                                                              W.E.Hollies b
b W.E.Hollies   0   226   1   0   8   0   56-0
262. Gloucestershire v Lancashire, Old Trafford, July 25, 26, 27 (Lancashire won by 103 runs)
not out   9   184   46   10 115   2   J.L.Hopwood c C.C.R.Dacre   324-3d
                                                              J.Iddon c G.W.Parker
b R.Pollard   9   102   2   0   11   0   65-0d
263. Gloucestershire v Worcestershire, Dudley, July 28, 30, 31 (Gloucestershire won by an innings and 34 runs)
b A.P.Singleton   1   625-6d   54   13 125   2   H.H.I.H.Gibbons b   326
                                                              S.H.Martin lbw
                                        28.1   4   105   7   C.F.Walters c D.A.C.Page   265   1
                                                              C.H.Bull c B.O.Allen
                                                              S.H.Martin c W.R.Hammond
                                                              R.Howorth lbw
                                                              C.J.Lyttelton b
                                                              R.T.D.Perks c B.O.Allen
                                                              E.S.Baker b
264. Gloucestershire v Australians, Bristol, August 1, (2), 3 (Match drawn)
c and b L.O.Fleetwood-Smith 4 184   60   20 93   0   308-2d

265. Gloucestershire v Hampshire, Bristol, August 4, 6, 7 (Match drawn)
not out   0   206   38.1   12   73   4   R.H.Moore   c and b   292   2
                                                                  C.P.Mead   lbw
                                                                  G.S.Boyes   c V.Hopkins
                                                                  G.Hill   c and b
did not bat   -   79-5   23   11   31   2   R.H.Moore   lbw   129-6d   1
                                                                  C.P.Mead   c D.A.C.Page

266. Gloucestershire v Glamorgan, Bristol, August 8, 9, 10 (Match drawn)
did not bat   -   603-6d   46   13   69   3   A.H.Dyson   lbw   324-5
                                                                  D.E.Davies b
                                                                  M.J.L.Turnbull b

267. Gloucestershire v Worcestershire, Cheltenham, August 11, 13, 14 (Match drawn)
b M.E.White   8   254   7   5   5   0   126
did not bat   -   234-6d   21   7   47   1   C.H.Bull   b   263-3

268. Gloucestershire v Sussex, Cheltenham, August 15, 16, 17 (Gloucestershire won by seven wickets)
did not bat   -   608-7d   28.4   6   83   5   J.Langridge   c C.J.Barnett 442
                                                                  H.W.Parks   lbw
                                                                  G.Cox   c B.O.Allen
                                                                  G.S.Pearce   c B.H.Lyon
                                                                  M.W.Tate   b
did not bat   -   52-3   21.5   4   71   6   T.E.R.Cook   lbw   217
                                                                  J.Langridge   st C.C.R.Dacre
                                                                  W.L.Cornford c R.A.Sinfield
                                                                  H.W.Parks   c B.O.Allen
                                                                  G.S.Pearce   c W.L.Neale
                                                                  M.W.Tate   c W.R.Hammond

269. Gloucestershire v Surrey, Cheltenham, August 18, 20, 21 (Gloucestershire won by 279 runs)
c H.M.Garland-Wells
       b E.R.T.Holmes   7   305   14   1   67   1   L.B.Fishlock c D.A.C.Page   261
did not bat   -   353-6d   13   2   62   3   H.T.Barling   c C.J.Barnett 118
                                                                  E.R.T.Holmes c B.O.Allen
                                                                  H.M.Garland-Wells b

270. Gloucestershire v Yorkshire, Scarborough, August 22, 23, 24 (Gloucestershire won by nine wickets)
not out   14   348   32   14   58   4   L.Hutton   lbw   143   3
                                                                  A.B.Sellers   b
                                                                  A.Wood   c and b
                                                                  T.F.Smailes   c and b
did not bat   -   58-1   41.3   16   101   5   L.Hutton   b   262
                                                                  A.B.Sellers   b
                                                                  A.Wood   b
                                                                  T.F.Smailes   c G.W.Parker
                                                                  H.S.Hargreaves b

271. Gloucestershire v Essex, Gloucester, August 25, 27, 28 (Match drawn)
b L.C.Eastman   4   210   19   5   44   0   312
did not bat   -   43-1   -   -   -   -   337-4d

SEASON'S AVERAGES

Batting and Fielding	M	I	NO	Runs	HS	Ave	50	Ct
Championship	23	33	8	230	30	9.20	-	19
Other Glos matches	2	3	0	11	4	3.66	-	-
Season	25	36	8	241	30	8.60	-	19
Career	271	361	109	2253	71	8.94	1	165

Bowling	O	M	R	W	BB	Ave	5i	10m	Strike	RunR
Championship	1088.2	288	2822	119	9-37	23.71	9	4	54.87	43.21
Other Glos matches	97	26	209	7	4-96	29.85	-	-	83.14	35.91
Season	1185.2	314	3031	126	9-37	24.05	9	4	56.44	42.61
Career (6b)	9722.1	2623	23539	1114	9-21	21.13	82	27	52.36	40.35

1935

Goddard reached the 200 wickets mark for the first time in 1935 but he had to bowl a lot of overs to do it, 1553 in all, more than any one else in the country. Only Freeman and Verity took more wickets in the season. He was often over-bowled and this no doubt affected his average which was 20.36 overall. For Gloucestershire, in the Championship alone, he bowled 1453.4 overs, nearly 600 more overs than any other player, but as the County's main wicket taker he took 189 Championship wickets at 20.10. Eighteen times did he take five wickets in an innings, six times he took ten wickets in a match. He often got badly punished because of the number of overs he had to bowl an example being the match against Warwickshire at Gloucester when, although he took five wickets he conceded 170 runs in 31.5 overs. This was the start of a magnificent run by Goddard which saw him take 915 wickets in five English seasons up to the Second World War, reaching 200 wickets on three occasions. As a batsman he scored 407 runs in 44 innings and he held sixteen catches.

	Own Team Total	O	M	R	W		Opp Total	Ct
272. Gloucestershire v Warwickshire, Edgbaston, May 4, 6, 7 (Match drawn)								
c L.T.A.Bates b W.E.Hollies	24 360	40	10	87	3	N.Kilner c V.Hopkins	228	
						H.E.Dollery b		
						J.H.Mayer lbw		
did not bat	- 165-4	41	9	132	4	N.Kilner c W.L.Neale	388-7d	
						F.R.Santall c E.J.Stephens		
						R.E.S.Wyatt b		
						L.T.A.Bates b		
273. Gloucestershire v Oxford University, The Parks, May 8, 9, 10 (Match drawn)								
c J.W.Seamer b T.G.L.Ballance	27 460	35.1	11	110	4	J.G.Halliday b	386	1
						T.G.L.Ballance b		
						N.S.Mitchell-Innes c W.L.Neale		
						A.P.Singleton c W.L.Neale		
did not bat	- 240-7d	15	4	28	2	N.S.Mitchell-Innes c C.J.Barnett	126-5	1
						D.F.Walker c and b		
274. Gloucestershire v Nottinghamshire, Trent Bridge, May 11, 13, 14 (Match drawn)								
c C.B.Harris b W.Voce	4 288	36.1	8	97	2	C.B.Harris c W.L.Neale	250	
						A.Staples c V.Hopkins		
did not bat	- 13-0	37.3	10	109	5	S.D.Rhodes c C.C.R.Dacre	270	
						J.Hardstaff b		
						A.Staples c W.L.Neale		
						G.F.H.Heane lbw		
						H.J.Butler c C.J.Barnett		
275. Gloucestershire v Yorkshire, Gloucester, May 18, 20, 21 (Yorkshire won by eight wickets)								
b C.Turner	0 128	16.4	6	45	3	C.Turner lbw	166	1
						T.F.Smailes b		
						E.P.Robinson c W.R.Hammond		
c T.F.Smailes b H.Verity	2 116	10	1	38	1	H.Sutcliffe c E.J.Stephens	79-2	
276. Gloucestershire v Lancashire, Gloucester, May 22, 23, 24 (Lancashire won by eight wickets)								
c G.Duckworth b F.S.Booth c G.E.Tydesley b F.B.Watson	1 163 25 260	32 9	8 1	79 34	1 1	F.S.Booth lbw C.Washbrook c C.J.Barnett	341 84-2	
277. Gloucestershire v Surrey, Bristol, May 25, 27, 28 (Match drawn)								
b R.J.Gregory	0 308	30.2	7	87	2	E.W.Whitfield lbw	338	
						A.R.Gover c B.H.Lyon		
did not bat	- 190-8	23	4	69	4	E.R.T.Holmes c and b	243-8d	2
						H.S.Squires c W.R.Hammond		
						H.T.Barling c V.Hopkins		
						L.B.Fishlock b		
278. Gloucestershire v Surrey, Kennington Oval, May 29, 30, 31 (Match drawn)								
b R.J.Gregory	28 265	36	9	76	0		344	
did not bat	- 192-7	21	2	92	2	R.J.Gregory c E.J.Stephens	252-4d	
						L.B.Fishlock c C.J.Barnett		

279. Gloucestershire v Middlesex, Lord's, June 1, 3, 4 (Match drawn)
    absent   -   136   23.1   6   54   4   J.H.Human   lbw   143   2
                                                            R.W.V.Robins   c C.C.R.Dacre
                                                            C.I.J.Smith   b
                                                            B.L.Muncer   c and b
    did not bat   -   103-4   -   -   -   -   195-8d

280. Gloucestershire v Kent, Bristol, June 8, 10, 11 (Kent won by six wickets)
    c B.H.Valentine
       b C.S.Marriott   15 305   49.1   5   147   7   A.E.Fagg   lbw   372
                                                            F.E.Woolley   c W.R.Hammond
                                                            B.H.Valentine   lbw
                                                            C.P.Hamilton   lbw
                                                            W.H.V.Levett   lbw
                                                            A.P.Freeman   b
                                                            C.S.Marriott   c B.H.Lyon
    c W.H.Ashdown
       b A.P.Freeman   1   156   14   2   40   4   W.H.Ashdown   lbw   90-4
                                                            A.E.Fagg   b
                                                            F.E.Woolley   c W.L.Neale
                                                            L.E.G.Ames   c V.Hopkins

281. Gloucestershire v Somerset, Bristol, June 12, 13, 14 (Gloucestershire won by nine wickets)
    did not bat   -   294-6d   17.4   3   38   5   J.W.Lee   c R.A.Sinfield   130
                                                            R.A.Ingle   b
                                                            H.D.Burrough   b
                                                            W.T.Luckes   c C.J.Barnett
                                                            H.L.Hazell   b
    did not bat   -   60-1   49   22   69   5   C.J.P.Barnwell   b   223
                                                            J.C.White   lbw
                                                            C.C.C.Case   lbw
                                                            R.A.Ingle   c W.R.Hammond
                                                            H.F.T.Buse   b

282. Gloucestershire v Hampshire, Portsmouth, June 19, 20, 21 (Hampshire won by six wickets)
    not out   30 282   18.3   4   40   3   W.C.L.Creese   b   170
                                                            G.Hill   b
                                                            W.L.Budd   c E.J.Stephens
    did not bat   -   190-7d   41   13   99   3   A.K.Judd   c C.C.R.Dacre   305-4
                                                            C.P.Mead   c C.C.R.Dacre
                                                            W.G.L.F.Lowndes   b

283. Gloucestershire v Glamorgan, Bristol, June 22, 24 (Gloucestershire won by an innings and 5 runs)
    b D.E.Davies   7   293   29   12   36   6   D.Davies   b   93
                                                            M.J.L.Turnbull   b
                                                            R.G.Duckfield   b
                                                            T.L.Brierley   lbw
                                                            D.A.Davies   b
                                                            J.F.Roberts   lbw
                                 29   9   55   3   D.E.Davies   c and b   195   2
                                                            G.Lavis   b
                                                            J.Mercer   b

284. Gloucestershire v Essex, Bristol, June 26, 27 (Essex won by nine wickets)
    b H.D.Read   0   163   35.1   9   79   4   J.O'Connor   c D.A.C.Page   206
                                                            L.C.Eastman   c C.C.R.Dacre
                                                            V.J.Evans   c W.L.Neale
                                                            H.D.Read   st H.Smith
    c J.O'Connor b H.D.Read 0 102 -   -   -   -   62-8

285. Gloucestershire v Somerset, Bath, June 29, July 1, 2 (Somerset won by one wicket)
    c W.T.Luckes
       b A.W.Wellard   6   218   11   3   25   0   244
    not out   2   126   6   1   20   2   W.H.R.Andrews   b
                                                            c C.J.Barnett   101-9
                                                            W.T.Luckes   c E.J.Stephens

286. Gloucestershire v Worcestershire, Worcester, July 3, 4 (Gloucestershire won by an innings and 117 runs)
    did not bat   -   434-8d   19   8   25   5   C.H.Bull   c W.R.Hammond   81
                                                            F.B.Warne   b
                                                            B.W.Quaife   b
                                                            R.Howorth   lbw
                                                            L.Oakley   st H.Smith
                                 20   4   62   2   C.A.Humphries   st H.Smith   236
                                                            F.B.Warne   c C.J.Barnett

39

287. Gloucestershire v Sussex, Hove, July 6, 8 (Sussex won by an innings and 96 runs)
    c and b M.W.Tate   0   39   34   14   65   1   A.Melville c W.L.Neale   412-3d
    c A.F.Wensley b J.Langridge   1   277

288. Gloucestershire v Derbyshire, Bristol, July 10, 11, 12 (Gloucestershire won by 68 runs)
    c A.E.Alderman b A.V.Pope   11   250   34.3   8   62   6   T.S.Worthington lbw   233
                                                                                                      L.F.Townsend c D.A.C.Page
                                                                                                      E.Carrington b
                                                                                                      A.V.Pope b
                                                                                                      H.Elliott lbw
                                                                                                      W.H.Copson c W.R.Hammond
    b A.V.Pope   8   208   25   9   60   4   T.S.Worthington lbw   157   1
                                                                                                      L.F.Townsend c H.Smith
                                                                                                      W.W.H.Hill-Wood b
                                                                                                      A.V.Pope b

289. Gloucestershire v Hampshire, Bristol, July 13, 15, 16 (Hampshire won by three wickets)
    b G.S.Boyes   2   133   29   5   76   5   N.T.McCorkell lbw   201
                                                                                                        A.E.Pothecary lbw
                                                                                                      G.S.Boyes st H.Smith
                                                                                                      W.C.L.Creese lbw
                                                                                                      W.Lancashire b
    c W.C.L.Creese b G.S.Boyes   4   183   17.3   6   45   4   N.T.McCorkell c H.Smith   117-7
                                                                                                      A.E.Pothecary c C.I.Monks
                                                                                                      C.P.Mead lbw
                                                                                                      W.G.L.F.Lowndes b

290. Gloucestershire v Lancashire, Old Trafford, July 17, 18, 19 (Lancashire won by 111 runs)
    c P.T.Eckersley
        b F.M.Sibbles   9   68   18   8   30   6   F.B.Watson c C.J.Barnett   106
                                                                                                        N.Oldfield c W.L.Neale
                                                                                                        W.Farrimond b
                                                                                                       W.E.Phillipson c C.J.Barnett
                                                                                                       F.M.Sibbles b
    b W.E.Phillipson   2   154   32   9   71   3   P.T.Eckersley b
                                                                                                        N.Oldfield c C.J.Barnett   227-8d
                                                                                                       W.E.Phillipson c D.A.C.Page
                                                                                                       R.Pollard b

291. Gloucestershire v Derbyshire, Burton-on-Trent, July 20, 22, 23 (Derbyshire won by ten wickets)
    b W.H.Copson   0   234   39.1   8   97   4   D.Smith b   325
                                                                                                         L.F.Townsend c C.C.R.Dacre
                                                                                                        A.V.Pope c W.L.Neale
                                                                                                        W.H.Copson c D.A.C.Page
    b W.H.Copson   0   171   5   0   21   0   81-0

292. Gloucestershire v Yorkshire, Hull, July 24, 25, 26 (Yorkshire won by 197 runs)
    c W.E.Bowes b T.F.Smailes   0   203   28   3   70   1   A.B.Sellers b   260
    c A.B.Sellers b M.Leyland   35   154   38   11   99   5   W.Barber st H.Smith   294-9d   1
                                                                                                        M.Leyland c H.Smith
                                                                                                       C.Turner c E.J.Stephens
                                                                                                       H.Verity lbw
                                                                                                       E.P.Robinson b

293. Gloucestershire v Sussex, Bristol, July 27, 29, 30 (Sussex won by six wickets)
    c J.G.Langridge
        b A.F.Wensley   8   187   54.4   13   111   3   J.Langridge c E.J.Stephens   382
                                                                                                         A.F.Wensley c W.L.Neale
                                                                                                         W.L.Cornford b
    c H.E.Hammond
        b J.Langridge   6   290   21   4   43   2   J.H.Parks lbw   99-4   1
                                                                                                         T.E.R.Cook c and b

294. Gloucestershire v Kent, Canterbury, August 3, 5, 6 (Kent won by 60 runs)
    c B.H.Valentine
        b C.S.Marriott   2   316   41   14   102   5   F.E.Woolley
                                                                                                        c W.R.Hammond   335   1
                                                                                                        L.E.G.Ames c C.J.Barnett
                                                                                                        C.H.Knott c C.C.R.Dacre
                                                                                                        A.E.Watt c C.C.R.Dacre
                                                                                                        A.P.Freeman b

c A.E.Watt b C.S.Marriott	17	94	15.4	3	49	5	W.H.Ashdown lbw	135
							L.J.Todd c D.A.C.Page	
							B.H.Valentine c E.J.Stephens	
							C.H.Knott c W.R.Hammond	
							C.S.Marriott c R.A.Sinfield	

295. Gloucestershire v Worcestershire, Cheltenham, August 7, 8 (Worcestershire won by eight wickets)

c A.P.Singleton								
b R.T.D.Perks	8	171	16	0	94	3	S.H.Martin b	200
							R.H.C.Human c C.W.L.Parker	
							A.P.Singleton c H.Smith	
c G.E.B.Abell b R.T.D.Perks	0	70	6.3	2	22	1	H.H.I.H.Gibbons c and b	42-2	1

296. Gloucestershire v South Africans, Cheltenham, August 10, 12, 13 (Gloucestershire won by 87 runs)

b R.J.Crisp	0	279	29	8	70	2	E.A.B.Rowan b	289	1
							I.J.Siedle c and b		
c D.S.Tomlinson								
b C.L.Vincent	0	298	20	7	65	3	A.D.Nourse b	201
							E.L.Dalton b	
							R.J.Crisp c C.J.Barnett	

297. Gloucestershire v Middlesex, Cheltenham, August 14, 15, 16 (Middlesex won by four wickets)

b J.A.Young	1	344	34.4	6	139	8	W.F.F.Price	
							c W.R.Hammond	300	1
							G.E.Hart c and b	
							J.W.Hearne lbw	
							R.W.V.Robins b	
							J.H.Human c E.J.Stephens	
							B.L.Muncer c W.L.Neale	
							J.A.Young c E.J.Stephens	
							L.H.Gray c W.R.Hammond	
c J.H.Human								
b H.G.O.Owen-Smith	27	180	27	3	86	2	G.E.Hart lbw	226-6
							H.G.O.Owen-Smith c C.J.Barnett	

298. Gloucestershire v Essex, Southend-on-Sea, August 17, 19, 20 (Essex won by 63 runs)

c R.Smith b T.P.B.Smith	32	228	37	9	132	4	J.A.Cutmore lbw	317
							B.H.Belle lbw	
							N.G.Wykes c R.A.Sinfield	
							H.T.O.Smith c R.A.Sinfield	
not out	12	177	19.2	4	49	7	J.A.Cutmore lbw	151
							B.H.Belle b	
							J.O'Connor b B.H.Lyon	
							N.G.Wykes c R.A.Sinfield	
							A.G.Powell lbw	
							H.T.O.Smith c V.Hopkins	
							T.P.B.Smith c W.L.Neale	

299. Gloucestershire v Glamorgan, Cardiff, August 21, 22, 23 (Gloucestershire won by an innings and 63 runs)

b D.E.Davies	21	440-9d	48	14	90	4	D.Davies lbw	238
							R.G.Duckfield lbw	
							C.C.Smart c D.A.C.Page	
							D.W.Hughes b	
					30	8	61	5	A.H.Dyson b	139
							D.E.Davies c R.A.Sinfield	
							M.J.L.Turnbull lbw	
							D.W.Hughes b	
							J.Mercer b	

300. Gloucestershire v Nottinghamshire, Bristol, August (24), 26, 27 (Match drawn)

b H.Larwood	26	163	33.1	6	98	6	C.B.Harris c W.L.Neale	212
							W.Walker b	
							J.Hardstaff st V.Hopkins	
							J.Knowles lbw	
							H.Larwood c F.J.Seabrook	
							H.J.Butler b	
did not bat	-	79-1						

301. Gloucestershire v Leicestershire, Aylestone Road, Leicester, August 28, 29 (Gloucestershire won by an innings and 260 runs)

did not bat	-	459-7d	15.2	5	36	5	N.F.Armstrong lbw	74
							F.T.Prentice lbw	
							G.Geary b	
							W.E.Astill c W.R.Hammond	
							H.A.Smith c E.J.Stephens	

41

```
                         18    4    59   4   N.F.Armstrong
                                             c F.J.Seabrook      125
                                             G.S.Watson  b
                                             C.L.Edgson  c W.R.Hammond
                                             W.H.Marlow  c W.R.Hammond
302. Gloucestershire v Warwickshire, Gloucester, August (31), September 2, 3 (Match drawn)
    not out                6   280     31.5  2   170   5  N.Kilner  c W.R.Hammond   305
                                                          R.E.S.Wyatt  c B.O.Allen
                                                          F.R.Santall  c W.L.Neale
                                                          H.E.Dollery  st H.Smith
                                                          W.E.Fantham  b
                                     10   0    30   0                               113-2
```

SEASON'S AVERAGES

Batting and Fielding	M	I	NO	Runs	HS	Ave	50	Ct
Championship	29	41	4	383	35	10.35	-	13
Other Glos matches	2	3	0	27	24	9.00	-	3
Season	31	44	4	410	35	10.25	-	16
Career	302	405	113	2663	71	9.11	1	181

Bowling	O	M	R	W	BB	Ave	5i	10m	Strike	RunR
Championship	1453.4	354	3800	189	8-139	20.10	18	6	46.14	43.56
Other Glos matches	99.1	30	273	11	4-110	24.81	-	-	54.09	45.88
Season	1552.5	384	4073	200	8-139	20.36	18	6	46.58	43.71
Career (6b)	11275	3007	27612	1314	9-21	21.01	100	33	51.48	40.81

1936

Goddard took his first benefit in the 1936 season choosing the game against Nottinghamshire at Gloucester at the end of August. He suffered a strained side in August which restricted his effectiveness to some extent although it did not prevent him taking 8 for 64 against Essex and 7 for 66 against Sussex during the month. Altogether he took 143 Championship wickets, three less than Reg Sinfield who headed the Gloucestershire averages. Goddard's 153 wickets overall that season were taken at 20.30 each and he took five wickets or more in an innings 15 times and ten wickets in a match on threeoccasions. These figures included his 100th five wicket haul, against Oxford University in May. As a batsman he scored 376 runs in 36 innings including his second half-century, an innings of 67 against Sussex at Eastbourne. He held seventeen catches.

```
                                         Own Team    O    M    R    W                                 Opp       Ct
                                         Total                                                        Total
303. Gloucestershire v Oxford University, The Parks, May 2, 4, 5 (Oxford University won by 34 runs)
    c D.O.Hay b R.West          22   215    37.1   6  110   6  P.G.Foster  c D.A.C.Page         348
                                                               R.C.M.Kimpton  c W.L.Neale
                                                               N.S.Mitchell-Innes  c E.J.Stephens
                                                               M.H.Matthews  lbw
                                                               R.F.H.Darwall-Smith  b
                                                               R.West  c J.F.Crapp
    c N.S.Mitchell-Innes
             b J.H.Dyson     1   360    22   1   83   4  M.R.Barton  lbw                  261       2
                                                         N.S.Mitchell-Innes  c and b
                                                         D.O.Hay  c J.F.Crapp
                                                         A.P.Singleton  lbw
304. Gloucestershire v Kent, Gravesend, May 6, 7, 8 (Kent won by 153 runs)
    not out                     3   102    13.2   9   14   3  I.S.Akers-Douglas  lbw       180       1
                                                               W.H.V.Levett  lbw
                                                               A.P.Freeman  c C.J.Barnett
    c W.H.V.Levett b C.Lewis   0   196    32    4   101  4  W.H.Ashdown  lbw                271       1
                                                               F.E.Woolley  c R.W.Haynes
                                                               L.J.Todd  lbw
                                                               W.H.V.Levett  lbw
```

305. Gloucestershire v Surrey, Kennington Oval, May 9, 11, 12 (Surrey won by 274 runs)
c H.T.Barling b A.R.Gover   4   174   36   10   76   5   H.S.Squires c J.F.Crapp   229   1
                                                                    H.T.Barling b
                                                                    E.A.Watts   b
                                                                    K.C.W.King   c and b
                                                                    A.R.Gover   lbw
absent ill   -   119   29   7   84   4   A.Sandham   c V.Hopkins   338-8d   1
                                                                    R.J.Gregory lbw
                                                                    H.S.Squires lbw
                                                                    H.T.Barling c and b

306. Gloucestershire v Nottinghamshire, Trent Bridge, May 16, 18, 19 (Nottinghamshire won by ten wickets)
c J.Hardstaff b A.Staples   4   183   47   7   147   5   W.Walker   lbw   425   1
                                                                    J.Hardstaff lbw
                                                                    G.F.H.Heane c and b
                                                                    J.Knowles   c E.J.Stephens
                                                                    W.Voce   b
b H.Larwood   29   269   6.2   0   17   0   28-0

307. Gloucestershire v Kent, Gloucester, May 20, 21, 22 (Match drawn)
b A.P.Freeman   3   385   59   23   118   4   W.H.Ashdown c V.Hopkins   314
                                                                    B.H.Valentine c V.Hopkins
                                                                    D.V.P.Wright lbw
                                                                    C.Lewis   b
did not bat   -   72-2   29   4   83   1   F.E.Woolley c C.J.Barnett   306-6d

308. Gloucestershire v Glamorgan, Bristol, May 23, 25, 26 (Gloucestershire won by one wicket)
b J.Mercer   13   177   40   12   83   4   D.E.Davies   b   240   1
                                                                    M.J.L.Turnbull lbw
                                                                    R.G.Duckfield b
                                                                    A.J.P.Ling   c R.A.Sinfield
not out   11   183-9   27.1 10   43   5   D.E.Davies   b   116
                                                                    T.L.Brierley b
                                                                    A.J.P.Ling   b
                                                                    E.R.K.Glover c R.A.Sinfield
                                                                    J.Mercer   b

309. Gloucestershire v Derbyshire, Bristol, May 27, 28 (Derbyshire won by ten wickets)
b W.H.Copson   23   164   33   12   62   1   A.V.Pope   c C.I.Monks   193
c sub b A.V.Pope   4   123   10   3   29   0   95-0

310. Gloucestershire v Somerset, Taunton, May 30, June 1, (2) (Match drawn)
c H.L.Hazell b A.W.Wellard   0   287   39.1   10   96   3   H.Gimblett   lbw   329
                                                                    W.H.R.Andrews c R.A.Sinfield
                                                                    W.T.Luckes   b
                                             11   5   20   0   55-4

311. Gloucestershire v Hampshire, Bristol, June (3), 4, 5 (Match drawn)
not out   1   155   33   4   92   5   R.H.Moore   c E.J.Stephens 180   1
                                                                    W.C.L.Creese b
                                                                    N.T.McCorkell lbw
                                                                    G.Hill   c and b
                                                                    O.W.Herman   lbw
did not bat   -   266-3

312. Gloucestershire v Warwickshire, Bristol, June 6, 8, 9 (Gloucestershire won by an innings and 117 runs)
did not bat   -   453-8d   38.2   16   57   4   H.E.Dollery lbw   169   2
                                                                    T.Collin   b
                                                                    J.A.Smart   lbw
                                                                    W.E.Hollies lbw
                                             46.3   25   55   7   N.Kilner   b   167   1
                                                                    A.J.W.Croom c R.A.Sinfield
                                                                    W.A.Hill   b
                                                                    R.E.S.Wyatt c D.A.C.Page
                                                                    H.E.Dollery b
                                                                    T.Collin   b
                                                                    G.A.E.Paine c and b

313. Gloucestershire v Derbyshire, Derby, June 10, 11 (Derbyshire won by ten wickets)
b W.H.Copson   0   95   27   5   65   2   H.Elliott   c J.F.Crapp   200
                                                                    S.W.Hunt   b
c H.Elliott b A.V.Pope   29   194   -   -   -   -   91-0

43

314. Gloucestershire v Glamorgan, Newport, June 13, 15, 16 (Gloucestershire won by 97 runs)
c E.R.K.Glover b C.C.Smart 21   313   34   11   61   5   D.E.Davies st V.Hopkins   182   1
                                                                T.L.Brierley c E.J.Stephens
                                                                R.G.Duckfield c R.G.Ford
                                                                C.C.Smart c W.L.Neale
did not bat   -   69-1d   19.5   6   31   3   D.Davies c and b   103
                                                                A.H.Dyson lbw
                                                                D.Davies lbw
                                                                G.Lavis b

315. Gloucestershire v Worcestershire, Gloucester, June 17, 18, 19 (Worcestershire won by eight wickets)
b R.T.D.Perks   11   88   54   22   81   2   B.W.Quaife lbw   237
not out   0   182   -   -   -   -   B.P.King c J.F.Crapp   34-2

316. Gloucestershire v Leicestershire, Gloucester, June 20, 22, 23 (Gloucestershire won by 61 runs)
not out   11   305   30   8   60   6   G.L.Berry b   189   1
                                                                N.F.Armstrong lbw
                                                                F.T.Prentice c and b
                                                                C.S.Dempster c D.A.C.Page
                                                                G.Geary st V.Hopkins
                                                                H.A.Smith c R.W.Haynes
c W.A.Smith b W.E.Astill   3   174   27.1   8   64   1   N.F.Armstrong c C.I.Monks   229

317. Gloucestershire v Middlesex, Lord's, June 24, 25, (26) (Match drawn)
run out   10   249   12   0   59   1   W.F.F.Price c C.J.Barnett   317
                                          2.3   0   11   1   L.H.Gray c V.Hopkins   329

318. Gloucestershire v Yorkshire, Bramall Lane, June 27, (29), 30 (Match drawn)
b W.E.Bowes   0   66   38   14   67   6   H.Sutcliffe c W.L.Neale   190
                                                                L.Hutton b
                                                                J.R.S.Raper lbw
                                                                A.Wood b
                                                                T.F.Smailes c D.A.C.Page
                                                                E.P.Robinson c C.I.Monks
did not bat   -   248-2d   9   0   23   1   L.Hutton hit wkt   31-1

319. Gloucestershire v Lancashire, Preston, July 1, 2, 3 (Gloucestershire won by 175 runs)
b F.M.Sibbles   10   138   12   7   15   6   F.B.Watson lbw   45
                                                                J.L.Hopwood b
                                                                J.Iddon c V.Hopkins
                                                                E.Paynter b
                                                                C.Washbrook c W.R.Hammond
                                                                R.Pollard b
c J.Iddon b R.Pollard   2   214   50   24   57   5   J.L.Hopwood b   132
                                                                N.Oldfield lbw
                                                                W.H.L.Lister lbw
                                                                F.S.Booth b
                                                                G.Duckworth lbw

320. Gloucestershire v Essex, Bristol, July 4, 6, 7 (Match drawn)
b J.W.A.Stephenson   9   156   37   10   70   5   M.S.Nichols lbw   175   1
                                                                J.O'Connor b
                                                                T.N.Pearce st V.Hopkins
                                                                T.P.B.Smith b
                                                                J.W.A.Stephenson b
did not bat   -   68-4   16   2   46   2   T.P.B.Smith c E.J.Stephens   190-8d
                                                                J.W.A.Stephenson lbw

321. Gloucestershire v Yorkshire, Bristol, July 8, (9), (10) (Match drawn)
did not bat   -   57-5   14.4   7   23   5   M.Leyland c W.L.Neale   56   1
                                                                H.Verity lbw
                                                                A.B.Sellers b
                                                                T.F.Smailes b
                                                                W.E.Bowes c and b

322. Gloucestershire v Warwickshire, Edgbaston, July (11), (13), 14 (Match drawn)
run out   5   145-7   16   5   24   3   R.E.S.Wyatt c R.W.Haynes   67
                                                                T.Collin b
                                                                J.Buckingham c D.A.C.Page

323. Gloucestershire v Worcestershire, Worcester, July 15, 16, 17 (Match drawn)
not out   8   134   37   18   55   1   R.Howorth c C.I.Monks   249
did not bat   -   83-2   26   8   54   1   B.W.Quaife c V.Hopkins   147-8d

324. Gloucestershire v Lancashire, Bristol, July 22, (23), (24) (Match drawn)
did not bat   - 116-4   40   17   58   0   278-2d

325. Gloucestershire v Leicestershire, Aylestone Road, Leicester, July 25, 27, 28 (Match drawn)
    b G.Geary   14   236   49   13   110   3   G.L.Berry b   419-8d
                                                                                                                                                     N.F.Armstrong lbw
                                                                                                                                                     G.S.Watson b
    did not bat   -   292-6

326. Gloucestershire v Somerset, Bristol, August 1, 3, 4 (Match drawn)
    c J.W.Seamer b R.J.O.Meyer   0   281   22   5   41   1   J.H.Cameron b   133
    did not bat   -   159-5d   -   -   -   -   99-5

327. Gloucestershire v Sussex, Cheltenham, August 15, 17, 18 (Gloucestershire won by three wickets)
    not out   15   257   41   6   90   2   J.H.Parks lbw   266
                                                                                                                                                        A.J.Holmes b
    did not bat   -   174-7   27   5   66   7   J.H.Parks c V.Hopkins   164
                                                                                                                                                        H.E.Hammond lbw
                                                                                                                                                        T.E.R.Cook b
                                                                                                                                                        J.Langridge lbw
                                                                                                                                                        B.L.Cumming lbw
                                                                                                                                                        W.L.Cornford b
                                                                                                                                                        J.K.Nye lbw

328. Gloucestershire v Hampshire, Portsmouth, August 19, 20, 21 (Match drawn)
    b H.M.Lawson   27   298   56.4   17   140   3   W.Lancashire lbw   422
                                                                                                                                         A.S.Kennedy c J.F.Crapp
                                                                                                                                            O.W.Herman b
    did not bat   -   98-4   -   -   -   -   108-3d

329. Gloucestershire v Sussex, Eastbourne, August 22, 24, 25 (Gloucestershire won by an innings and 16 runs)
    b T.E.R.Cook   67   586   46   13   115   0   439
                                                                                12.2   3   42   2   A.J.Holmes b   131
                                                                                                                                   J.H.Cornford c J.F.Crapp

330. Gloucestershire v Essex, Clacton-on-Sea, August 26, 27 (Gloucestershire won by 153 runs)
    b K.Farnes   4   146   21.2   5   64   8   D.R.Wilcox c C.J.Barnett   171
                                                                                                                            M.S.Nichols c J.F.Crapp
                                                                                                                                  J.O'Connor lbw
                                                                                                                                  J.R.Sheffield lbw
                                                                                                                                  R.M.Taylor c J.F.Crapp
                                                                                                                                  A.B.Quick c D.A.C.Page
                                                                                                                                 J.W.A.Stephenson c D.A.C.Page
                                                                                                                                 V.J.Evans b
    run out   11   299   6   1   24   1   K.Farnes c R.W.Haynes   121

331. Gloucestershire v Nottinghamshire, Gloucester, August 29, 31, September 1 (Gloucestershire won by an innings and 70 runs)
    b G.F.H.Heane   1   485   28.1   9   49   4   W.Walker c C.J.Barnett   200   1
                                                                                                                            G.V.Gunn b
                                                                                                                           A.B.Wheat c E.J.Stephens
                                                                                                                           H.J.Butler lbw
                                                                            25   6   71   1   G.V.Gunn b   215

SEASON'S AVERAGES

Batting and Fielding	M	I	NO	Runs	HS	Ave	50	Ct
Championship	28	34	7	353	67	13.07	1	15
Other Glos match	1	2	0	23	22	11.50	-	2
Season	29	36	7	376	67	12.96	1	17
Career	331	441	120	3039	71	9.46	2	198

Bowling	O	M	R	W	BB	Ave	5i	10m	Strike	RunR
Championship	1366.3	416	2913	143	8-64	20.37	14	2	57.33	35.52
Other Glos match	59.1	7	193	10	6-110	19.30	1	1	35.50	54.36
Season	1425.4	423	3106	153	8-64	20.30	15	2	55.90	36.31
Career (6b)	12700.4	3430	30118	1467	9-21	20.53	115	36	51.94	39.52

1937

Goddard had a quite magnificent season in 1937 taking 248 wickets overall at an average of 16.76 which put him in fourth place in the national averages, although no-one else took more than 202 wickets in the season. For Gloucestershire, alone, he captured 222 wickets in all games, beating by three Charlie Parker's record haul for a season for the County. Amongst many notable feats was his taking of all ten second innings of Worcestershire at Cheltenham – this after he had already taken six wickets in the first innings. He was recalled to the England side for the Tests against New Zealand at Old Trafford and Kennington Oval, bowling England to victory at Lancashire's headquarters by taking 6 for 29 in the New Zealand second innings. He took five wickets in an innings on no less than 32 occasions and in thirteen matches he took ten wickets or more. At the end of the season he was voted one of the Five Cricketers of the Year by *Wisden*. At the age of 37 he had reached his peak. As a batsman he hit 421 runs in 41 innings which included an innings of 61 not out against Somerset at Taunton, his third half-century. He held 21 catches.

	Own Team	O	M	R	W		Opp	Ct
	Total						Total	

332. Gloucestershire v Oxford University, The Parks, May 1, 3, 4 (Oxford University won by eight wickets)
c R.E.Whetherley
  b R.F.H.Darwall-Smith 2 224   23   5   57 0   384   1
c J.N.Grover
  b D.H.Macindoe   24 190   6.5   2   15 1   M.M.Walford c R.W.Haynes 32-2

333. Gloucestershire v Hampshire, Southampton, May 5, 6, 7 (Gloucestershire won by 297 runs)
  b W.C.L.Creese   13 204   35.5 18 66 4   W.C.L.Creese c and b   172   1
                                                       W.Lancashire c J.F.Crapp
                                                       G.Hill c J.F.Crapp
                                                       H.M.Lawson b
did not bat   -   339-7d -   -   -   -   74

334. Gloucestershire v Glamorgan, Bristol, May 8, 10, 11 (Match drawn)
lbw b D.E.Davies   10 336   5   1   5   2   G.Lavis b   71   2
                                                       J.C.Clay c and b
not out   15 173-6d 1   1   0   0   48-0

335. Gloucestershire v Somerset, Taunton, May 15, 17, 18 (Gloucestershire won by nine wickets)
not out   61 415-9d 29   11 65 6   F.S.Lee c C.J.Barnett   219
                                                       H.D.Burrough c W.L.Neale
                                                       G.M.Bennett b
                                                       A.W.Wellard c J.F.Crapp
                                                       R.A.Ingle b
                                                       W.H.R.Andrews c J.F.Crapp
did not bat   -   29-1   23   12 36 0   221

336. Gloucestershire v Middlesex, Bristol, May 19, 20, 21 (Gloucestershire won by 85 runs)
c E.H.Hendren b W.T.Nevell 6 246   27.2   6   73 5   R.E.Butterworth c and b   176   2
                                                       W.J.Edrich b
                                                       R.W.V.Robins c E.J.Stephens
                                                       W.T.Nevell b
                                                       I.A.R.Peebles c C.J.Barnett
c W.J.Edrich
  b R.E.Butterworth   17 215-9d 24.5 2   115 5   R.E.Butterworth lbw   200   1
                                                       W.J.Edrich c and b
                                                       E.H.Hendren lbw
                                                       R.W.V.Robins b
                                                       W.T.Nevell b

337. Gloucestershire v Surrey, Bristol, May 22, 24, 25 (Match drawn)
  b E.R.T.Holmes   2   389   48.4 7   136 4   R.J.Gregory lbw   399-9d
                                                       E.W.Whitfield c J.W.Burrough
                                                       L.B.Fishlock c sub
                                                       K.C.W.King b
                                     12   2   22 0   259-7

338. Gloucestershire v Yorkshire, Headingley, May 26, 27, 28 (Yorkshire won by 140 runs)
c and b E.P.Robinson   2   77   24   8   57   6   A.Mitchell c V.Hopkins   157   2
                                                    G.A.Wilson c J.F.Crapp
                                                    T.F.Smailes st V.Hopkins
                                                    A.Wood c E.J.Stephens
                                                    H.S.Hargreaves c F.J.Sewell
                                                    C.Turner c and b
b E.P.Robinson   5   87   34   8   85   7   A.Mitchell b   147
                                                    W.Barber c E.J.Stephens
                                                    H.Sutcliffe c E.J.Stephens
                                                    J.A.Richardson c B.O.Allen
                                                    T.F.Smailes c W.L.Neale
                                                    A.B.Sellers c W.L.Neale
                                                    G.A.Wilson lbw

339. Gloucestershire v Nottinghamshire, Trent Bridge, May 29, 31, June 1 (Match drawn)
b A.Staples   1 350   57 15 110   4   C.B.Harris c V.Hopkins   396
                                                    W.Walker b
                                                    J.Hardstaff lbw
                                                    A.B.Wheat lbw
did not bat   - 107-2 24   4 102   3   C.B.Harris b   204-4d 1
                                                    W.Walker c B.O.Allen
                                                    G.V.Gunn c and b

340. Gloucestershire v Leicestershire, Gloucester, June 2, 3, 4 (Match drawn)
not out   4 471 44.4 11 108   5   C.S.Dempster c J.F.Crapp 351
                                                    G.S.Watson st V.Hopkins
                                                    G.Geary b
                                                    H.A.Smith c C.I.Monks
                                                    P.Corrall c W.R.Hammond
                             21   1   63   0   299-3

341. Gloucestershire v Warwickshire, Gloucester, June 5, 7, 8 (Warwickshire won by six wickets)
b R.E.S.Wyatt   19 322   51 14 130   3   A.J.W.Croom b   518   3
                                                    G.A.E.Paine c and b
                                                    J.H.Mayer c R.A.Sinfield
not out   14 263   -   -   -   -   68-4

342. Gloucestershire v Sussex, Horsham, June 9, 10, 11 (Sussex won by five wickets)
c J.G.Langridge
  b H.E.Hammond   6 230   38   5 124   0   443
not out   8 287 12.3 2   42   2   J.H.Parks lbw   75-5
                                                    G.Cox c J.F.Crapp

343. Gloucestershire v Essex, Brentwood, June 12, 14 (Gloucestershire won by eight wickets)
did not bat   - 283-6d 29   5   84   7   S.Proffitt lbw   212   1
                                                    T.N.Pearce lbw
                                                    J.O'Connor b
                                                    M.S.Nichols c W.R.Hammond
                                                    C.T.Ashton lbw
                                                    F.S.Unwin st B.T.L.Watkins
                                                    T.P.B.Smith c B.T.L.Watkins
did not bat   -   18-2 14.2 3   42   5   S.Proffitt b   88
                                                    T.N.Pearce lbw
                                                    J.O'Connor c E.J.Stephens
                                                    F.S.Unwin c B.O.Allen
                                                    V.J.Evans c W.R.Hammond

344. Gloucestershire v Surrey, Kennington Oval, June 19, 21 (Gloucestershire won by 109 runs)
c E.W.J.Brooks b A.R.Gover 0 174   23   7   57   3   R.J.Gregory lbw   127
                                                        L.B.Fishlock c B.H.Lyon
                                                        E.W.J.Brooks c E.J.Stephens
c R.J.Gregory b A.R.Gover   3 119 11.4   3   26   6   R.J.Gregory b   57
                                                        H.S.Squires st B.T.L.Watkins
                                                        L.B.Fishlock b
                                                        J.F.Parker lbw
                                                        E.A.Watts b
                                                        E.W.J.Brooks b

47

345. Gloucestershire v Kent, Victoria Park, Cheltenham, June 23, 24 (Gloucestershire won by an innings and 31 runs)
not out   31   279   19   6   26   6   W.H.Ashdown c sub   104
                                                       P.R.Sunnucks c sub
                                                       L.E.G.Ames b
                                                       L.J.Todd c W.R.Hammond
                                                       J.G.W.Davies b
                                                       R.T.Bryan b
                                  28.1   9   67   6   W.H.Ashdown
                                                           c R.W.Haynes   144
                                                       P.R.Sunnucks b
                                                       J.G.W.Davies b
                                                       R.T.Bryan b
                                                       P.M.W.Whitehouse lbw
                                                       F.G.Foy b

346. Gloucestershire v Derbyshire, Buxton, June 26, 28 (Derbyshire won by an innings and 133 runs)
c A.F.Townsend
     b T.R.Armstrong   2   106   39.2   9   119 5   L.F.Townsend c W.L.Neale 372
                                                       A.F.Townsend lbw
                                                       H.Elliott c J.F.Crapp
                                                       A.V.Pope b
c T.S.Worthington   A.E.G.Rhodes c sub
     b L.F.Townsend   18   133

347. Gloucestershire v Worcestershire, Dudley, June 30, July 1, 2 (Worcestershire won by 82 runs)
lbw b R.Howorth   3   154   25   6   84   7   C.H.Bull c W.L.Neale   163
                                                       F.B.Warne b
                                                       E.Cooper lbw
                                                       S.H.Martin b
                                                       R.Howorth c J.F.Crapp
                                                       J.S.Buller lbw
                                                       R.T.D.Perks lbw
b S.H.Martin   16   137   36   11   109   6   E.Cooper c and b   210   1
                                                       H.H.I.H.Gibbons c E.J.Stephens
                                                       S.H.Martin b
                                                       J.Horton c J.F.Crapp
                                                       R.Howorth c J.F.Crapp
                                                       R.T.D.Perks c B.T.L.Watkins

348. Gloucestershire v New Zealanders, Bristol, July 3, 5, 6 (Match drawn)
b A.W.Roberts   0   335   33.3 10   96   4   W.M.Wallace b   362
                                                       M.P.Donnelly c G.M.Emmett
                                                       M.L.Page c L.M.Cranfield
                                                       J.A.Dunning c L.M.Cranfield
                                  11   3   32   2   H.G.Vivian c C.J.Barnett   91-4
                                                       J.R.Lamason c R.A.Sinfield

349. Gloucestershire v Hampshire, Bristol, July 7, 8, 9 (Gloucestershire won by 57 runs)
c N.T.McCorkell
     b G.E.M.Heath   6   305   39   10   80   8   R.H.Moore c B.H.Lyon   221   2
                                                       N.T.McCorkell c B.T.L.Watkins
                                                       A.E.Pothecary c B.O.Allen
                                                       J.Arnold c W.R.Hammond
                                                       G.L.Jones b
                                                       G.Hill c and b
                                                       W.L.Budd c and b
c G.E.M.Heath   O.W.Herman c J.F.Crapp
     b O.W.Herman   15   145   23.5   5   66   6   R.H.Moore c W.R.Hammond 172
                                                       A.E.Pothecary lbw
                                                       J.Arnold c L.M.Cranfield
                                                       D.F.Walker c L.M.Cranfield
                                                       A.G.Holt lbw
                                                       G.E.M.Heath b

350. Gloucestershire v Warwickshire, Edgbaston, July 10, 12 (Warwickshire won by an innings and 32 runs)
c and b G.A.E.Paine 12   107   24   3   82   5   R.E.S.Wyatt c R.A.Sinfield 222
                                                       H.E.Dollery b
                                                       P.Cranmer c R.A.Sinfield
                                                       G.A.E.Paine c B.O.Allen
                                                       J.H.Mayer st B.T.L.Watkins
b J.H.Mayer   2   83

48

351. Players v Gentleman, Lord's, July 14, 15 (Players won by eight wickets)
```
     c C.R.N.Maxwell b K.Farnes   0    229         5.5   1    10   2   C.R.N.Maxwell
                                                                          st L.E.G.Ames         165
                                                                       A.B.Sellers  st L.E.G.Ames
     did not bat                   -  121-2        17    2    58   3   R.C.M.Kimpton
                                                                          c L.E.G.Ames          184
                                                                       F.R.Brown  c J.Hardstaff
                                                                       C.R.N.Maxwell  b
```

352. Gloucestershire v Middlesex, Lord's, July 17, 19 (Middlesex won by eight wickets)
```
     b H.G.O.Owen-Smith            0    200       23.3   3    91   3   D.C.S.Compton  c V.Hopkins  352
                                                                       J.M.Sims  c W.R.Hammond
                                                                       C.I.J.Smith  c B.H.Lyon
     c R.W.V.Robins
     b H.G.O.Owen-Smith           16    204         -    -    -    -                                56-2
```

353. Gloucestershire v Essex, Bristol, July 21, 22, 23 (Gloucestershire won by 119 runs)
```
     not out                      21    150       32.2  13    58   6   L.C.Eastman
                                                                          c B.T.L.Watkins         170
                                                                       R.M.Taylor  c B.T.L.Watkins
                                                                       J.H.Pawle  lbw
                                                                       T.P.B.Smith  lbw
                                                                       R.Smith  b
                                                                       S.Proffitt  c R.W.Haynes
     not out                       1  205-5d      20.2   8    22   5   D.R.Wilcox  b                66
                                                                       T.H.Wade  b
                                                                       R.M.Taylor  c B.O.Allen
                                                                       J.O'Connor  lbw
                                                                       S.Proffitt  c B.T.L.Watkins
```

354. ENGLAND V NEW ZEALAND, Old Trafford, July 24, 26, 27 (England won by 130 runs)
```
     not out                       4  358-9d      18     5    48   0                              281
     not out                       1   187        14.4   5    29   6   W.M.Wallace  b             134
                                                                       W.A.Hadlee  b
                                                                       M.L.Page  b
                                                                       N.Gallichan  c A.W.Wellard
                                                                       J.A.Dunning  b
                                                                       J.Cowie  c A.W.Wellard
```

355. Gloucestershire v Glamorgan, Newport, July 28, 29, 30 (Gloucestershire won by 255 runs)
```
     c E.C.Jones b C.C.Smart       9   319        31     8    58   5   A.H.Dyson  c and b         135   1
                                                                       D.Davies  c B.T.L.Watkins
                                                                       M.J.L.Turnbull  c B.T.L.Watkins
                                                                       T.L.Brierley  c J.F.Crapp
                                                                       A.D.G.Matthews  c B.T.L.Watkins
     did not bat                   - 162-2d       27.1  15    41   8   A.H.Dyson  c B.L.Watkins    91
                                                                       D.E.Davies  c W.L.Neale
                                                                       D.Davies  c R.A.Sinfield
                                                                       R.G.Duckfield  c B.H.Lyon
                                                                       C.C.Smart  c W.R.Hammond
                                                                       G.Lavis  c J.F.Crapp
                                                                       T.L.Brierley  b
                                                                       J.C.Clay  c C.J.Barnett
```

356. Gloucestershire v Somerset, Bristol, July 31, August 2, 3 (Gloucestershire won by 198 runs)
```
     b J.H.Cameron                 9   452        37    12   116   6   F.S.Lee  c W.R.Hammond     264   1
                                                                       E.F.Longrigg  c C.J.Barnett
                                                                       J.H.Cameron  c and b
                                                                       W.H.R.Andrews  lbw
                                                                       A.W.Wellard  c W.L.Neale
                                                                       R.A.Ingle  c R.W.Haynes
     did not bat                   - 187-4d       21     4    59   2   H.Gimblett  b              177
                                                                       H.D.Burrough  c B.H.Lyon
```

357. Gloucestershire v Lancashire, Old Trafford, August 4, 5, 6 (Lancashire won by six wickets)
```
     c W.H.L.Lister b A.J.Birtwell 8   287        27     6    85   0                              454
     not out                       3   311         -     -    -    -                              147-4
```

358. Gloucestershire v Worcestershire, Cheltenham, August 7, 9, 10 (Gloucestershire won by three wickets)
```
     c R.T.D.Perks b S.H.Martin    4   196        18     4    68   6   C.H.Bull  st B.T.L.Watkins 310
                                                                       H.H.I.H.Gibbons  b
                                                                       R.H.C.Human  c C.J.Barnett
                                                                       B.W.Quaife  b
                                                                       R.Howorth  c G.W.Parker
                                                                       R.T.D.Perks  b
```

49

not out		0	317-7	28.4	4	113	10	C.H.Bull st B.T.L.Watkins	202
								J.S.Buller c W.R.Hammond	
								E.Cooper b	
								R.H.C.Human c B.O.Allen	
								S.H.Martin c W.R.Hammond	
								B.W.Quaife b	
								R.C.M.Kimpton c G.W.Parker	
								R.Howorth c G.W.Parker	
								R.T.D.Perks c J.F.Crapp	
								P.F.Jackson c J.F.Crapp	

359. Gloucestershire v Derbyshire, Cheltenham, August 11, 12 (Gloucestershire won by an innings and 84 runs)

c A.F.Skinner								
b L.F.Townsend	12	392	25.1	3	104	7	D.Smith lbw	228
							L.F.Townsend lbw	
							A.F.Skinner c B.O.Allen	
							A.E.G.Rhodes b	
							H.Elliott c J.F.Crapp	
							A.V.Pope c G.W.Parker	
							T.B.Mitchell c B.O.Allen	
		12	1	41	5	T.S.Worthington b	80
							L.F.Townsend c E.D.R.Eagar	
							G.H.Pope st B.T.L.Watkins	
							A.E.G.Rhodes c J.F.Crapp	
							H.Elliott b	

360. ENGLAND V NEW ZEALAND, Kennington Oval, August 14, 16, 17 (Match drawn)

did not bat	-	254-7d	10	2	25	0		249
did not bat	-	31-1	18	8	41	2	G.L.Weir c C.J.Barnett	187
							A.W.Roberts lbw	

361. Gloucestershire v Kent, Dover, August 18, 19, 20 (Kent won by eight wickets)

c L.E.G.Ames b F.E.Woolley	6	434	23.1	2	77	1	D.V.P.Wright	
							c B.T.L.Watkins	399
c and b N.W.Harding	9	182	8.2	0	98	0		219-2

362. Gloucestershire v Lancashire, Gloucester, August 21, 23, 24 (Gloucestershire won by 215 runs)

b F.M.Sibbles	0	427	29	6	106	4	W.Place lbw	230
							W.H.L.Lister c C.J.Barnett	
							W.E.Phillipson c B.T.L.Watkins	
							G.Duckworth lbw	
did not bat	-	204-4d	30.2	7	65	7	E.Paynter c C.J.Barnett	186
							N.Oldfield c J.F.Crapp	
							J.Iddon lbw	
							W.Place lbw	
							W.E.Phillipson c G.W.Parker	
							G.Duckworth b	
							F.M.Sibbles c J.F.Crapp	

363. Gloucestershire v Nottinghamshire, Bristol, August 28, 30, 31 (Gloucestershire won by an innings and 185 runs)

b G.V.Gunn	1	572-9d	23.3	7	74	6	C.B.Harris lbw	194
							A.Staples c W.R.Hammond	
							G.F.H.Heane c B.O.Allen	
							E.A.Marshall lbw	
							R.J.Giles lbw	
							F.G.Woodhead c G.W.Parker	
		19	2	73	8	W.W.Keeton cW.L.Neale	193
							C.B.Harris lbw	
							J.Knowles lbw	
							G.V.Gunn b	
							E.A.Marshall c C.J.Barnett	
							A.Staples c G.W.Parker	
							G.F.H.Heane b	
							R.J.Giles b	

364. Over Thirty v Under Thirty, Folkestone, September 4, 6, 7 (Over Thirty won by an innings and 8 runs)

not out	0	530	27	7	95	6	W.J.Edrich lbw	256	1
							J.F.Crapp c and b		
							R.C.M.Kimpton c J.Langridge		
							B.H.Valentine b		
							W.H.R.Andrews c L.J.Todd		
							L.H.Gray c W.R.Hammond		

32.4	4	122	7	H.Gimblett c and b		266	1
				W.J.Edrich b			
				J.F.Crapp st L.E.G.Ames			
				R.C.M.Kimpton c L.E.G.Ames			
				B.H.Valentine c J.H.Parks			
				W.H.R.Andrews c R.J.Gregory			
				T.P.B.Smith c W.R.Hammond			

SEASON'S AVERAGES

Batting and Fielding	M	I	NO	Runs	HS	Ave	50	Ct
Test Matches	2	2	2	5	4*	-	-	-
Players v Gentlemen	1	1	0	0	0	0.00	-	-
Championship	27	41	10	390	61*	12.58	1	18
Other Glos matches	2	3	0	26	24	8.66	-	1
Other match	1	1	1	0	0*	-	-	2
Season	33	48	13	421	61*	12.02	1	21
Career	364	489	133	3460	71	9.71	3	219

Bowling	O	M	R	W	BB	Ave	5i	10m	Strike	RunR
Test Matches	60.4	20	143	8	6-29	17.87	1	-	45.50	39.28
Players v Gentlemen	22.5	3	68	5	3-58	13.60	-	-	27.40	49.63
Championship	1261.4	310	3530	215	10-113	16.41	29	12	35.20	46.63
Other Glos matches	74.2	20	200	7	4-96	28.57	-	-	63.71	44.84
Other match	59.4	11	217	13	7-122	16.69	2	1	27.53	60.61
Season	1479.1	364	4158	248	10-113	16.76	32	13	35.78	46.85
Career (6b)	14179.5	3794	34276	1715	10-113	19.98	147	49	49.60	40.28

1938

Having broken through into the Test team in 1937 Goddard could have reasonably expected to stay there against the Australians the following year. The 1938 season, though, turned out to be an unlucky one for him. He fractured his thumb in May and missed a number of Gloucestershire's games. He also missed selection for the first Test – his County colleague Reg Sinfield played and got Bradman out. Selected in the squad to play at Old Trafford in the third Test, the match never got under way with all four days being washed out. Although in the squad for the fourth Test at Headingley, Goddard did not make the final eleven which may have been a mistake as Australia's spinners won the match. All this meant that Goddard played in only 20 Championship games and his wickets dropped from 248 for the season to 114 with his average increasing from 16.76 to 23.02. He still had some outstanding performances taking thirteen wickets in the matches against Kent and Worcestershire and twelve against Hampshire and Middlesex. As a batsman he scored only 133 runs in 27 innings. He made eight catches. At the end of the season he was selected to tour South Africa with the MCC team in the winter of 1938/39.

	Own Team Total	O	M	R	W		Opp Total	Ct
365. Gloucestershire v Oxford University, The Parks, April 30, May 2, (3) (Match drawn)								
c D.H.Macindoe b R.F.H.Darwall-Smith	0 445	24.5	6	73	2	R.C.M.Kimpton c R.A.Sinfield D.H.Macindoe st A.E.Wilson	229	
		9	3	14	0		69-0	
366. Gloucestershire v Hampshire, Portsmouth, May 4, 5, 6 (Hampshire won by 30 runs)								
absent ill	- 271	39	13	91	3	J Arnold c W.L.Neale G.Hill c B.O.Allen G.E.M.Heath b	279	1
absent ill	- 352	-	-	-	-		374-7d	

51

367. Gloucestershire v Middlesex, Lord's, May 11, 12, 13 (Middlesex won by three wickets)
not out		4	478	45.5	1	182	7	W.J.Edrich c B.O.Allen	478
							S.M.Brown b
							D.C.S.Compton lbw
							R.W.V.Robins c R.W.Haynes
							J.M.Sims c L.M.Cranfield
							R.Felton c W.R.Hammond
							W.T.Nevell b
did not bat		-	243-7d	20	2	94	5	W.H.Webster
							c W.R.Hammond	244-7
							D.C.S.Compton c C.J.Barnett
							R.W.V.Robins c W.R.Hammond
							W.F.F.Price c R.W.Haynes
							R.Felton c W.R.Hammond

368. Gloucestershire v Yorkshire, Gloucester, May 14, 16, 17 (Match drawn)
lbw b L.Hutton		6	428-9d	54	13	128	4	H.Sutcliffe c W.L.Neale	266
							W.Barber lbw
							T.F.Smailes b
							E.P.Robinson c J.F.Crapp
			6	0	27	0		58-0

369. Gloucestershire v Kent, Gillingham, May 18, 19 (Gloucestershire won by 169 runs)
c A.E.Fagg b D.V.P.Wright	0	221	24.3	4	57	7	A.E.Fagg c and b	133	2
							F.G.H.Chalk lbw
							L.E.G.Ames c R.W.Haynes
							L.J.Todd c W.R.Hammond
							P.R.Sunnucks b
							T.W.Spencer lbw
							N.W.Harding b
did not bat		-	208-9d	17	3	50	6	F.E.Woolley
							c W.R.Hammond	127
							L.E.G.Ames b
							A.P.F.Chapman b
							P.R.Sunnucks lbw
							T.W.Spencer c G.M.Emmett
							D.V.P.Wright lbw

370. Gloucestershire v Surrey, Kennington Oval, May 25, 26, 27 (Match drawn)
not out		1	443-8d	36	10	73	3	H.S.Squires lbw	334
							H.T.Barling b
							E.W.Whitfield lbw
			5	1	15	0		59-0

371. Gloucestershire v Warwickshire, Bristol, May 28, 30, (31) (Match drawn)
did not bat		-	324-5d	15	0	72	0		148-1

372. Gloucestershire v Warwickshire, Edgbaston, June 25, 27, 28 (Warwickshire won by ten wickets)
c F.R.Santall b G.A.E.Paine	22	148	11	1	47	0		305
c J.Buckingham b J.H.Mayer	0	190	-	-	-	-		34-0

373. Gloucestershire v Essex, Brentwood, June 29, 30 (Essex won by an innings and 40 runs)
b M.S.Nichols	0	96	26.4	5	71	1	J.O'Connor c C.J.Scott	309
b M.S.Nichols	4	173					

374. Gloucestershire v Glamorgan, Neath, July 2, 4, (5) (Match drawn)
run out	0	183	23.3	9	51	4	T.L.Brierley lbw	113
							D.Davies c W.L.Neale
							W.E.Jones c W.L.Neale
							J.C.Clay st A.E.Wilson
			27	7	89	2	A.H.Dyson c J.F.Crapp	151-3	1
							D.Davies c and b

375. Gloucestershire v Sussex, Hove, July 13, 14, 15 (Sussex won by ten wickets)
b H.E.Hammond	19	207	44	13	78	4	J.G.Langridge c V.Hopkins	414-9d
							H.W.Parks b
							G.Cox lbw
not out		1	225	-	-	-	-	J.Langridge b	21-0

376. Gloucestershire v Lancashire, Bristol, July 16, 18, 19 (Match drawn)
    not out   6   561   65   12 144   6   E.Paynter   c J.F.Crapp   426-9d
                                                          J.Iddon   c B.O.Allen
                                                          N.Oldfield lbw
                                                          J.L.Hopwood c G.M.Emmett
                                                          A.E.Nutter lbw
                                                          E.W.Greenhalgh b
                                 -    -   -   -   105-1

377. Gloucestershire v Nottinghamshire, Trent Bridge, July 27, 28, (29) (Match drawn)
    c C.B.Harris b W.Voce   24 227   27   3   80   0   332
                                         20   5   37   1   W.W.Keeton c W.L.Neale   97-2

378. Gloucestershire v Somerset, Bristol, July 30, August 1, 2 (Match drawn)
    b A.W.Wellard   4 233   60 15 160   2   H.Gimblett c G.M.Emmett   501-7d
                                                           W.H.R.Andrews b
    did not bat   - 250-4

379. Gloucestershire v Glamorgan, Bristol, August 3, 4, 5 (Gloucestershire won by an innings and 214 runs)
    c M.J.L.Turnbull b J.C.Clay 0 503-9d   24   6   54   2   D.Davies c C.Tyler   173   1
                                                                J.C.Clay c B.O.Allen
                                             19.4 7   33   5   D.E.Davies b   116
                                                                D.Davies lbw
                                                                M.J.L.Turnbull c C.J.Scott
                                                                C.C.Smart lbw
                                                                W.M.Jones lbw

380. Gloucestershire v Hampshire, Cheltenham, August 6, 8, 9 (Gloucestershire won by 44 runs)
    b C.J.Knott   11 134   27   6   61   5   C.G.A.Paris c G.M.Emmett   172
                                                              D.F.Walker b
                                                              J.W.J.Steele b
                                                              G.S.Boyes b
                                                              O.W.Herman lbw
    lbw b W.C.L.Creese   2 140   17   4   26   7   N.T.McCorkell c C.J.Barnett 58
                                                              C.G.A.Paris lbw
                                                              O.W.Herman c J.F.Crapp
                                                              W.C.L.Creese c B.O.Allen
                                                              J.D.Eggar lbw
                                                              J.W.J.Steele b
                                                              G.S.Boyes c C.J.Barnett

381. Gloucestershire v Worcestershire, Cheltenham, August 13, 15, 16 (Gloucestershire won by two wickets)
    not out   0 204   29.1   5   77   4   B.P.King b   270
                                                              C.H.Palmer c G.M.Emmett
                                                              J.S.Buller b
                                                              P.F.Jackson b
    did not bat   - 250-8   21.2   1   86   4   S.H.Martin lbw   180
                                                              R.Howorth c G.W.Parker
                                                              R.T.D.Perks c J.F.Crapp
                                                              P.F.Jackson c W.R.Hammond

382. Gloucestershire v Yorkshire, Scarborough, August 17, 18 (Yorkshire won by an innings and 80 runs)
    b H.Verity   11 119   40   4 136   2   A.B.Sellers c G.M.Emmett   346   1
                                                              H.Verity st A.E.Wilson
    not out   4 147

383. Gloucestershire v Leicestershire, Bristol, August 24, 25, 26 (Gloucestershire won by 12 runs)
    b H.A.Smith   0 160   32.2   6   73   5   C.S.Dempster b   202
                                                              N.F.Armstrong c V.Hopkins
                                                              F.T.Prentice lbw
                                                              P.R.Cherrrington b
                                                              W.H.Flamson b
    b W.H.Flamson   0 214   29.2   8   62   8   G.L.Berry c V.Hopkins   160   1
                                                              C.S.Dempster b
                                                              F.T.Prentice lbw
                                                              P.R.Cherrington b
                                                              G.O.Dawkes c R.A.Sinfield
                                                              W.E.Astill c and b
                                                              G.Lester b
                                                              W.H.Flamson b

384. Gloucestershire v Essex, Gloucester, August 31, September 1, 2 (Essex won by an innings and 65 runs)

c and b M.S.Nichols		2	97	43.3	9	127	4	T.P.B.Smith	
								c W.R.Hammond	553	1
								N.Vere-Hodge c A.E.Wilson	
								R.Smith c B.O.Allen	
not out		8	391					K.Farnes c J.F.Crapp	

385. Gloucestershire v Sussex, Gloucester, September 3, 5, 6 (Sussex won by seven wickets)

b J.H.Cornford		4	488	26	6	60	3	G.Cox b	341
								A.J.Holmes b J.H.Cornford b	
did not bat		-	156-5d	27	4	98	3	J.G.Langridge lbw	306-3
								J.H.Parks lbw G.Cox b	

386. Players v Gentlemen, Scarborough, September 7, 8, 9 (Players won by five wickets)

not out		0	429	25.3	9	58	4	B.O.Allen b	325
								H.M.Garland-Wells c H.Sutcliffe	
								S.C.Griffith c A.W.Wellard	
								G.O.B.Allen c T.F.Smailes	
did not bat		-	133-5	9	0	41	1	B.O.Allen c C.J.Barnett	233-6d

SEASON'S AVERAGES

Batting and Fielding	M	I	NO	Runs	HS	Ave	50	Ct	
Players v Gentlemen	1	1	1	0	0*	-	-	-	
Championship	20	25	7	133	24	7.38	-	8	
Other Glos match	1	1	0	0	0	0.00	-	-	
Season	22	27	8	133	24	7.00	-	8	
Career	386	516	141	3590	71	9.57	3	227	

Bowling	O	M	R	W	BB	Ave	5i	10m	Strike	RunR
Players v Gentlemen	34.3	9	99	5	4-58	19.80	-	-	41.40	47.82
Championship	902.5	183	2439	107	8-62	22.79	10	4	50.62	45.02
Other Glos match	33.5	9	87	2	2-73	43.50	-	-	101.50	42.85
Season	971.1	201	2625	114	8-62	23.02	10	4	51.11	45.04
Career (6b)	15151	3995	37501	1829	10-113	20.50	157	53	49.70	41.25

1938/39 – MCC in South Africa

Undoubtedly the highlight of Goddard's second tour to South Africa was the hat-trick he took in the Test match at Johannesburg on Boxing Day 1938. They were the only wickets he took in the match. He played in two other Tests, taking another five wickets, giving him eight in the series at an average of 35.25. Bowlers in the main struggled on perfect batting wickets in a high scoring series. On the tour as a whole Goddard took 31 wickets at an average of 26.35 which put him third in the averages although four bowlers took more wickets. His best performance was the 6 for 38 he took against Rhodesia at Salisbury, his only five wicket haul. As a batsman he only batted eight times in the ten games he appeared in scoring 76 runs at an average of 9.14. He took one catch, a vital one as it was the wicket of A.D.Nourse the first victim of his Johannesburg hat-trick. Goddard also took a hat-trick in the game against Rhodesia.

	Own Team Total	O	M	R	W		Opp Total	Ct

387. MCC v Western Province, Cape Town, November 12, 14, 15 (MCC won by eight wickets)

c J.G.B.Brinkhaus b B.M.Roscoe	16	276	17	7	38	1	K.G.Dimbleby	
							c W.R.Hammond	174
did not bat	-	69-2	12	0	26	0		169

388. MCC v Griqualand West, Kimberley, November 19, 21, 22 (MCC won by an innings and 289 runs)

b E.V.Franz	1	676	10	2	26	1	L.E.Macnamara b	114

54

```
                                         24    6   66   3   A.P.C.Steyn  b              273      1
                                                             F.Nicholson  c sub
                                                             LE.Macnamara  c W.R.Hammond
```
389. MCC v North Eastern Transvaal, Pretoria, December 10, 12, 13 (MCC won by an innings and 76 runs)
```
     did not bat                    -  379-6d   14   3   49   3   M.A.Wright  c P.A.Gibb        161
                                                             N.J.Reid  c P.A.Gibb
                                                             R.S.Martin  c P.A.Gibb
                                          5    1   11   1   T.E.Cook  st P.A.Gibb         142
```
390. MCC v Transvaal, Johannesburg, December 16, 18, 19 (Match drawn)
```
     c A.W.Briscoe b E.Q.Davies     3   268    30   4   67   0                            428-8d
                                                10   1   28   0                            174-2
```
391. ENGLAND v SOUTH AFRICA, Johannesburg, December 24, 26, 27, 28 (Match drawn)
```
     not out                        0   422    27   5   54   3   A.D.Nourse  c and b          390      1
                                                             N.Gordon  st L.E.G.Ames
                                                             W.W.Wade  b
     did not bat                    -  291-4d  11   3   31   0                            108-1
```
392. ENGLAND v SOUTH AFRICA, Cape Town, December 31, January 2, 3, 4 (Match drawn)
```
     did not bat                    -  559-9d  38  15   64   3   A.W.Briscoe  lbw             286
                                                             A.C.B.Langton  lbw
                                                             N.Gordon  st L.E.G.Ames
                                         11    1   68   1   P.G.van der Bijl  hit wkt    201-2
```
393. MCC v Border, East London, January 13, 14, 16 (MCC won by nine wickets)
```
     not out                       14   320     9   5   19   1   C.D.White  b                 121
     did not bat                    -   79-1    9   5   14   0                             275
```
394. MCC v Combined Transvaal XI, Johannesburg, January 27, 28, 30 (Match drawn)
```
     b S.F.Viljoen                  1   434    22   2   71   4   E.A.B.Rowan  lbw             304
                                                             B.Mitchell  c H.T.Bartlett
                                                             S.F.Viljoen  b
                                         15    2   60   1   L.S.Brown  b
                                                             D.G.Helfrich  c P.A.Gibb    220-2
```
395. MCC v Rhodesia, Salisbury, February 10, 11, 13 (Match drawn)
```
     c F.Davidson b J.H.Charsley   33   180    17   3   38   6   J.H.F.Fuller  b               96
                                                             D.S.Tomlinson  lbw
                                                             M.Napier  b
                                                             P.N.F.Mansell  b
                                                             J.H.Charsley  c B.H.Valentine
                                                             H.K.S.Evans  b
     did not bat                    -  174-2d  12   3   22   2   F.Davidson  b                95-6
                                                             A.Hyde  lbw
```
396. ENGLAND v SOUTH AFRICA, Johannesburg, February 18, 20, (21), 22 (Match drawn)
```
     c P.G.van der Bijl
            b A.C.B.Langton         8   215    18   2   65   1   P.G.van der Bijl  lbw       349-8d
     did not bat                    -  203-4
```

SEASON'S AVERAGES

Batting and Fielding	M	I	NO	Runs	HS	Ave	50	Ct
Test Matches	3	2	1	8	8	8.00	-	1
Other matches	7	6	1	68	33	13.60	-	1
Tour	10	8	2	76	33	12.66	-	2
Career	396	524	143	3669	71	9.62	3	229

Bowling	O	M	R	W	BB	Ave	5i	10m	Strike	RunR
Test Matches	105	26	282	8	3-54	35.25	-	-	105.00	33.57
Other matches	206	46	535	23	6-38	23.26	1	-	71.65	32.46
Tour (8b)	311	72	817	31	6-38	26.35	1	-	80.25	32.83
Career (6b)	15151	3995⎱	38318	1860	10-113	20.60	158	53	50.21	41.02
(8b)	311	72 ⎰								

1939

Goddard had another wonderful season in this last summer before the war. For the third time in five seasons he reached the 200 wicket mark, the only bowler in the country to do so, and he took them at the very low cost of 14.86 runs each. He finished fourth in the national averages. In this season the number of balls in an over was increased to eight. Amongst other feats he took 84 wickets at Bristol in seven matches at a cost of eight runs each including two world records, seventeen wickets in a day against Kent which, following thirteen wickets against Yorkshire, made thirty during the week. He played against West Indies in the Old Trafford and Kennington Oval Tests taking four wickets at 28.50. He took five wickets or more in an innings twenty times and ten wickets in a match on eight occasions. In the course of the summer he took his total of first-class wickets past 2000. Against Somerset at Bristol he made his fourth half-century, (56 not out), and followed up by taking 5 for 15 and 9 for 44 when Somerset batted. He made 215 runs in 33 innings and took fourteen catches. Sadly his career, along with many others, was now to be interrupted for six long years.

	Own Team Total	O	M	R	W		Opp Total	Ct
397. Gloucestershire v Oxford University, The Parks, April 29, May 1, 2 (Gloucestershire won by five wickets)								
c E.J.H.Dixon b G.Evans	4 213-8d	17.6	5	42	5	E.J.H.Dixon c J.F.Crapp	286	
						R.Sale lbw		
						G.Evans b		
						D.E.Warburton b		
						C.W.S.Lubbock c W.L.Neale		
not out	11 206-5	11.4	1	58	4	R.Sale lbw	132-8d	
						E.D.R.Eagar c G.M.Emmett		
						G.Evans b		
						D.E.Warburton c C.J.Scott		
398. Gloucestershire v Lancashire, Gloucester, May 6, 8, 9 (Lancashire won by ten wickets)								
b A.E.Nutter	19 267	31	9	61	2	N.Oldfield lbw	308	
						A.E.Nutter c W.R.Hammond		
c W.Farrimond b W.E.Phillipson	7 79	-	-	-	-		39-0	
399. Gloucestershire v Worcestershire, Bristol, May 13, 15 (Gloucestershire won by three wickets)								
c R.O.Jenkins b R.Howorth	2 165	14	2	55	9	C.H.Bull lbw	149	
						B.P.King lbw		
						E.Cooper b		
						H.H.I.H.Gibbons b		
						A.F.T.White b		
						R.Howorth b		
						C.J.Lyttelton c R.A.Sinfield		
						J.S.Buller lbw		
						R.O.Jenkins c A.E.Wilson		
did not bat	- 90-7	12.2	2	44	7	C.H.Bull c J.F.Crapp	105	
						E.Cooper st A.E.Wilson		
						H.H.I.H.Gibbons c J.F.Crapp		
						J.S.Buller c J.F.Crapp		
						S.H.Martin c R.W.Haynes		
						C.J.Lyttelton c R.W.Haynes		
						R.T.D.Perks st A.E.Wilson		
400. Gloucestershire v Yorkshire, Bradford, May 17, 18, 19 (Gloucestershire won by six wickets)								
c E.P.Robinson b H.Verity	1 227	22	4	76	5	H.Sutcliffe c J.F.Crapp	253	1
						A.B.Sellers b		
						T.F.Smailes c E.A.Wilson		
						A.Wood c V.Hopkins		
						E.P.Robinson c A.E.Wilson		
did not bat	- 190-4	7	0	49	1	T.F.Smailes st A.E.Wilson	162-7d	
401. Gloucestershire v Middlesex, Lord's, May 20, 22, 23 (Gloucestershire won by three wickets)								
b C.I.J.Smith	0 207	24	1	83	5	W.J.Edrich lbw	236	
						D.C.S.Compton b		
						J.M.Sims c C.J.Scott		
						C.I.J.Smith b		
						I.A.R.Peebles b		

```
         did not bat              -   239-7   18.2   0   68   6   J.D.B.Robertson  b            207
                                                                 W.J.Edrich  c G.E.E.Lambert
                                                                 N.S.Hotchkin  c J.F.Crapp
                                                                 W.F.F.Price  b
                                                                 C.I.J.Smith  c C.J.Barnett
                                                                 I.A.R.Peebles  b
```

402. Gloucestershire v Warwickshire, Bristol, May 24, 25 (Gloucestershire won by an innings and 16 runs)
```
   b F.R.Santall                  0   353     17     1   62   3   W.A.Hill  c J.F.Crapp         181
                                                                 R.E.S.Wyatt  c R.A.Sinfield
                                                                 K.Wilmot  b
                                            13.5   0   66   6   F.R.Santall  b                 156
                                                                 J.S.Ord  c C.J.Scott
                                                                 J.Buckingham  c B.O.Allen
                                                                 P.Cranmer  c W.L.Neale
                                                                 K.Wilmot  lbw
                                                                 J.H.Mayer  c J.F.Crapp
```

403. Gloucestershire v Somerset, Taunton, May 27, 29, 30 (Match drawn)
```
         not out              18  265     21    8   43   1   H.Gimblett  b                247
         did not bat           -  192-5  19.6   2  110   4   H.Gimblett  lbw              344-6d
                                                              H.F.T.Buse  c J.F.Crapp
                                                              J.W.Seamer  c G.M.Emmett
                                                              E.F.Longrigg  c W.R.Hammond
```

404. Gloucestershire v Glamorgan, Newport, May 31, June 1, 2 (Match drawn)
```
         did not bat              -   505-5d  22.6   7   45   4   D.E.Davies  lbw            196
                                                                 W.Wooller  b
                                                                 P.F.Judge  c W.L.Neale
                                                                 J.Mercer  b
                                            38     7  123   1   T.L.Brierley
                                                                     c W.R.Hammond            577-4
```

405. Gloucestershire v Surrey, Gloucester, June 7, 8, 9 (Gloucestershire won by an innings and 57 runs)
```
   c H.S.Squires b E.A.Watts     4   464     10     2   33   2   H.M.Garland-Wells
                                                                     c G.M.Emmett            236    1
                                                                 A.J.W.McIntyre  b
                                            10.7   2   31   1   L.B.Fishlock  c V.Hopkins   171    1
```

406. Gloucestershire v Essex, Gloucester, June 10, 12 (Gloucestershire won by an innings and 93 runs)
```
         not out                  1   425     13    4   40   5   J.O'Connor  lbw            150
                                                                 J.W.A.Stephenson  c C.J.Scott
                                                                 T.P.B.Smith  b
                                                                 F.H.Rist  c V.Hopkins
                                             8    1   31   1   F.H.Rist  c G.M.Emmett      182
```

407. Gloucestershire v Sussex, Worthing, June 17, 19 (Gloucestershire won by four wickets)
```
   c C.Oakes b J.Langridge       3   191     22    6   86   4   J.G.Langridge  c J.F.Crapp   225
                                                                 J.H.Parks  c V.Hopkins
                                                                 C.Oakes  b
                                                                 W.L.Cornford  lbw
         did not bat              -   162-6  11.3   1   53   5   J.H.Parks  c W.R.Hammond    124    1
                                                                 G.Cox  lbw
                                                                 H.T.Bartlett  c C.J.Barnett
                                                                 A.J.Holmes  c W.L.Neale
                                                                 W.L.Cornford  c and b
```

408. Gloucestershire v Worcestershire, Worcester, June 24, 26, 27 (Worcestershire won by five wickets)
```
   b S.H.Martin                  3   236     27.6   4  133   4   B.P.King  lbw              386
                                                                 S.H.Martin  c R.W.Haynes
                                                                 R.O.Jenkins  c G.E.E.Lambert
                                                                 R.T.D.Perks  c G.E.E.Lambert
         not out                  7   226     -     -    -   -                               79-5
```

409. Gloucestershire v Yorkshire, Bristol, June 28, 29, 30 (Gloucestershire won by seven wickets)
```
   c W.E.Bowes b H.Verity        0   168     28    6   61   6   H.Sutcliffe  b              176
                                                                 A.Mitchell  c G.E.E.Lambert
                                                                 N.W.D.Yardley  b
                                                                 A.B.Sellers  b
                                                                 A.Wood  st A.E.Wilson
                                                                 W.E.Bowes  b
```

| | | | did not bat | | - | 114-3 | 18 | 6 | 38 | 7 | H.Sutcliffe lbw
L.Hutton lbw
W.Barber b
N.W.D.Yardley b
A.B.Sellers lbw
T.F.Smailes b
A.Wood b | 105 | |

410. Gloucestershire v Kent, Bristol, July 1, 3 (Gloucestershire won by an innings and 40 runs)

| | lbw b D.V.P.Wright | 0 | 284 | 15.4 | 2 | 38 | 9 | A.E.Fagg b
F.G.H.Chalk c W.L.Neale
B.H.Valentine c J.F.Crapp
L.J.Todd b
T.W.Spencer b
T.C.Longfield b
D.V.P.Wright b
W.J.V.Levett b
C.Lewis b | 120 | |
| | | | | 16.2 | 1 | 68 | 8 | A.E.Fagg c W.R.Hammond
L.E.G.Ames c R.W.Haynes
L.J.Todd c C.J.Barnett
T.W.Spencer lbw
T.C.Longfield c G.M.Emmett
D.V.P.Wright st A.E.Wilson
N.W.Harding c G.M.Emmett
C.Lewis c R.W.Haynes | 124 | |

411. Gloucestershire v Essex, Westcliff-on-Sea, July 8, 10, 11 (Gloucestershire won by 234 runs)

| | c F.S.Unwin b R.M.Taylor | 6 | 432 | 21 | 3 | 95 | 3 | F.H.Vigar c C.J.Scott
F.S.Unwin c W.R.Hammond
F.H.Rist c G.E.E.Lambert | 300 | 1 |
| | did not bat | | - | 241-7d | 9 | 4 | 22 | 3 | F.H.Vigar c J.F.Crapp
N.Vere-Hodge b
T.P.B.Smith c W.L.Neale | 139 | |

412. Gloucestershire v Surrey, Kennington Oval, July 12, 13, 14 (Surrey won by seven wickets)

| | not out | 0 | 210 | 20.2 | 5 | 91 | 7 | L.B.Fishlock lbw
H.S.Squires lbw
J.F.Parker c V.Hopkins
H.M.Garland-Wells c G.E.E.Lambert
F.R.Brown c V.Hopkins
E.A.Watts c G.E.E.Lambert
A.R.Gover b | 259 | |
| | not out | 13 | 349-9d | 18 | 1 | 86 | 1 | H.M.Garland-Wells b | 301-3 | |

413. Gloucestershire v Kent, Maidstone, July 15, 17 (Kent won by 98 runs)

| | b D.V.P.Wright | 0 | 170 | 18.2 | 1 | 70 | 4 | L.E.G.Ames c J.F.Crapp
L.J.Todd c W.R.Hammond
T.C.Longfield c W.R.Hammond
W.H.V.Levett c E.D.R.Eagar | 182 | 1 |
| | c F.G.H.Chalk
   b N.W.Harding | 8 | 103 | 13 | 0 | 76 | 4 | F.G.H.Chalk b
L.E.G.Ames c G.E.E.Lambert
B.H.Valentine c and b
L.J.Todd b | 189 | 1 |

414. Gloucestershire v Hampshire, Bristol, July 19, (20), 21 (Gloucestershire won by five wickets)

| | did not bat | | - | 104-6d | 19.5 | 7 | 36 | 4 | N.T.McCorkell c C.J.Scott
J.Bailey c V.Hopkins
A.E.Pothecary c C.J.Scott
G.E.M.Heath b | 103 | |
| | did not bat | | - | 66-5 | 9 | 2 | 36 | 8 | N.T.McCorkell b
J.Bailey b
J.P.Blake b
D.F.Walker lbw
J.Arnold c G.M.Emmett
A.E.Pothecary st A.E.Wilson
P.A.Mackenzie lbw
G.R.Taylor c R.W.Haynes | 66 | 1 |

415. ENGLAND v WEST INDIES, Old Trafford, July 22, 24, 25 (Match drawn)

| | did not bat | | - | 164-7d | 4 | 0 | 43 | 2 | R.S.Grant c A.E.Fagg
J.B.Stollmeyer c and b | 133 | 1 |
| | did not bat | | - | 128-6d | 4.6 | 1 | 15 | 1 | G.E.Gomez b | 43-4 | |

416. Gloucestershire v Hampshire, Bournemouth, July 26, 27, 28 (Gloucestershire won by 43 runs)
    not out   18   212   20.2   2   77   7   R.H.Moore   c G.M.Emmett   167
                                                          J.Bailey   lbw
                                                          J.P.Blake   b
                                                          W.C.L.Creese c J.F.Crapp
                                                          D.F.Walker   c G.M.Emmett
                                                          P.A.Mackenzie c V.Hopkins
                                                          A.E.G.Baring c V.Hopkins
    b W.C.L.Creese   2   160-7d   16.4   2   65   5   R.H.Moore   b   162
                                                          J.Bailey   c J.F.Crapp
                                                          J.P.Blake   lbw
                                                          G.S.Boyes   c R.A.Sinfield
                                                          A.E.G.Baring c E.D.R.Eagar

417. Gloucestershire v Lancashire, Old Trafford, July (29), 31, August (1) (Match drawn)
    did not bat   -   14-1

418. Gloucestershire v Derbyshire, Chesterfield, August 2, 3, (4) (Match drawn)
    not out   9   198   10   1   29   0   121
                                     12   2   37   1   D.Smith   lbw   120-2

419. Gloucestershire v Somerset, Bristol, August 5, 7, 8 (Gloucestershire won by an innings and 109 runs)
    not out   56   329   10   3   15   5   H.D.Burrough b   106
                                                          F.M.McRae   c W.R.Hammond
                                                          E.F.Longrigg b
                                                          W.H.R.Andrews b
                                                          H.L.Hazell   c R.A.Sinfield
                                     13.5   4   44   9   F.S.Lee   c G.M.Emmett   114
                                                          H.Gimblett   c A.E.Wilson
                                                          H.F.T.Buse   c E.D.R.Eagar
                                                          R.J.O.Meyer   c C.J.Scott
                                                          H.D.Burrough b
                                                          W.T.Luckes   lbw
                                                          E.F.Longrigg c A.H.Broadhurst
                                                          W.H.R.Andrews c G.E.E.Lambert
                                                          H.L.Hazell   c G.E.E.Lambert

420. Gloucestershire v Glamorgan, Bristol, August 9, 10, 11 (Glamorgan won by six wickets)
    did not bat   -   223-7d   19   3   60   2   T.L.Brierley lbw   235-7d
                                                          D.Davies   c C.J.Scott
    b A.D.G.Matthews 6   128-3d   6.2   0   50   1   H.G.Davies   c J.F.Crapp   120-4

421. Gloucestershire v West Indians, Cheltenham, August 12, 14, 15 (Gloucestershire won by seven wickets)
    not out   3   152   10   0   45   3   K.H.Weekes   c C.J.Barnett   162   1
                                                          L.G.Hylton   b
                                                          E.A.Martindale c and b
    did not bat   -   231-3   17.3   3   60   3   G.E.Gomez   c and b   220   1
                                                          V.H.Stollmeyer lbw
                                                          E.A.Martindale b

422. Gloucestershire v Derbyshire, Cheltenham, August 16, 17, 18 (Derbyshire won by 1 run)
    c T.D.Hounsfield b A.V.Pope 3   81   8   0   32   0   193   1
    c A.F.Townsend
        b W.H.Copson 4   259   5   1   20   0   148

423. ENGLAND v WEST INDIES, Kennington Oval, August 19, 21, 22 (Match drawn)
    b C.B.Clarke   0   352   12   1   56   1   V.H.Stollmeyer st A.Wood   498   1
    did not bat   -   366-3d

424. Gloucestershire v Warwickshire, Edgbaston, August 23, 24, 25 (Warwickshire won by 110 runs)
    not out   7   187   12   3   28   1   W.A.Hill   lbw   165
    c P.Cranmer b W.E.Hollies 0   115   15   4   51   0   247

425. Gloucestershire v Nottinghamshire, Trent Bridge, August 26, 28, 29 (Gloucestershire won by an innings and
    56 runs)
    c C.B.Harris b F.G.Woodhead 0   395-9d   10.5   1   77   6   F.H.Winrow   b   199
                                                          J.Hardstaff   c W.R.Hammond
                                                          G.V.Gunn   c W.R.Hammond
                                                          R.J.Giles   c C.J.Scott
                                                          W.A.Sime   b
                                                          H.J.Butler   c W.R.Hammond
                                     14.7   1   70   5   C.B.Harris   c W.R.Hammond   140   1
                                                          J.Hardstaff   c C.J.Barnett
                                                          G.V.Gunn   c C.J.Barnett
                                                          H.J.Butler   b
                                                          F.G.Woodhead c G.M.Emmett

SEASON'S AVERAGES

Batting and Fielding	M	I	NO	Runs	HS	Ave	50	Ct
Test Matches	2	1	0	0	0	0.00	-	2
Championship	25	29	9	197	56*	9.85	1	10
Other Glos matches	2	3	2	18	11*	18.00	-	2
Season	29	33	11	215	56*	9.77	1	14
Career	425	557	154	3884	71	9.63	4	243

Bowling	O	M	R	W	BB	Ave	5i	10m	Strike	RunR
Test Matches	20.6	2	114	4	2-43	28.50	-	-	41.50	68.67
Championship	742.5	128	2654	181	9-38	14.66	19	8	32.82	44.67
Other Glos matches	56.5	9	205	15	5-42	13.66	1	-	30.20	45.25
Season (8b)	820	139	2973	200	9-38	14.86	20	8	32.80	45.32
Career (6b) (8b)	15151 1131	3995 ⎱ 211 ⎰	41291	2060	10-113	20.04	178	61	48.52	41.31

1946

Goddard was in his 46th year when cricket resumed after the war but he was still to take another 919 first-class wickets before he retired in 1952. In the 1946 season he took 150 wickets for Gloucestershire in the Championship and 177 in all fixtures, more than any one else in the country apart from Eric Hollies of Warwickshire. At times he was nearly unplayable and he took five wickets in an innings twelve times and ten in a match on six occasions. Highlights were 13 for 61 against Northamptonshire at Peterborough, 11 for 75 against Glamorgan at Bristol, 14 for 169 against Essex at Brentwood and 13 for 127 against Surrey at Cheltenham. As a batsman he scored 198 runs in 33 innings and he took seventeen catches.

	Own Team Total	O	M	R	W		Opp Total	Ct
426. Gloucestershire v Oxford University, The Parks, May 4, 6 (Gloucestershire won by an innings and 149 runs)								
did not bat	- 481-7d	17	3	59	6	R.Sale c J.F.Crapp	147	
						M.P.Donnelly c W.R.Hammond		
						C.D.Williams b		
						N.C.F.Bloy lbw		
						G.A.Wheatley b		
						D.H.Macindoe c C.J.Barnett		
		13	1	53	3	R.Sale b	185	
						J.O.Newton-Thompson c A.E.Wilson		
						D.H.Macindoe st A.E.Wilson		
427. Gloucestershire v Lancashire, Gloucester, May 11, 13, 14 (Lancashire won by 135 runs)								
lbw b R.Pollard	2 238	39.4	10	95	4	C.Washbrook c and b	264	1
						R.G.Garlick c C.Cook		
						R.Pollard b		
						W.B.Roberts c C.J.Scott		
not out	1 203	32.4	7	107	3	W.Place lbw	312-5d	
						B.P.King lbw		
						W.E.Phillipson b		
428. Gloucestershire v Nottinghamshire, Trent Bridge, May 18, 20, 21 (Gloucestershire won by eight wickets)								
b F.G.Woodhead	4 159-9d	14.1	6	27	4	J.Hardstaff c W.L.Neale	132	
						T.B.Reddick c C.Cook		
						I.Smithurst c G.E.E.Lambert		
						H.J.Butler lbw		
did not bat	- 145-2	24	7	70	3	G.F.H.Heane lbw	167	
						T.B.Reddick c A.E.Wilson		
						F.W.Stocks c J.F.Crapp		
429. Gloucestershire v Glamorgan, Bristol, May 22, 23 (Gloucestershire won by two wickets)								
not out	4 59	13.1	3	27	4	H.G.Davies c and b	95	1
						J.C.Clay b		
						A.D.G.Matthews b		
						P.F.Judge c C.Cook		

not out		0	153-8	24	6	48	7	A.H.Dyson b	115	1
								D.E.Davies lbw		
								W.Wooller lbw		
								G.Lavis lbw		
								C.C.Smart c G.M.Emmett		
								H.G.Davies b		
								A.D.G.Matthews b		

430. Gloucestershire v Warwickshire, Bristol, May 25, 27, 28 (Match drawn)
did not bat   - 274-4   28   5   67   0   287

431. Gloucestershire v Yorkshire, Bristol, June 1, 3, 4 (Match drawn)
b W.E.Bowes   4   369   48   15   104   2   L.Hutton c B.O.Allen   336-6
                                                      P.A.Gibb c A.E.Wilson

432. Gloucestershire v Somerset, Taunton, June 8, 10, (11) (Match drawn)
not out   8 364-9d   35   11   97   3   F.Castle c A.E.Wilson   313   2
                                                      H.F.T.Buse c and b
                                                      W.H.R.Andrews c J.F.Crapp
                      -     -   -   -   13-1

433. Gloucestershire v Northamptonshire, Peterborough, June 12, 13 (Gloucestershire won by nine wickets)
lbw b W.E.Merritt   5   105   13   0   38   7   C.P.Davis c G.E.E.Lambert   83
                                                      E.W.Whitfield b
                                                      J.E.Timms c C.J.Scott
                                                      R.G.Robinson c C.J.Scott
                                                      W.E.Merritt b
                                                      W.T.Nevell lbw
                                                      R.J.Partridge b
did not bat   -   19-1   16   6   23   6   C.P.Davis b   39
                                                      J.E.Timms lbw
                                                      W.E.Merritt b
                                                      W.T.Nevell b
                                                      P.E.Murray-Willis b
                                                      R.J.Partridge lbw

434. Gloucestershire v Kent, Gravesend, June 15, 17, 18 (Gloucestershire won by five wickets)
not out   1   241   31   17   47   3   T.A.Pearce b   171
                                                      B.H.Valentine c W.L.Neale
                                                      J.G.W.Davies b
did not bat   -   137-5   26   8   33   4   J.G.W.Davies b   206
                                                      T.W.Spencer c B.O.Allen
                                                      B.G.H.Gunn c A.E.Wilson
                                                      N.W.Harding c A.E.Wilson

435. Gloucestershire v Middlesex, Gloucester, June 22, 24, 25 (Middlesex won by 33 runs)
lbw b J.A.Young   0   163   33.4 8   72   6   S.M.Brown b   152
                                                      A.W.Thompson lbw
                                                      W.F.F.Price b
                                                      J.M.Sims c L.M.Cranfield
                                                      L.H.Gray c C.J.Scott
                                                      J.A.Young b
c S.M.Brown b L.H.Gray 8 157 29   14   44   3   S.M.Brown b   201
                                                      B.L.Muncer c B.O.Allen
                                                      W.F.F.Price b

436. Gloucestershire v Essex, Brentwood, June 26, 27, 28 (Gloucestershire won by an innings and 23 runs)
c R.M.Taylor b T.P.B.Smith 19 396 40.1 12 88 8   F.H.Vigar b   165
                                                      T.P.B.Smith b
                                                      R.M.Taylor c G.M.Emmett
                                                      R.F.T.Paterson lbw
                                                      T.C.Dodds c W.R.Hammond
                                                      D.F.Cock c C.Cook
                                                      T.H.Wade c B.O.Allen
                                                      F.W.Appleyard c C.Cook
                               33.2   7   81   6   F.H.Vigar lbw   208   1
                                                      R.F.T.Paterson b
                                                      R.M.Taylor c W.R.Hammond
                                                      D.F.Cock c L.M.Cranfield
                                                      R.Smith c C.Cook
                                                      F.W.Appleyard lbw

437. Gloucestershire v Oxford University, Bristol, June 29, July 1, 2 (Gloucestershire won by an innings and 101 runs)
b D.H.Macindoe   22   459   22.1   3   81   5   G.E.Beck   lbw   172   1
                                                                   N.C.F.Bloy   b
                                                                   J.D.Newton-Thompson   c and b
                                                                   D.H.Macindoe   b
                                                                   M.A.Sutton   b
                                           8   4   13   1   R.H.Maudsley   b   186

438. Gloucestershire v Glamorgan, Cardiff, July 6, 8, 9 (Glamorgan won by eight wickets)
c G.Lavis b P.F.Judge   23   175   28   10   62   2   A.H.Dyson   lbw   252
                                                                   C.C.Smart   b
b A.Porter   0   283   34   14   65   0   207-2

439. Gloucestershire v Leicestershire, Bristol, July 13, 15, 16 (Gloucestershire won by an innings and 112 runs)
did not bat   -   471-8d   37.5   19   65   5   G.Lester   b   224
                                                                   M.Tompkin   lbw
                                                                   G.S.Watson   c G.E.E.Lambert
                                                                   A.Riddington   b
                                                                   J.Sperry   b
                                          22   7   39   3   G.Lester   c B.O.Allen   135
                                                                   G.S.Watson   c J.F.Crapp
                                                                   J.M.Josephs   lbw

440. Gloucestershire v Hampshire, Bristol, July 17, 18, 19 (Gloucestershire won by an innings and 9 runs)
not out   4   331-9d   20.1   3   56   4   J.Arnold   lbw   132
                                                                   J.Bailey   b
                                                                   N.T.McCorkell   b
                                                                   E.D.R.Eagar   lbw
                                          28.3   11   66   4   A.G.Holt   c W.L.Neale   190   3
                                                                   E.D.R.Eagar   c and b
                                                                   T.A.Dean   c and b
                                                                   G.E.M.Heath   b

441. Gloucestershire v Middlesex, Lord's, July 20, 22 (Gloucestershire won by eight wickets)
lbw b J.M.Sims   3   132   28.5   8   59   7   J.D.B.Robertson   c C.J.Scott   138
                                                                   S.M.Brown   c J.F.Crapp
                                                                   J.P.Mann   c B.O.Allen
                                                                   L.H.Compton   b
                                                                   J.M.Sims   b
                                                                   W.F.F.Price   c C.J.Scott
                                                                   L.H.Gray   c W.L.Neale
did not bat   -   177-2   18   3   59   3   R.W.V.Robins   c and b   169   1
                                                                   J.P.Mann   c J.F.Crapp
                                                                   L.H.Compton   c B.O.Allen

442. Gloucestershire v Sussex, Bristol, July 24, 25, 26 (Match drawn)
not out   13   497-8   39   10   87   2   C.Oakes   c J.F.Crapp   552
                                                                   H.T.Bartlett   lbw

443. Gloucestershire v Worcestershire, Worcester, July 27, 29, 30 (Worcestershire won by 101 runs)
not out   4   269   44   11   97   4   A.F.T.White   c C.J.Scott   414
                                                                   J.S.Buller   b
                                                                   R.T.D.Perks   lbw
                                                                   P.F.Jackson   c A.E.Wilson
b R.Howorth   3   226   18.2   1   61   2   R.Howorth   c A.E.Wilson   182-5d
                                                                   R.T.D.Perks   c G.E.E.Lambert

444. Gloucestershire v Leicestershire, Grace Road, Leicester, July 31, August 1, 2 (Gloucestershire won by four wickets)
c P.Corrall b F.T.Prentice 0   348   19   5   36   1   A.Riddington   c G.M.Emmett   211
not out   4   227-6   38.1   11   76   4   A.Riddington   c C.J.Scott   360
                                                                   J.Howard   c C.Cook
                                                                   J.E.Walsh   st A.E.Wilson
                                                                   K.G.Peake   b

445. Gloucestershire v Somerset, Bristol, August 3, 5, 6 (Match drawn)
did not bat   -   550-5d   53   21   87   3   E.F.Longrigg   c C.Cook   372
                                                                   J.Lawrence   b
                                                                   W.H.R.Andrews   lbw
did not bat   -   150-4

446. Gloucestershire v Hampshire, Southampton, August 7, 8 (Gloucestershire won by seven wickets)
b C.J.Knott   1   226-8d   20.2   6   51   3   A.G.Holt   b   171
                                                                   N.H.Rogers   lbw
                                                                   O.W.Herman   b

did not bat		-	60-3	17.4	4	61	4	J.Arnold c and b	113	2
								G.Hill b		
								N.H.Rogers b		
								G.E.M.Heath c J.F.Crapp		

447. Gloucestershire v Indians, Cheltenham, August (10), 12, 13 (Match drawn)

did not bat	-	132-3d	23	2	81	7	M.H.Mankad c B.O.Allen	135-8d
							R.S.Modi lbw	
							L.Amarnath c A.E.Wilson	
							V.S.Hazare b	
							A.H.Kardar b	
							Gul Mahommad st A.E.Wilson	
							S.W.Sohoni b	
lbw b C.T.Sarwate	12	187	22	4	66	4	R.S.Modi b	177-9
							Gul Mahommad b	
							S.W.Sohoni b	
							R.B.Nimbalkar lbw	

448. Gloucestershire v Surrey, Cheltenham, August 14, 15, 16 (Gloucestershire won by 55 runs)

c E.A.Watts b J.F.Parker	4	132	22	8	45	4	L.B.Fishlock c C.J.Barnett	140	
							R.J.Gregory lbw		
							J.F.Parker lbw		
							E.A.Bedser lbw		
did not bat	-	299-7d	33.3	11	82	9	R.J.Gregory c A.E.Wilson	236	1
							H.S.Squires c and b		
							H.T.Barling lbw		
							J.F.Parker c J.F.Crapp		
							E.A.Bedser lbw		
							E.A.Watts b		
							N.H.Bennett b		
							A.R.Gover b		
							A.V.Bedser c C.J.Barnett		

449. Gloucestershire v Worcestershire, Cheltenham, August 17, 19, 20 (Worcestershire won by ten wickets)

c J.S.Buller b P.F.Jackson	0	139	26	11	41	3	R.E.Bird lbw	144	
							D.M.Young lbw		
							R.T.D.Perks c C.J.Barnett		
not out	2	74	7	2	18	0		70-0	

450. Gloucestershire v Yorkshire, Headingley, August 21, 22 (Yorkshire won by nine wickets)

b L.Hutton	4	106	40	12	76	2	N.W.D.Yardley b	188	
							K.Fiddling lbw		
c A.Coxon b E.P.Robinson	0	89	1	0	7	0		8-1	

451. Gloucestershire v Derbyshire, Derby, August 24, 26 (Gloucestershire won by 81 runs)

lbw b A.E.G.Rhodes	22	227	27	10	47	3	C.S.Elliott c and b	147	2
							A.E.G.Rhodes c and b		
							C.Gladwin lbw		
c W.H.Copson b T.R.Armstrong	2	67	9	3	8	3	D.Smith st A.E.Wilson	66	
							T.S.Worthington b		
							A.C.Revill b		

452. Gloucestershire v Sussex, Hove, August 28, 29, (30) (Match drawn)

c J.G.Langridge b D.J.Wood	15	193	30	7	109	0		250
did not bat		-	44-4					

453. Gloucestershire v Essex, Gloucester, August 31, September 2, (3) (Match drawn)

did not bat		-	24-1	25	4	55	2	T.E.Bailey c W.L.Neale	197	1
							R.F.T.Paterson c J.F.Crapp		

454. South of England v Indians, Hastings, September 4, 5, 6 (Indians won by 10 runs)

did not bat		-	218-9d	22	4	65	1	V.M.Merchant c L.E.G.Ames	241	
run out	4	266	22	2	94	0		253-3d	

SEASON'S AVERAGES

Batting and Fielding	M	I	NO	Runs	HS	Ave	50	Ct
Championship	25	30	10	160	22	8.00	-	16
Other Glos matches	3	2	0	34	22	17.00	-	1
Other match	1	1	0	4	4	4.00	-	-
Season	29	33	10	198	22	8.60	-	17
Career	454	590	164	4082	71	9.58	4	260

Bowling	O	M	R	W	BB	Ave	5i	10m	Strike	RunR
Championship	1168.1	354	2583	150	9-82	17.22	9	5	46.72	36.85
Other Glos matches	105.1	17	353	26	7-81	13.57	3	1	24.26	55.94
Other match	44	6	159	1	1-65	159.00	-	-	264.00	60.22
Season (6b)	1317.2	377	3095	177	9-82	17.48	12	6	44.65	39.15
Career (6b)	16468.2	4372 ⎫	44386	2237	10-113	19.84	190	67	48.21	41.15
(8b)	1131	211 ⎭								

1947

Goddard had a wonderful season in 1947, an "Indian summer" which saw him, in his 47th year, pick up 238 first-class wickets at an average of 17.30. The next highest wicket-taker in the country was Doug. Wright of Kent and he was well behind with 177 victims. Goddard took 222 wickets for his County, alone, in all matches equalling the record he had set back in 1937. No bowler has approached this figure since and, with the reduction in County matches since Goddard's day this record is likely to stand for all time. A few outstanding performances must be mentioned – 15 for 81 against Nottinghamshire, 15 for 134 against Leicestershire, 15 for 156 against Middlesex, and 12 for 65 against Somerset. He took hat-tricks against Glamorgan at Swansea and against Somerset at Bristol. He finished third in the national bowling averages. Probably his age weighed against his Test selection this year – he could hardly be seen as a long-term prospect. As a batsman he scored 326 runs in 47 innings and he held 13 catches.

		Own Team Total	O	M	R	W		Opp Total	Ct

455. Gloucestershire v Oxford University, The Parks, May 3, 5, 6 (Match drawn)
    c M.A.Sutton
        b A.W.H.Mallett   0   245   26   5   90   6   M.P.Donnelly st A.E.Wilson   234
                                                                  H.A.Pawson b
                                                                  C.J.R.Whittle c G.E.E.Lambert
                                                                  A.H.Kardar c B.H.Lyon
                                                                  N.C.F.Bloy c C.J.Scott
                                                                  A.W.H.Mallett c W.L.Neale
    did not bat   -   205-5d   15   4   46   2   M.P.Donnelly c A.E.Wilson   120-6
                                                                  N.C.F.Bloy c A.E.Wilson

456. Gloucestershire v Middlesex, Lord's, May 14, 15 (Middlesex won by an innings and 178 runs)
    not out   2   122   39.5   4   101   3   F.G.Mann c G.M.Emmett   388
                                                                  J.M.Sims b
    run out   2   88   R.A.Shaddick c J.F.Crapp

457. Gloucestershire v Hampshire, Bristol, May 17, 19 (Gloucestershire won by an innings and 141 runs)
    run out   20   378   21   9   25   5   N.H.Rogers b   77
                                                                  G.Hill c B.O.Allen
                                                                N.T.McCorkell c B.O.Allen
                                                                E.D.R.Eagar lbw
                                                                G.E.M.Heath b
                                               22   4   82   1   J.Bailey b   160

458. Gloucestershire v Nottinghamshire, Bristol, May 21, 22 (Gloucestershire won by an innings and 167 runs)

b A.Jepson	2	393-9d	21.4	8	41	9	W.W.Keeton c W.L.Neale	129
							R.T.Simpson c J.F.Crapp	
							J.Hardstaff b	
							T.B.Reddick b	
							F.W.Stocks c B.O.Allen	
							W.Voce b	
							W.A.Sime lbw	
							A.Jepson st A.E.Wilson	
							E.A.Meads b	
		9.1	2	40	6	R.T.Simpson c B.O.Allen	97	1
							F.W.Stocks c C.J.Barnett	
							W.Voce c W.L.Neale	
							A.Jepson c and b	
							H.J.Butler b	
							E.A.Meads b	

459. Gloucestershire v Somerset, Taunton, May 24, 26, 27 (Gloucestershire won by 78 runs)

lbw b J.Lawrence	6	231	20	6	62	1	R.J.O.Meyer c W.L.Neale	206
not out	16	334-9d	28	7	85	3	F.S.Lee c B.O.Allen	281	1
							G.E.S.Woodhouse c B.O.Allen	
							M.Coope c J.F.Crapp	

460. Gloucestershire v Yorkshire, Bristol, May 31, June 2 (Gloucestershire won by nine wickets)

c and b T.F.Smailes	16	176	21	6	48	0		128
did not bat	-	72-1	12.5	3	35	6	W.Watson c A.G.S.Wilcox	119	1
							F.Jakeman c A.E.Wilson	
							A.B.Sellers c W.L.Neale	
							T.F.Smailes st A.E.Wilson	
							E.P.Robinson b	
							W.E.Bowes c J.F.Crapp	

461. Gloucestershire v Cambridge University, Fenner's, June 4, 5, 6 (Match drawn)

c D.J.Insole								
b M.R.G.Earls-Davis	8	372	33	11	63	3	H.E.Watts lbw	401-7d
							S.N.Roberts c B.O.Allen	
							R.D.Pearsall c J.F.Crapp	
		-	-	-	-			60-5

462. Gloucestershire v Leicestershire, Gloucester, June 7, 9, 10 (Gloucestershire won by six wickets)

b G.Lester	13	363	17	7	26	8	G.L.Berry lbw	142	1
							M.Tompkin lbw	
							V.E.Jackson c C.J.Scott	
							G.Lester b	
							A.Riddington c and b	
							T.A.Chapman c J.F.Crapp	
							P.Corrall c C.J.Scott	
							J.S.Perry st A.E.Wilson	
did not bat	-	89-4	41.3	9	108	7	G.S.Watson c C.J.Scott	308
							M.Tompkin b	
							A.Riddington lbw	
							V.E.Jackson c W.L.Neale	
							T.A.Chapman c B.O.Allen	
							J.Howard b	
							P.Corrall c J.F.Crapp	

463. Gloucestershire v Warwickshire, Edgbaston, June 11, 12, 13 (Match drawn)

not out	12	327	44	14	106	7	F.C.Gardner b	401-9d
							P.Cranmer b	
							K.A.Taylor st A.E.Wilson	
							J.S.Ord c G.E.E.Lambert	
							W.E.Fantham c G.E.E.Lambert	
							T.L.Pritchard b	
							A.Woodroffe lbw	
not out	1	252-9	31.3	6	77	4	W.A.Hill b	234
							J.S.Ord b	
							A.Woodroffe c B.O.Allen	
							V.H.D.Cannings c J.F.Crapp	

464. Gloucestershire v Glamorgan, Swansea, June (14), 16, 17 (Match drawn)
   c A.J.Watkins b B.L.Muncer 8   153   19   8   40   6   A.H.Dyson lbw   90
                                                              M.Robinson lbw
                                                              A.Porter b
                                                              H.G.Davies b
                                                              W.E.Jones lbw
                                                              G.Lavis st A.E.Wilson
   did not bat   - 152-5d   23   7   35   1   A.Porter lbw   129-7
465. Gloucestershire v Worcestershire, Worcester, June 18, 19, 20 (Gloucestershire won by six wickets)
   c R.E.Bird b R.Howorth   4   248   4   1   13   0   172
   did not bat   -   149-4   22   6   56   2   A.F.T.White lbw   221
                                                              L.F.Outschoorn b
466. Gloucestershire v Kent, Bristol, June 21, 23, 24 (Gloucestershire won by an innings and 37 runs)
   c N.W.Harding b R.R.Dovey 11   507   30   12   71   5   L.J.Todd b   228
                                                              B.R.Edrich lbw
                                                              L.E.G.Ames c A.G.S.Wilcox
                                                              B.H.Valentine c B.O.Allen
                                                              R.Mayes lbw
                                         35   8   99   5   L.J.Todd b   242
                                                              A.J.B.Marsham lbw
                                                              B.R.Edrich c G.E.E.Lambert
                                                              N.W.Harding c A.G.S.Wilcox
                                                              W.H.V.Levett c G.E.E.Lambert
467. Gloucestershire v Nottinghamshire, Trent Bridge, June 24, 26, 27 (Match drawn)
   b A.Jepson   0   249   43   11   95   1   T.B.Reddick
                                                              c G.E.E.Lambert   482   1
   did not bat   -   132-3
468. Gloucestershire v Surrey, Kennington Oval, June 28, 30, July 1 (Gloucestershire won by eight wickets)
   lbw b A.R.Gover   12   358   28   10   55   7   E.A.Bedser c G.M.Emmett   128
                                                              H.S.Squires c G.M.Emmett
                                                              H.T.Barling c L.M.Cranfield
                                                              E.R.T.Holmes b
                                                              A.V.Bedser c C.J.Scott
                                                              J.W.J.McMahon c J.F.Crapp
                                                              A.R.Gover c A.E.Wilson
   did not bat   -   47-2   47.5 10 113   4   H.T.Barling b   276
                                                              J.F.Parker c B.O.Allen
                                                              J.W.J.McMahon b
                                                              A.R.Gover b
469. Gloucestershire v Derbyshire, Bristol, July 2, 3, 4 (Gloucestershire won by two wickets)
   b C.Gladwin   0   289   35   4 106   3   C.S.Elliott b   292
                                                              E.J.Gothard lbw
                                                              A.C.Revill c J.F.Crapp
   not out   0 155-8   11.2 1   32   2   R.M.Watson b   151
                                                              W.H.Copson b
470. Gloucestershire v Sussex, Bristol, July 5, 7, 8 (Match drawn)
   not out   4   311   28.1 8   63   3   J.G.Langridge c B.O.Allen 203
                                                              J.Y.Oakes c B.O.Allen
                                                              J.H.Cornford st A.E.Wilson
                                         34   6 104   4   R.G.Hunt c A.E.Wilson   397-7
                                                              H.W.Parks c C.J.Scott
                                                              G.Cox b
                                                              J.Y.Oakes lbw
471. Gloucestershire v Essex, Westcliff-on-Sea, July 12, 14, 15 (Gloucestershire won by eight wickets)
   b F.H.Vigar   22   336   43   13 110   2   A.V.Avery c G.M.Emmett   300
                                                              F.H.Vigar b
   did not bat   -   191-2   29   11   92   4   A.V.Avery c J.F.Crapp   226
                                                              F.H.Vigar c G.M.Emmett
                                                              D.J.Insole b
                                                              L.S.Clark lbw
472. Gloucestershire v Worcestershire, Gloucester, July 16, 17, 18 (Gloucestershire won by 65 runs)
   c R.E.S.Wyatt b R.Howorth   3   223   24   6   66   5   A.F.T.White c G.M.Emmett 149   1
                                                              E.Cooper lbw
                                                              R.E.S.Wyatt c and b
                                                              L.F.Outschoorn lbw
                                                              H.Horton b

not out	4	133	21.3	6	54	6	R.Howorth c C.Cook R.E.S.Wyatt lbw L.F.Outschoorn b H.Horton b R.T.D.Perks c C.Cook H.Yarnold b	142

473. Gloucestershire v Northamptonshire, Gloucester, July 19, (21), 22 (Gloucestershire won by 84 runs)

b C.B.Clarke	0	261	16.3	2	61	4	D.Brookes c C.J.Scott A.L.Cox lbw R.J.Partridge b C.B.Clarke c J.F.Crapp	133
did not bat	-	71-4d	16	4	44	5	J.E.Timms lbw W.Barron c G.M.Emmett V.Broderick b E.Davis b R.J.Partridge b	115

474. Gloucestershire v Leicestershire, Grace Road, Leicester, July 26, 28, 29 (Gloucestershire won by 71 runs)

c J.E.Walsh b A.Riddington	0	267	18.1	6	25	4	F.T.Prentice c C.Cook V.E.Jackson b G.Lester lbw P.Corrall c C.Cook	206
did not bat	-	198-3d	23.1	6	66	5	G.L.Berry lbw G.S.Watson b G.Lester b J.E.Walsh c J.K.R.Graveney P.Corrall lbw	188

475. Gloucestershire v Somerset, Bristol, August 2, 4 (Gloucestershire won by 316 runs)

lbw b R.J.O.Meyer	5	244	10.4	1	61	7	M.M.Walford st A.E.Wilson H.E.Watts c C.J.Scott J.Lawrence c C.J.Scott H.F.T.Buse b F.S.Lee b A.W.Wellard c C.J.Scott R.J.O.Meyer b	98
not out	1	195-9d	3	1	4	5	F.S.Lee b M.F.Tremlett c G.M.Emmett G.R.Langdale b A.W.Wellard c G.W.Parker R.J.O.Meyer lbw	25

476. Gloucestershire v Lancashire, Old Trafford, August 6, 7, 8 (Lancashire won by ten wickets)

st A.Barlow b W.B.Roberts	23	415	40.4	7	121	6	B.J.Howard lbw G.A.Edrich c G.E.E.Lambert A.Wharton c A.E.Wilson R.Pollard c G.E.E.Lambert A.Barlow c and b W.B.Roberts b	341	1
run out		0	106	10	0	38	0	183-0

477. Gloucestershire v Yorkshire, Bradford, August 9, 11, 12 (Gloucestershire won by 8 runs)

c sub b E.P.Robinson	4	182	25	8	75	3	G.A.Smithson c J.F.Crapp E.I.Lester c C.J.Barnett N.W.D.Yardley lbw	228
b J.P.Whitehead	11	281	36.2	4	116	6	W.Watson c B.O.Allen W.G.Keighley c C.J.Scott A.B.Sellers b J.H.Wardle c B.O.Allen D.V.Brennan c J.F.Crapp E.P.Robinson c B.O.Allen	227

478. Gloucestershire v South Africans, Cheltenham, August 13, 14, 15 (South Africans won by 133 runs)

c K.G.Viljoen b A.M.B.Rowan	4	185	28	7	73	3	K.G.Viljoen b A.M.B.Rowan lbw L.Tuckett c and b	225	1
run out		0	155	28	5	80	2	A.Melville c J.F.Crapp K.G.Viljoen st A.E.Wilson	248	1

479. Gloucestershire v Middlesex, Cheltenham, August 16, 18 (Middlesex won by 68 runs)
    c and b J.M.Sims   26   153   20.3   4   70   7   F.G.Mann c J.F.Crapp   180
                                                                                                                   R.W.V.Robins c C.J.Scott
                                                                                                                   A.W.Thompson b
                                                                                                                   L.H.Compton lbw
                                                                                                                   J.P.Mann c G.E.E.Lambert
                                                                                                                   J.M.Sims c B.O.Allen
                                                                                                                   J.A.Young b
    c W.J.Edrich b J.A.Young   0   100   22   4   86   8   S.M.Brown b   141
                                                                                                                  W.J.Edrich lbw
                                                                                                                  F.G.Mann st A.E.Wilson
                                                                                                                   R.W.V.Robins c C.I.Monks
                                                                                                                  A.W.Thompson lbw
                                                                                                                  L.H.Compton c C.J.Barnett
                                                                                                                  J.M.Sims c W.L.Neale
                                                                                                                  H.P.H.Sharp c C.J.Barnett

480. Gloucestershire v Glamorgan, Cheltenham, August 20, 21 (Gloucestershire won by 29 runs)
    b A.D.G.Matthews   5   172   16   2   57   1   G.Lavis c C.J.Scott   156
    c P.B.Clift b B.L.Muncer 0   138   12.3 0   61   8   D.E.Davies c J.F.Crapp   125
                                                                                                                       G.Lavis c C.J.Scott
                                                                                                                 W.Wooller c C.J.Scott
                                                                                                                 A.J.Watkins c J.F.Crapp
                                                                                                                 B.L.Muncer st A.E.Wilson
                                                                                                                 P.B.Clift c A.E.Wilson
                                                                                                                 H.G.Davies c L.M.Cranfield
                                                                                                                 W.H.Griffiths c W.L.Neale

481. Gloucestershire v Hampshire, Bournemouth, August 23, 25, 26 (Match drawn)
    did not bat   -   424-6d   41.5 10   132   5   N.T.McCorkell b   472   1
                                                                                                                 E.D.R.Eagar lbw
                                                                                                                 G.Hill c J.F.Crapp
                                                                                                                 L.Harrison c and b
    did not bat   -   298-5   O.W.Herman c G.M.Emmett

482. Gloucestershire v Sussex, Hove, August 27, 28, 29 (Sussex won by nine wickets)
    not out   11   293   26.3 10   64   3   J.G.Langridge st A.E.Wilson 426
                                                                                                                 H.T.Bartlett c B.O.Allen
                                                                                                                 J.K.Nye c J.F.Crapp
    c P.A.H.Carey b J.K.Nye   9   259   -   -   -   -   127-1

483. Gloucestershire v Essex, Bristol, August 31, September 1, 2 (Gloucestershire won by 317 runs)
    b T.P.B.Smith   17   324   29.3 5   106   5   F.H.Vigar c A.E.Wilson   215
                                                                                                                 R.Smith c W.L.Neale
                                                                                                                 W.J.Dines lbw
                                                                                                                 T.H.Wade b
                                                                                                                 W.T.Greensmith b
    c F.H.Vigar b R.Smith   21   365   20.3 4   57   4   T.P.B.Smith c and b   157   2
                                                                                                                 W.T.Dines c and b
                                                                                                                 T.H.Wade b
                                                                                                                 W.B.Morris c C.Cook

484. South of England v South Africans, Hastings, September 3, 4, 5 (South Africans won by nine wickets)
    not out   1   341-9d   35   7   136   2   B.Mitchell c B.H.Valentine 510-8d
                                                                                                                  N.B.F.Mann b
    not out   0   199   3   0   13   1   J.D.Lindsay b   31-1

485. South of England v Sir Pelham Warner's XI, Hastings, September 6, 8, 9 (Sir Pelham Warner's XI won by 26 runs)
    run out   0   199   23   3   102   4   T.E.Bailey lbw   306   1
                                                                                                                 W.Barron c J.H.Cornford
                                                                                                                 M.F.Tremlett c and b
                                                                                                                 S.C.Griffith b
    b J.C.Laker   0   265   16.4 5   53   5   J.D.B.Robertson lbw   184
                                                                                                                 T.E.Bailey b
                                                                                                                 J.C.Laker c B.O.Allen
                                                                                                                 M.F.Tremlett c M.M.Walford
                                                                                                                 S.C.Griffith c B.O.Allen

486. Rest of England v Middlesex (Champion County), Kennington Oval, September 13, 15, 16, 17 (Middlesex won by nine wickets)
st W.F.F.Price
    b D.C.S.Compton   8   246   46.3   6   179   4   W.J.Edrich st T.G.Evans   543-9d
                                                                   D.C.S.Compton st T.G.Evans
                                                                    R.W.V.Robins c H.J.Butler
                                                                    W.F.F.Price c A.V.Bedser
c and b L.H.Gray   14   317   -   -   -   -   21-1

SEASON'S AVERAGES

Batting and Fielding	M	I	NO	Runs	HS	Ave	50	Ct	
Championship	26	37	9	291	26	10.39	-	10	
Other Glos matches	3	4	0	12	8	3.00	-	2	
Other matches	3	6	2	23	14	5.75	-	1	
Season	32	47	11	326	26	9.05	-	13	
Career	486	637	175	4408	71	9.54	4	273	

Bowling	O	M	R	W	BB	Ave	5i	10m	Strike	RunR
Championship	1196.1	291	3284	206	9-41	15.94	24	8	34.83	45.75
Other Glos matches	130	32	352	16	6-90	22.00	1	-	48.75	45.12
Other matches	124.1	21	483	16	5-53	30.18	1	-	46.56	64.83
Season (6b)	1450.2	344	4119	238	9-41	17.30	26	8	36.56	47.33
Career (6b) (8b)	17918.4 1131	4716 ⎱ 211 ⎰	48505	2475	10-113	19.59	216	75	47.09	41.61

1948

After the brilliance of the 1947 season Goddard had a fairly ordinary season in 1948. Perhaps some falling off was inevitable. His wickets fell from 238 to 125 and his average increased from 19.59 to 21.49. Nevertheless these were still very good returns for a man in his 48th year and it was the fourteenth consecutive season in which he had taken 100 wickets. There were still some outstanding analyses. He took 11 for 165 against Sussex at Eastbourne and 11 for 133 against the same County at Bristol. He took 6 for 16 in Nottinghamshire's second innings at Cheltenham and, altogether, he captured five wickets in an innings on ten occasions and ten wickets in a match twice. As a batsman he scored 263 runs in 35 innings and he held eleven catches. At the end of the season he had taken 2600 wickets in his career and those who thought his powers were waning would have been surprised to know that he would take a further 379 before he hung up his boots for the last time.

	Own Team Total	O	M	R	W		Opp Total	Ct
487. Gloucestershire v Oxford University, The Parks, May 1, 3, (4) (Match drawn)								
st W.W.Davidson b A.H.Kardar	1 156	33	8	109	3	W.G.Keighley c B.O.Allen H.A.Pawson b P.A.Whitcombe b	305	
		-	-	-	-		51-8	
488. Gloucestershire v Worcestershire, Gloucester, May 8, 10, 11 (Match drawn)								
c D.M.Young b L.F.Outschoorn	8 132	51.5	20	112	4	D.Kenyon c A.E.Wilson R.Howorth st A.E.Wilson R.O.Jenkins c B.O.Allen R.T.D.Perks c B.O.Allen	411	
did not bat	- 315-5							

489. Gloucestershire v Somerset, Taunton, May 15, 17, 18 (Gloucestershire won by an innings and 58 runs)
c E.Hill b M.F.Tremlett	28	522	32.2	12	65	6	N.S.Mitchell-Innes	
							c T.W.Graveney	245
							H.Gimblett c J.F.Crapp	
							M.F.Tremlett c G.E.E.Lambert	
							E.Hill b	
							A.W.Wellard c C.J.Scott	
							P.A.O.Graham c G.M.Emmett	
		17	4	38	1	S.S.Rogers b	219

490. Gloucestershire v Sussex, Bristol, May 19, 20, 21 (Gloucestershire won by 57 runs)
b J.Y.Oakes	5	224	27.2	11	40	5	C.Oakes c J.F.Crapp	153
							P.A.H.Carey b	
							J.Y.Oakes b	
							H.T.Bartlett c C.J.Barnett	
							J.H.Cornford c C.J.Barnett	
b J.H.Cornford	19	225	39.2	9	93	6	H.W.Parks c B.O.Allen	239
							J.G.Langridge b	
							D.V.Smith b	
							C.Oakes c B.O.Allen	
							J.Y.Oakes st A.E.Wilson	
							A.S.M.Oakman c G.E.E.Lambert	

491. Gloucestershire v Yorkshire, Bristol, May 22, 24, 25 (Gloucestershire won by six wickets)
c A.Coxon b J.H.Wardle	4	171	38	14	63	1	H.Halliday lbw	312-7d	
did not bat	-	392-4	31	4	80	5	J.V.Wilson c G.M.Emmett	247-8d	1
							W.Watson st A.E.Wilson		
							A.Coxon c C.Cook		
							T.F.Smailes c C.J.Barnett		
							J.H.Wardle c T.W.Graveney		

492. Gloucestershire v Surrey, Kennington Oval, May (29), (31), June 1 (Surrey won by 2 runs)
not out	0	131	20	2	57	4	H.S.Squires lbw	133	1
							J.F.Parker c J.F.Crapp		
							A.J.W.McIntyre st A.E.Wilson		
							B.Constable c and b		

493. Gloucestershire v Northamptonshire, Northampton, June (2), 3, 4 (Match drawn)
did not bat	-	229-7d	19	7	42	1	W.Barron b	135
did not bat	-	48-2d	13	3	54	2	D Brookes b	99-9
							W.Barron c C.J.Scott	

494. Gloucestershire v Hampshire, Gloucester, June 5, 7, 8 (Hampshire won by 137 runs)
b C.J.Knott	1	114	30	9	72	3	G.W.Dawson c B.O.Allen	258	1
							H.Dawson b		
							L.Harrison c G.M.Emmett		
run out	9	174	20	4	72	3	E.D.R.Eagar b	167	
							G.Hill lbw		
							C.J.Andrews b		

495. Gloucestershire v Essex, Ilford, June 9, 10, 11 (Essex won by an innings and 37 runs)
c R.Horsfall b K.C.Preston	27	251	32	5	92	2	S.J.Cray lbw	405	1
							F.H.Rist c J.F.Crapp		
c R.Horsfall b K.C.Preston	4	117							

496. Gloucestershire v Middlesex, Lord's, June 12, 14, 15 (Match drawn)
c A.W.Thompson b L.H.Gray	1	361	26	14	28	3	J.D.B.Robertson b	224	1
							A.Fairbairn b		
							F.G.Mann c and b		
			26	8	43	2	S.M.Brown c A.E.Wilson	327-7	
							H.P.H.Sharp b		

497. Gloucestershire v Warwickshire, Edgbaston, June 16, 17, 18 (Match drawn)
b T.L.Pritchard	9	223	25	6	60	3	F.C.Gardner lbw	167
							J.S.Ord c W.L.Neale	
							R.T.Spooner lbw	
did not bat	-	142-4d	14	2	35	2	C.W.C.Grove b	123-5
							T.L.Pritchard lbw	

498. Gloucestershire v Leicestershire, Bristol, June 19, 21 (Gloucestershire won by ten wickets)
b J.E.Walsh	1	367	21	3	54	0		252
did not bat	-	5-0	3	0	8	1	P.Corrall b	117

499. Gloucestershire v Lancashire, Old Trafford, June 26, (28), 29 (Match drawn)
b K.Cranston	3	150	15.1	0	29	2	T.L.Brierley lbw	170
							R.Pollard b	
			4	2	6	0		50-2

500. Gloucestershire v Warwickshire, Bristol, June 30, July 1, 2 (Gloucestershire won by 8 runs)
b T.L.Pritchard   6   178   46   13   73   2   F.C.Gardner   lbw   271
                                                              K.A.Taylor   lbw
lbw b W.E.Hollies   0   332   32.3 3   119 5   F.C.Gardner   b   231
                                                              K.A.Taylor   c J.F.Crapp
                                                              A.Townsend   lbw
                                                              T.L.Pritchard c C.Cook
                                                              W.E.Hollies c G.M.Emmett

501. Gloucestershire v Australians, Bristol, July 3, 5, 6 (Australians won by an innings and 363 runs)
c R.A.Saggers
         b I.W.G.Johnson   0   279   32   3   186 0   774-7d
not out   10   132

502. Gloucestershire v Derbyshire, Chesterfield, July 7, 8, 9 (Derbyshire won by two wickets)
c G.O.Dawkes b G.H.Pope   0   242   26   10   41   4   C.S.Elliott b   180
                                                              P.Vaulkhard b
                                                              A.C.Revill   lbw
                                                              G.O.Dawkes   c L.M.Cranfield
c A.C.Revill b C.Gladwin   21   215   19   5   53   1   A.E.G.Rhodes c and b   280-8   1

503. Gloucestershire v Lancashire, Bristol, July 10, 12, 13 (Match drawn)
not out   5   347-8d   23   3   76   2   A.Wharton   c C.I.Monks   350
                                                              P.Greenwood st A.E.Wilson
did not bat   -   139-4

504. Gloucestershire v Derbyshire, Bristol, July 14, 15, 16 (Derbyshire won by 87 runs)
c P.Vaulkhard b H.L.Jackson 0   202   18   7   43   2   G.H.Pope   lbw   207
                                                              G.O.Dawkes   c T.W.Graveney
not out   12   128   12   3   51   1   D.Smith   c G.E.E.Lambert   210

505. Gloucestershire v Worcestershire, Worcester, July 17, 19, 20 (Gloucestershire won by ten wickets)
not out   3   324-9d   8   3   17   0   143   1
did not bat   -   4-0   12.3 3   23   4   D.Kenyon   c G.E.E.Lambert   184
                                                              R.T.D.Perks c B.O.Allen
                                                              H.Yarnold   b
                                                              P.F.Jackson b

506. Gloucestershire v Hampshire, Bournemouth, July 24, 26, 27 (Hampshire won by eight wickets)
b C.J.Knott   7   187   31   4   88   5   G.W.Dawson   b   231
                                                              N.T.McCorkell b
                                                              G.Hill   c C.J.Scott
                                                              J.R.Gray   c A.G.S.Wilcox
                                                              O.W.Herman   c A.G.S.Wilcox
b O.W.Herman   14   225   9   1   37   0   182-2

507. Gloucestershire v Somerset, Bristol, July 31, August 2, 3 (Match drawn)
not out   18   379-8d   18   7   55   1   H.E.Watts   c A.E.Wilson   190
                                         18   5   31   2   E.Hill   c and b   135-5   1
                                                              H.E.Watts   c G.E.E.Lambert

508. Gloucestershire v Glamorgan, Ebbw Vale, August 4, 5, (6) (Match drawn)
c H.G.Davies b A.J.Watkins 1   148   63-4

509. Gloucestershire v Northamptonshire, Cheltenham, August 7, 9, 10 (Northamptonshire won by 20 runs)
not out   1   168   37.2 14   61   5   W.Barron   lbw   177
                                                              N.Oldfield   lbw
                                                              E.Davis   c B.O.Allen
                                                              V.Broderick b
                                                              R.G.Garlick lbw
b R.W.Clarke   1   197   27.4 4   71   2   D.Brookes   lbw   208-4d
                                                              E.Davis   b

510. Gloucestershire v Nottinghamshire, Cheltenham, August 11, 12, 13 (Gloucestershire won by an innings and 98 runs)
did not bat   -   354-5d   28   9   49   3   F.W.Stocks   b   168
                                                              A.Jepson   b
                                                              H.J.Butler   lbw
                                         11.4 5   16   6   W.W.Keeton   c B.O.Allen   88   1
                                                              F.H.Winrow   c and b
                                                              E.A.Meads   b
                                                              J.Hardstaff c B.O.Allen
                                                              F.W.Stocks   lbw
                                                              H.J.Butler   b

511. Gloucestershire v Surrey, Cheltenham, August 14, 16, 17 (Match drawn)
```
c E.A.Bedser b J.C.Laker    13   145        41.3   9   84   5   L.B.Fishlock  c C.J.Barnett    260
                                                                E.A.Bedser  b
                                                                A.J.W.McIntyre  b
                                                                T.H.Clark  b
                                                                J.W.J.McMahon  c G.M.Emmett
   not out                    0   124-9     -      -   -    -                                   175
```
512. Gloucestershire v Sussex, Eastbourne, August 21, 23, 24 (Gloucestershire won by an innings and 26 runs)
```
   run out                    7   443       29.1   5   115  4   J.G.Langridge  lbw              278
                                                                J.Langridge  lbw
                                                                P.D.S.Blake  lbw
                                                                R.T.Webb  b
                                            19     7   50   7   J.G.Langridge  c B.O.Allen      139    1
                                                                C.Oakes  c and b
                                                                G.Cox  b
                                                                J.Langridge  c L.M.Cranfield
                                                                P.D.S.Blake  c B.O.Allen
                                                                H.T.Bartlett  c T.W.Graveney
                                                                D.J.Wood  b
```
513. Gloucestershire v Kent, Gloucester, August 28, 30, 31 (Gloucestershire won by nine wickets)
```
   c H.J.Pocock b F.Ridgway  20   286       20.1   0   43   2   L.E.G.Ames  c and b              252    1
                                                                F.Ridgway  lbw
   did not bat                -   201-1     23     8   53   3   A.H.Phebey  hit wkt              233
                                                                B.H.Valentine  b
                                                                T.G.Evans  st A.E.Wilson
```

SEASON'S AVERAGES

Batting and Fielding	M	I	NO	Runs	HS	Ave	50	Ct
Championship	25	32	7	248	28	9.92	-	11
Other Glos matches	2	3	1	11	10*	5.50	-	-
Season	27	35	8	259	28	9.59	-	11
Career	513	672	183	4667	71	9.54	4	284

Bowling	O	M	R	W	BB	Ave	5i	10m	Strike	RunR
Championship	1015.3	267	2392	122	7-50	19.60	10	2	49.94	39.25
Other Glos matches	65	11	295	3	3-109	98.33	-	-	130.00	75.64
Season (6b)	1080.3	278	2687	125	7-50	21.49	10	2	51.86	41.44
Career (6b) (8b)	18999.1 1131	4994 } 211 }	51192	2600	10-113	19.68	226	57	47.32	41.60

1949

Goddard was back to his venomous best in 1949 taking 160 wickets in all matches at an average of 19.18, more than anyone else in the country apart from Eric Hollies who bowled more than 400 more overs for his 166 victims. Thirteen times did Goddard take five wickets in an innings and on five occasions he took ten wickets in a match. Outstanding performances were 13 for 111 against Lancashire at Old Trafford, 15 for 107, (including 9 for 61 in the second innings), against Derbyshire at Bristol, 11 for 141 against Kent at Bristol and 11 for 138 against Yorkshire at Huddersfield. He also took eight Warwickshire second innings wickets for 70 at Gloucester. As a batsman he scored 226 runs in 40 innings and he held fourteen catches.

```
                            Own Team    O    M    R    W                              Opp      Ct
                            Total                                                      Total
514. Gloucestershire v Oxford University, The Parks, April 30, May 2, 3 (Match drawn)
   c K.A.Shearwood
     b G.H.Chesterton        1   259     25   3    72   1   K.A.Shearwood  c C.I.Monks  328      1
   c C.R.D.Rudd b R.V.Divecha 0  253-9    -   -    -    -                               215-9d
515. Gloucestershire v Warwickshire, Edgbaston, May 7, 9, 10 (Warwickshire won by six wickets)
   b C.W.C.Grove              7   84      36   14   79   2   F.C.Gardner  lbw            269
                                                             R.T.Spooner  b
   c D.Flint b A.Townsend     5   347     11   1    28   0                               166-4
```

516. Gloucestershire v Sussex, Chichester, May 11, 12, 13 (Match drawn)
   not out   2   366   36   3   154   2   H.T.Bartlett
                                                              c G.E.E.Lambert   552-6d
                                                              S.C.Griffith c J.F.Crapp
   did not bat   -   280-4

517. Gloucestershire v Nottinghamshire, Trent Bridge, May 14, 16, 17 (Match drawn)
   did not bat   -   334-5   30   7   75   0   402   1

518. Gloucestershire v Sussex, Gloucester, May 21, 23, 24 (Gloucestershire won by four wickets)
   c J.Langridge b J.Y.Oakes 14 341   34   15 51   4   D.V.Smith c J.F.Crapp   241
                                                              J.Langridge c B.O.Allen
                                                              G.T.Hurst b
                                                              J.H.Cornford b
   did not bat   -   74-6   31   14 64   3   J.G.Langridge c A.E.Wilson 171
                                                              G.Cox b
                                                              G.T.Hurst c J.F.Crapp

519. Gloucestershire v Hampshire, Bristol, May 28, 30, 31 (Match drawn)
   c C.Walker b J.Bailey   1   260   32   3   133   4   N.H.Rogers c D.M.Young 256-8
                                                              N.T.McCorkell c C.A.Milton
                                                              J.Bailey c T.W.Graveney
                                                              D.R.Guard c C.A.Milton

520. Gloucestershire v Somerset, Taunton, June 4, 6 (Somerset won by eight wickets)
   c M.F.Tremlett b H.L.Hazell 7 123   24   6   110   7   H.Gimblett c A.E.Wilson 221   2
                                                              F.L.Angell c and b
                                                              M.Coope J.F.Crapp
                                                              G.E.S.Woodhouse b
                                                              S.S.Rogers c G.E.E.Lambert
                                                              M.F.Tremlett c T.W.Graveney
                                                              J.Lawrence c T.W.Graveney
   c and b H.L.Hazell   3   189   4   1   34   0   95-2

521. Gloucestershire v Lancashire, Old Trafford, June 8, 9, 10 (Gloucestershire won by nine wickets)
   hit wkt b K.J.Grieves   13 306   27   11 54   6   C.Washbrook c J.F.Crapp 204
                                                              N.D.Howard b
                                                              J.T.Ikin c J.F.Crapp
                                                              K.J.Grieves c T.W.Graveney
                                                              P.Greenwood lbw
                                                              W.B.Roberts b
   did not bat   -   54-1   28.5 6   57   7   W.Place c B.O.Allen   155   1
                                                              N.D.Howard b
                                                              J.T.Ikin b
                                                              P.Greenwood c T.W.Graveney
                                                              R.Pollard b
                                                              W.B.Roberts st A.E.Wilson
                                                              M.J.Hilton c C.A.Milton

522. Gloucestershire v Surrey, Kennington Oval, June 11, 13, 14 (Gloucestershire won by 40 runs)
   b J.C.Laker   0   232   19   4   48   2   G.J.Whittaker c and b   178   2
                                                              J.F.Parker c and b
   c H.S.Squires b P.Westerman 1 239   25   10 59   4   G.J.Whittaker c G.M.Emmett 253   1
                                                              J.F.Parker lbw
                                                              A.J.W.McIntyre c J.F.Crapp
                                                              J.C.Laker c B.O.Allen

523. Gloucestershire v Derbyshire, Bristol, June 18, 20 (Gloucestershire won by an innings and 1 run)
   b A.E.G.Rhodes   4   320   22.4 9   46   6   H.L.Johnson b   177   1
                                                              A.E.G.Rhodes c and b
                                                              F.E.Marsh lbw
                                                              K.A.Shearwood b
                                                              W.H.Copson b
                                                              H.L.Jackson c A.E.Wilson
                                         29.1 9   61   9   C.S.Elliott st A.E.Wilson 142
                                                              A.C.Revill lbw
                                                              H.L.Johnson lbw
                                                              A.E.G.Rhodes b
                                                              W.H.Copson b
                                                              D.A.Skinner c A.E.Wilson
                                                              F.E.Marsh c B.O.Allen
                                                              C.Gladwin c B.O.Allen
                                                              K.A.Shearwood st A.E.Wilson

524. Gloucestershire v Middlesex, Bristol, June 22, 23, 24 (Middlesex won by nine wickets)
    not out   14   189   60   13   137   3   W.J.Edrich lbw   357
                                                                          D.C.S.Compton c C.A.Milton
                                                                          A.W.Thompson lbw
    not out   9   246   10   2   40   1   J.D.B.Robertson
                                                                              st A.E.Wilson   82-1

525. Gloucestershire v Worcestershire, Dudley, June 25, 27, 28 (Match drawn)
    not out   10   337   38   12   92   1   R.O.Jenkins
                                                                              c J.K.R.Graveney   427-8d
    did not bat   -   163-6

526. Gloucestershire v Kent, Tunbridge Wells, June 29, 30 (Gloucestershire won by an innings and 102 runs)
    c P.Hearn b B.R.Edrich   0   417   -   -   -   -   182
                                                      14   2   37   4   R.Mayes st A.E.Wilson   133
                                                                                   B.R.Edrich lbw
                                                                                   E.Crush c C.A.Milton
                                                                                   D.G.Clark b

527. Gloucestershire v New Zealanders, Bristol, July 2, 4, 5 (New Zealanders won by seven wickets)
    not out   5   232   45.3   11   131   5   J.R.Reid c G.M.Emmett   252
                                                                                 M.P.Donnelly c C.A.Milton
                                                                                 W.A.Hadlee lbw
                                                                                 W.M.Wallace c G.M.Emmett
                                                                                 F.L.H.Mooney c B.O.Allen
    b T.B.Burtt   0   155   14.2   3   39   2   B.Sutcliffe b   138-3
                                                                                  G.O.Rabone hit wkt

528. Gloucestershire v Kent, Bristol, July 6, 7 (Gloucestershire won by seven wickets)
    not out   13   205   13.5   2   53   7   P.Hearn b   121
                                                                                  B.R.Edrich b
                                                                                  T.G.Evans c C.Cook
                                                                                 D.G.Clark b
                                                                                 A.F.H.Debnam c C.Cook
                                                                                  E.Crush b
                                                                                  R.R.Dovey b
    did not bat   -   129-3   21.2   3   88   4   L.E.G.Ames c and b   209   1
                                                                                  B.R.Edrich lbw
                                                                                  T.G.Evans c C.A.Milton
                                                                                  F.Ridgway c C.Cook

529. Gloucestershire v Hampshire, Portsmouth, July 9, 11, 12 (Match drawn)
    c and b C.J.Knott   9   489   41.1   13   99   4   G.W.Dawson lbw   365
                                                                                  G.Hill c G.E.E.Lambert
                                                                                  L.Harrison c A.E.Wilson
                                                                                  V.J.Ransom c J.F.Crapp
    did not bat   -   158-8d   17   6   40   3   J.Bailey c C.A.Milton   138-7   1
                                                                                  E.D.R.Eagar b
                                                                                  D.Shackleton b

530. Gloucestershire v Worcestershire, Gloucester, July 16, 18, 19 (Match drawn)
    c R.E.Bird b R.Howorth   1   193   5   1   22   0   224
    did not bat   -   113-5   18   1   48   6   D.Kenyon b   151-9d
                                                                                  R.O.Jenkins lbw
                                                                                  R.E.Bird b
                                                                                  R.E.S.Wyatt lbw
                                                                                  R.Howorth c D.M.Young
                                                                                  A.F.T.White c C.A.Milton

531. Gloucestershire v Warwickshire, Gloucester, July 20, 21, 22 (Warwickshire won by 112 runs)
    run out   6   288   25   3   86   2   J.S.Ord b   400-9d
                                                                                 H.E.Dollery c J.F.Crapp
    not out   0   157   14.3   3   70   8   K.A.Taylor c J.F.Crapp   157-9d
                                                                                  F.C.Gardner lbw
                                                                                  J.S.Ord lbw
                                                                                  H.E.Dollery c T.W.Graveney
                                                                                  A.V.G.Wolton b
                                                                                  A.H.Kardar c B.O.Allen
                                                                                  C.W.C.Grove b
                                                                                  T.L.Pritchard lbw

532. Gloucestershire v Lancashire, Bristol, July 23, 25, 26 (Gloucestershire won by ten wickets)
lbw b J.T.Ikin   7   305   38   18   59   5   J.M.Kelly b   220
                                                                A.Wharton lbw
                                                                N.D.Howard lbw
                                                                P.Greenwood lbw
                                                                A.Barlow b
did not bat   -   55-0   14   3   47   3   J.T.Ikin c T.W.Graveney   139   1
                                                                P.Greenwood lbw
                                                                R.Pollard c and b

533. Gloucestershire v Somerset, Bristol, July 30, August 1, 2 (Match drawn)
c M.Coope b H.L.Hazell   1   342   45.3   13   94   4   H.E.Watts b   224
                                                                H.F.T.Buse c C.A.Milton
                                                                M.Coope c C.Cook
                                                                H.W.Stephenson c G.M.Emmett
not out   3   101   20   7   55   1   M.M.Walford c C.Cook   132-6

534. Gloucestershire v Derbyshire, Chesterfield, August 3, 4, 5 (Gloucestershire won by 184 runs)
run out   20   198   9   2   24   3   J.D.Eggar lbw   149
                                                                D.A.Skinner b
                                                                G.O.Dawkes b
st G.O.Dawkes b D.B.Carr 13 302   5   0   21   0   167   1

535. Gloucestershire v Essex, Cheltenham, August 6, 8, 9 (Gloucestershire won by 253 runs)
c T.H.Wade b R.Smith   0   349   25   3   51   4   F.H.Vigar lbw   148
                                                                S.C.Eve b
                                                                D.J.Insole c C.Cook
                                                                T.P.B.Smith b
not out   3   250-8d   31   5   79   2   S.C.Eve c B.O.Allen   198
                                                                T.P.B.Smith c B.O.Allen

536. Gloucestershire v Surrey, Cheltenham, August 10, 11, 12 (Surrey won by an innings and 10 runs)
not out   18   168   37.1 8   98   3   E.A.Bedser c A.E.Wilson   374
                                                                M.R.Barton c A.E.Wilson
                                                                A.V.Bedser c A.E.Wilson
b A.V.Bedser   1   196

537. Gloucestershire v Glamorgan, Cheltenham, August 13, 15, 16 (Match drawn)
c P.B.Clift b W.Wooller 4   340   34   19   31   2   M.Robinson c A.E.Wilson   170
                                                                J.R.Pleass c A.E.Wilson
not out   7   180-8d   18   9   31   1   M.Robinson c C.A.Milton   180-3

538. Gloucestershire v Leicestershire, Grace Road, Leicester, August 17, 18, 19 (Gloucestershire won by an innings and 82 runs)
did not bat   -   449-8d   22.3 11   26   2   T.A.Chapman c G.M.Emmett   195   1
                                                                P.Corrall c and b
                                      19.1 8   40   4   T.A.Chapman lbw   172
                                                                G.Evans st A.E.Wilson
                                                                J.E.Walsh c C.J.Scott
                                                                P.Corrall b

539. Gloucestershire v Northamptonshire, Northampton, August 20, 22, 23 (Northamptonshire won by an innings and 13 runs)
not out   3   253   46.2 11   133   5   W.Barron c J.F.Crapp   448
                                                                F.Jakeman c A.E.Wilson
                                                                E.Davis c T.W.Graveney
                                                                A.E.Nutter st A.E.Wilson
                                                                K.Fiddling c G.E.E.Lambert
not out   4   182

540. Gloucestershire v Yorkshire, Huddersfield, August 24, 25, 26 (Yorkshire won by three wickets)
c D.B.Close b C.W.Foord 1   77   24.1 8   55   6   W.Watson lbw   161
                                                                N.W.D.Yardley c B.O.Allen
                                                                D.B.Close c J.F.Crapp
                                                                A.Coxon b
                                                                J.H.Wardle b
                                                                D.V.Brennan c J.F.Crapp
c D.V.Brennan b D.B.Close 15 213   32   6   83   5   L.Hutton c A.E.Wilson   130-7
                                                                W.Watson b
                                                                J.V.Wilson c J.F.Crapp
                                                                D.B.Close c J.K.R.Graveney
                                                                A.Coxon lbw

541. Gloucestershire v Northamptonshire, Bristol, August 27, 29, 30 (Match drawn)
c N.Oldfield b F.R.Brown   1   366   6.1   1   17   3   D.Brookes lbw   460-6d
                                                                  D.W.Barrrick b
                                                                  F.R.Brown st A.E.Wilson
                                             9   3   18   0   164-4

SEASON'S AVERAGES

Batting and Fielding	M	I	NO	Runs	HS	Ave	50	Ct
Championship	26	36	12	220	20	9.16	-	13
Other Glos matches	2	4	1	6	5*	2.00	-	1
Season	28	40	13	226	20	8.37	-	14
Career	541	712	176	4893	71	9.12	4	298

Bowling	O	M	R	W	BB	Ave	5i	10m	Strike	RunR
Championship	1103.3	309	2827	152	9-61	18.59	12	5	43.55	42.69
Other Glos matches	84.5	17	242	8	5-131	30.25	1	-	63.62	47.54
Season (6b)	1188.2	326	3069	160	9-61	19.18	13	5	44.56	43.04
Career (6b)	20187.3	5320 ⎫	54261	2760	10-113	19.65	239	82	47.16	41.68
(8b)	1131	211 ⎭								

1950

Goddard took 100 wickets for the sixteenth and last time in the 1950 season bowling, as usual, more overs than anybody else for Gloucestershire and taking 131 wickets in the Championship and 137 in all first-class matches at an average of 19.99. At Bristol between 17th and 23rd June he took 20 wickets in the matches against Derbyshire and Hampshire at an average of 12.45. Against Sussex at Worthing he took 13 for 95 including an analysis of 8 for 37 as Sussex were dismissed in their second innings for 82. In all he took five wickets in an innings nine times and ten wickets in a match on three occasions. As a batsman he scored 168 runs in 34 innings and he held five catches to take his career total beyond 300.

	Own Team Total	O	M	R	W		Opp Total	Ct
542. Gloucestershire v Oxford University, The Parks, April (29), May 1, 2 (Match drawn)								
not out	8	155	30.5	6	73	3	M.B.Hofmeyr	
							c T.W.Graveney	264
							P.D.S.Blake c B.O.Allen	
							D.C.Candler c B.O.Allen	
did not bat	-	106-2						
543. Gloucestershire v Warwickshire, Gloucester, May 6, (8), 9 (Match drawn)								
did not bat	-	197-5d	33.2	17	45	6	A.V.G.Wolton b	165	1
							H.E.Roberts c G.M.Emmett	
							A.H.Kardar c J.F.Crapp	
							C.W.C.Grove c and b	
							T.L.Pritchard c C.J.Scott	
							W.E.Hollies c T.W.Graveney	
	4	1	10	0				25-0
544. Gloucestershire v Kent, Bristol, May 13, 15, 16 (Match drawn)								
lbw b D.V.P.Wright	13	379	23	8	42	1	T.G.Evans c J.K.R.Graveney	193
not out	0	193-9	23	3	62	1	A.H.Phebey c C.Cook	386-9d
545. Gloucestershire v Yorkshire, Bristol, May 17, 18, 19 (Match drawn)								
not out	1	269	40.3	11	108	2	F.A.Lowson lbw	404
							F.S.Trueman c C.J.Scott	
not out	2	229-8	2	0	11	1	J.H.Wardle c A.E.Wilson	141-5d
546. Gloucestershire v Worcestershire, Worcester, May 20, 22, 23 (Gloucestershire won by ten wickets)								
b R.Howorth	4	352	24	12	40	2	G.Dews lbw	164
							L.F.Outschoorn lbw	
did not bat	-	36-0	26.1	10	43	3	L.F.Outschoorn lbw	223
							H.Yarnold b	
							P.F.Jackson b	

547. Gloucestershire v Somerset, Taunton, May 27, 29, 30 (Match drawn)
    b J.Lawrence   2   375   31   11   62   3   S.S.Rogers   lbw   382   1
                                                              H.L.Hazell   c G.E.E.Lambert
                                                              E.P.Robinson   c T.W.Graveney
    not out   0   197-8d   8   1   23   2   F.L.Angell   lbw   121-6
                                                              J.Lawrence   c J.F.Crapp

548. Gloucestershire v Nottinghamshire, Bristol, June 3, 5, 6 (Match drawn)
    not out   1   518-8d   37.2 13   65   4   F.H.Winrow
                                                                c G.E.E.Lambert   321
                                                              F.W.Stocks   c C.J.Scott
                                                              W.A.Sime   b
                                                              E.A.Meads   c G.M.Emmett
                                          11   5   17   0   119-3

549. Gloucestershire v Lancashire, Gloucester, June 7, 8, 9 (Lancashire won by 82 runs)
    not out   12   131   20   9   42   0   164
    not out   0   114   21.2   7   43   2   R.Tattersall c D.M.Young   163
                                                              A.Barlow   lbw

550. Gloucestershire v Glamorgan, Gloucester, June 10, 12, 13 (Glamorgan won by 22 runs)
    b B.L.Muncer   0   331   25   7   54   1   M.Robinson b   400
    lbw b B.L.Muncer   3   184   11.5   3   31   5   W.G.A.Parkhouse
                                                                c G.E.E.Lambert   137
                                                              W.E.Jones   c C.J.Scott
                                                              J.E.McConnon lbw
                                                              H.G.Davies b
                                                              N.G.Hever   b

551. Gloucestershire v Lancashire, Old Trafford, June 14, 15, 16 (Match drawn)
    b M.J.Hilton   29   239   14   4   55   2   A.Wharton   c C.A.Milton   214
                                                              J.G.Lomax   c T.W.Graveney
    did not bat   -   106-3   32.4   6   109   4   J.T.Ikin   st A.E.Wilson   294-8d
                                                              K.J.Grieves   c C.Cook
                                                              R.Tattersall st A.E.Wilson
                                                              M.J.Hilton   c G.E.E.Lambert

552. Gloucestershire v Derbyshire, Bristol, June 17, 19, 20 (Gloucestershire won by 81 runs)
    c C.S.Elliott b H.L.Jackson   2   104   44.3 13   100   4   J.M.Kelly   lbw   314
                                                              A.E.G.Rhodes   c J.F.Crapp
                                                              P.Vaulkhard   b
                                                              D.C.Morgan   c C.A.Milton
    c G.O.Dawkes
      b A.E.G.Rhodes   16   381   15   5   42   7   J.M.Kelly   lbw   90
                                                              A.C.Revill   c A.E.Wilson
                                                              G.O.Dawkes   c J.F.Crapp
                                                              D.Smith   c J.F.Crapp
                                                              H.L.Johnson   c T.W.Graveney
                                                              A.E.G.Rhodes   c J.F.Crapp
                                                              P.Vaulkhard   lbw

553. Gloucestershire v Hampshire, Bristol, June (21), 22, 23 (Hampshire won by 83 runs)
    did not bat   -   186-2d   28   6   67   5   N.H.Rogers   lbw   169   1
                                                              J.R.Gray   lbw
                                                              E.D.R.Eagar   c and b
                                                              D.Shackleton   b
                                                              R.A.Dare   lbw
    b C.J.Knott   0   53   14.5   3   40   4   N.H.Rogers   b   153   1
                                                              J.R.Gray   lbw
                                                              E.D.R.Eagar   b
                                                              R.A.Dare   c J.K.R.Graveney

554. Gloucestershire v Essex, Colchester, June 24, 26, 27 (Gloucestershire won by six wickets)
    not out   8   292   18   6   33   3   F.H.Vigar   lbw   253
                                                              S.J.Cray   lbw
                                                              J.M.Leiper   c J.F.Crapp
    did not bat   -   141-4   28   10   45   1   T.P.B.Smith   b   176

555. Gloucestershire v Cambridge University, Bristol, July 1, 3, 4 (Match drawn)
    not out   18   373   34   11   63   3   J.G.Dewes   c C.J.Scott   335-8
                                                              M.H.Stevenson   b
                                                              T.U.Wells   st R.B.Wood

556. Gloucestershire v Sussex, Worthing, July 5, 6, 7 (Gloucestershire won by an innings and 102 runs)
b J.H.Cornford   4   383   34   17   58   5   D.V.Smith   c J.F.Crapp   199
                                                              G.Cox   c A.E.Wilson
                                                              J.Langridge   lbw
                                                              J.Y.Oakes   c C.A.Milton
                                                              K.G.Suttle   c B.O.Allen
                                       29   14   37   8   J.G.Langridge   lbw   82
                                                              D.V.Smith   b
                                                              C.Oakes   c C.J.Scott
                                                              G.Cox   lbw
                                                              J.Y.Oakes   lbw
                                                              K.G.Suttle   c G.E.E.Lambert
                                                              J.H.Cornford   c C.Cook
                                                              D.J.Wood   b
557. Gloucestershire v Glamorgan, Llanelli, July 8, 10, 11 (Match drawn)
st H.G.Davies b N.G.Hever   5   195   42   12   97   4   D.E.Davies   c G.M.Emmett   405
                                                              W.G.A.Parkhouse   c sub
                                                              A.J.Watkins   b
did not bat   -   85-1   J.E.Pleass   lbw
558. Gloucestershire v Surrey, Kennington Oval, July 12, 13, 14 (Surrey won by 183 runs)
c E.A.Bedser b A.V.Bedser   5   147   28   6   54   3   E.A.Bedser   b   278
                                                              T.H.Clark   b
                                                              B.Constable   c A.E.Wilson
b J.C.Laker   1   210   23   2   80   2   A.J.W.McIntyre
                                                                   c D.M.Young   262
                                                              J.C.Laker   c D.M.Young
559. Gloucestershire v Sussex, Bristol, July (15), (17), 18 (Gloucestershire won by two wickets)
not out   4   189-8 27   8   95   2   D.S.Sheppard
                                                                   c T.W.Graveney   188-3d
                                                              G.H.G.Doggart   c A.E.Wilson
560. Gloucestershire v Surrey, Bristol, July 19, 20, 21 (Surrey won by five wickets)
c G.J.Whittaker b J.C.Laker   0   187 28   7   72   4   P.B.H.May   b   151
                                                              A.J.W.McIntyre   lbw
                                                              J.C.Laker   b
                                                              W.S.Surridge   c A.E.Wilson
b G.A.R.Lock   0   173   28   7   74   2   B.Constable   lbw   211-5
                                                              G.J.Whittaker   b
561. Gloucestershire v Warwickshire, Edgbaston, July 22, 24, 25 (Match drawn)
c A.Townsend b A.H.Kardar   3   82   36   13   59   6   F.C.Gardner   b   171   1
                                                              J.B.Guy   c G.E.E.Lambert
                                                              A.V.G.Wolton   lbw
                                                              C.W.C.Grove   lbw
                                                              H.E.Dollery   c G.E.E.Lambert
did not bat   -   245-3   A.Townsend   c A.E.Wilson
562. Gloucestershire v Yorkshire, Hull, July 26, 27, 28 (Yorkshire won by an innings and 41 runs)
not out   3   198   42   14   89   2   W.H.H.Sutcliffe   lbw   348
                                                              J.H.Wardle   c C.A.Milton
c J.Firth b E.Leadbeater   2   109
563. Gloucestershire v Kent, Maidstone, July 29, 31, August 1 (Match drawn)
run out   5   199   19.1 6   30   2   B.R.Edrich   c G.M.Emmett   215
                                                              R.R.Dovey   c G.E.E.Lambert
c F.Ridgway b R.R.Dovey   6   236-9d 19   12   35   1   H.A.Pawson   c B.O.Allen   92-6
564. Gloucestershire v Northamptonshire, Bristol, August (2), 3, 4 (Match drawn)
c G.H.J.Brice b R.G.Garlick   5   200 34   10   89   4   L.Livingston   c C.J.Scott   180
                                                              W.Barron   c C.A.Milton
                                                              G.H.J.Brice   lbw
                                                              A.E.Nutter   c B.O.Allen
did not bat   -   78-4   19   4   45   1   N.Oldfield   lbw   178-1d

565. Gloucestershire v Somerset, Bristol, August 5, 7, 8 (Match drawn)
c H.W.Stephenson
          b J.Lawrence   5   276   25.2   9   50   5   M.M.Walford
                                                                c D.T.L.Bailey   275
                                                                M.F.Tremlett c C.A.Milton
                                                                H.W.Stephenson b
                                                                E.P.Robinson b
                                                                H.L.Hazell b
did not bat   -   40-1   33   11   69   2   H.Gimblett lbw   261-6d
                                                                H.F.T.Buse b

566. Gloucestershire v Derbyshire, Derby, August 9, 10, 11 (Match drawn)
did not bat   -   475-7d   34   10   77   2   A.C.Revill b   329
                                                                P.Vaulkhard b
did not bat   -   123-4d   10   3   29   2   C.S.Elliott st A.E.Wilson   164-5
                                                                P.Vaulkhard c T.W.Graveney

567. Gloucestershire v Middlesex, Cheltenham, August 12, 14, 15 (Match drawn)
c R.S.Cooper b J.J.Warr   1   440   23   3   76   0   296

568. Gloucestershie v Worcestershire, Cheltenham, August 16, 17, 18 (Match drawn)
did not bat   -   70-6d   28   12   54   1   R.Howorth c D.T.L.Bailey   205-9d
did not bat   1   111-5   -   -   -   -   71-5d

569. Gloucestershire v Hampshire, Bournemouth, September 2, 4, 5 (Gloucestershire won by nine wickets)
did not bat   -   304-7d   39.2   13   65   6   A.W.H.Rayment b   133
                                                                C.Walker c G.M.Emmett
                                                                J.R.Gray lbw
                                                                A.F.H.Debnam c G.E.E.Lambert
                                                                V.H.D.Cannings c J.F.Crapp
                                                                C.J.Knott c T.W.Graveney
did not bat   -   18-1   34.1   8   80   4   N.H.Rogers c G.E.E.Lambert 188
                                                                L.Harrison st A.E.Wilson
                                                                D.Shackleton c C.A.Milton
                                                                C.J.Knott c B.O.Allen

SEASON'S AVERAGES

Batting and Fielding	M	I	NO	Runs	HS	Ave	50	Ct
Championship	26	32	10	142	29	6.45	-	5
Other Glos matches	2	2	2	26	18*	-	-	-
Season	28	34	12	168	29	7.63	-	5
Career	569	746	208	5061	71	9.40	4	303

Bowling	O	M	R	W	BB	Ave	5i	10m	Strike	RunR
Championship	1171.3	372	2603	131	8-37	19.87	9	3	53.65	37.03
Other Glos matches	64.5	17	136	6	3-62	22.66	-	-	64.83	34.96
Season (6b)	1236.2	389	2739	137	8-37	19.99	9	3	54.14	36.92
Career (6b)	21424.1	5709	57000	2897	10-113	19.67	248	85	47.49	41.42
(8b)		1131	211							

1951

Goddard had the misfortune to contract pneumonia and pleurisy in July 1951 and because of this did not play after the middle of July. He only played in eleven of Gloucestershire's games and in these he took just 37 wickets at the much increased average of 28.45. On no occasion did he take more than five wickets in an innings and his best overall performance was against Derbyshire at the end of May when he took 4 for 42 in the first innings and 3 for 5 in 1.4 overs in the second. As a batsman he scored 63 runs in eighteen innings and he held four catches.

	Own Team Total	O	M	R	W		Opp Total	Ct

570. Gloucestershire v Derbyshire, Derby, May 26, 28, 29 (Gloucestershire won by 67 runs)
  b A.E.G.Rhodes   1 104   13   5   42   4   P.Vaulkhard c C.A.Milton   196   1
                                                             A.E.G.Rhodes c and b
                                                             D.C.Morgan b
                                                             G.O.Dawkes c C.A.Milton
  c J.M.Kelly b D.C.Morgan   0 251   1.4   1   5   3   G.L.Willatt c A.E.Wilson   92
                                                             G.O.Dawkes c C.A.Milton
                                                             B.H.Richardson c J.F.Crapp

571. Gloucestershire v Yorkshire, Bradford, May 30, 31, June 1 (Yorkshire won by nine wickets)
  c N.W.D.Yardley
           b R.Appleyard   4 257   39.1 13   96   2   H.Halliday lbw   349
                                                              R.Appleyard c C.Cook
  run out   0 109   -   -   -   -   18-1

572. Gloucestershire v Lancashire, Bristol, June 2, 4, 5 (Match drawn)
  c G.A.Edrich b M.J.Hilton   6 378   19   3   62   1   A.Barlow b   384   1
                                          4   0   20   0   144-1

573. Gloucestershire v Surrey, Kennington Oval, June 6, 7, 8 (Match drawn)
  b E.A.Bedser   2 438   28   5   82   3   L.B.Fishlock c A.E.Wilson   426
                                                             A.J.W.McIntyre b
                                                             J.W.J.McMahon c J.F.Crapp
  not out   2 252   18   2   79   3   T.H.Clark b T.W.Graveney   210-8
                                                             A.F.Brazier lbw
                                                             A.J.W.McIntyre b

574. Gloucestershire v Middlesex, Lord's, June 9, 11, 12 (Middlesex won by 144 runs)
  not out   6 249   -   -   -   -   234
  not out   0   95   10   1   37   1   A.W.Thompson b   254-6d

575. Gloucestershire v Hampshire, Gloucester, June 13, 14, 15 (Match drawn)
  b V.H.D.Cannings   1 200   30   4   89   3   E.D.R.Eagar b   472   1
                                                             C.Walker c G.E.E.Lambert
                                                             D.Shackleton b
  did not bat   - 235-3

576. Gloucestershire v Derbyshire, Gloucester, June 16, 18, 19 (Match drawn)
  lbw b H.L.Jackson   6 355   26.2 7   73   3   G.L.Willatt c A.E.Wilson   324   1
                                                             G.O.Dawkes c and b
                                                             H.L.Jackson c R.B.Nicholls
  not out   1 150-8d 15   5   45   4   P.Vaulkhard b   147-9
                                                             C.Gladwin c D.M.Young
                                                             G.O.Dawkes c C.J.Scott
                                                             B.H.Richardson c A.E.Wilson

577. Gloucestershire v Warwickshire, Bristol, June 23, 25, 26 (Warwickshire won by eight wickets)
  not out   2 330   42   11   97   3   F.C.Gardner lbw   374-9d
                                                             A.Townsend st A.E.Wilson
                                                             T.L.Pritchard lbw
  not out   15 163   5   0   25   0   121-2

578. Gloucestershire v Warwickshire, Coventry, June 30, July 2, 3 (Warwickshire won by three wickets)
  R.T.Spooner b T.L.Pritchard   1 163   12   3   49   0   313
  c R.T.Spooner
           b T.L.Pritchard   0 328   8.2   1   33   1   H.E.Dollery b   179-7

579. Gloucestershire v Sussex, Hove, July 7, 9, 10 (Sussex won by an innings and 14 runs)
  not out   0 103   24   4   68   2   J.Langridge c J.F.Crapp   376-8d
                                                             D.L.Bates b
  b D.J.Wood   16 259

580. Gloucestershire v Northamptonshire, Bristol, July 11, 12, 13 (Match drawn)
  did not bat   - 288-8d 32   10   85   3   D.Brookes b   212
                                                             E.Davis lbw
                                                             J.M.Warrington c G.M.Emmett
  did not bat   - 262-3d 14   1   66   1   V.Broderick c C.A.Milton   230-6

SEASON'S AVERAGES

Batting and Fielding	M	I	NO	Runs	HS	Ave	50	Ct
Championship	11	18	7	63	16	5.72	-	4
Career	580	764	215	5124	71	9.33	4	307

Bowling	O	M	R	W	BB	Ave	5i	10m	Strike	RunR
Championship	341.3	76	1053	37	4-42	28.45	-	-	55.37	51.39
Career (6b)	21765.4	5785 ⎫	58053	2934	10-113	19.78	248	85	47.59	41.57
(8b)		1131	211 ⎭							

1952

In Goddard's last season in 1952 he played in thirteen Championship matches taking 45 wickets at an average of 23.62. There were still some outstanding performances. His 44 overs against Somerset to take 7 wickets for 93 recalled his best days and he also took five wickets in an innings against Middlesex and Hampshire. In his 52nd year his stamina seemed as good as ever but, with new spinners coming through the ranks in John Mortimore and Brian Wells he felt it was time to finish. His 2979 first-class wickets are, and seem likely to remain, the fifth greatest number ever taken by a bowler. As a batsman in this final season he scored 110 runs in eleven innings and he held five catches.

	Own Team Total	O	M	R	W		Opp Total	Ct
581. Gloucestershire v Sussex, Bristol, May 28, 29, 30 (Match drawn)
did not bat	- 447-7d	8.4	2	19	1	D.J.Wood b	208	
		20	6	36	2	N.I.Thomson lbw	242-9	
						R.T.Webb lbw		
582. Gloucestershire v Yorkshire, Harrogate, June 11, 12, 13 (Yorkshire won by seven wickets)
c D.V.Brennan b N.W.D.Yardley	17 232	14	3	50	1	L.Hutton c and b	406-7d	1
b W.E.N.Holdsworth	0 286	-	-	-	-		113-3	
583. Gloucestershire v Worcestershire, Worcester, June 14, 16, 17 (Match drawn)
did not bat	- 345-5d	28	9	50	1	L.N.Devereux b	346-6d	
did not bat	- 273-3d	6	2	22	0		155-5	
584. Gloucestershire v Middlesex, Gloucester, June 25, 26, 27 (Middlesex won by 71 runs)
did not bat	- 331-5d	18	5	41	1	D.Bennett c A.E.Wilson	294-7d	
not out	0 144	24	3	63	5	J.D.B.Robertson		
						c A.E.Wilson	252-6d	1
						W.J.Edrich c D.M.Young		
						D.C.S.Compton b		
						W.Knightley-Smith c C.A.Milton		
						A.W.Thompson c and b		
585. Gloucestershire v Hampshire, Southampton, July 2, 3, 4 (Gloucestershire won by six wickets)
c J.R.Gray b D.Shackleton	7 231	7	1	25	2	V.H.D.Cannings b	188	
						R.A.Dare c C.A.Milton		
did not bat	- 148-4	33	5	79	4	J.R.Gray c C.J.Scott	188	
						E.D.R.Eagar b		
						C.Walker c D.T.L.Bailey		
						R.O.Prouton c J.F.Crapp		
586. Gloucestershire v Worcestershire, Bristol, July 5, 7, 8 (Gloucestershire won by four wickets)
did not bat	- 142-5d	22	8	38	0		337	1
did not bat	- 259-6	-	-	-	-		63-1d	
587. Gloucestershire v Glamorgan, Ebbw Vale, July 12, 14, 15 (Gloucestershire won by eight wickets)
c D.E.Davies b B.L.Muncer	18 184	25	4	59	3	W.G.A.Parkhouse		
						st A.E.Wilson	209	
						B.L.Muncer b		
						H.G.Davies b		
did not bat	- 191-2	7	2	19	0		165	
588. Gloucestershire v Sussex, Hove, July 16, 17, 18 (Gloucestershire won by an innings and 4 runs)
c J.G.Langridge b J.H.Cornford	13 348	-	-	-	-		139	
		25	11	41	3	D.V.Smith c C.A.Milton	205	
						A.E.James b		
						J.Langridge c C.J.Scott		

589. Gloucestershire v Hampshire, Bristol, July 19, 21, 22 (Hampshire won by seven wickets)
c R.A.Carty b D.Shackleton 16   256   37.4 12   79   5   N.H.Rogers c D.T.L.Bailey   240
                                                                    J.R.Gray c J.F.Crapp
                                                                    R.A.Dare b
                                                                    R.A.Carty c I.N.Mitchell
                                                                    R.O.Prouton b
lbw b R.A.Dare   0   115   12   5   30   0   135-3

590. Gloucestershire v Lancashire, Old Trafford, July 26, 28, 29 (Match drawn)
c A.Wilson b J.B.Statham   5   266   5   1   33   0   402-8d
did not bat   - 285-4d

591. Gloucestershire v Somerset, Bristol, August 2, 4, 5 (Match drawn)
did not bat   - 349-4d   7   4   16   3   G.G.Tordoff lbw   131
                                                                    R.Smith c D.T.L.Bailey
                                                                    E.P.Robinson b
did not bat   - 38-1   44   14   93   7   H.Gimblett c D.M.Young   265   1
                                                                    G.G.Tordoff c J.F.Crapp
                                                                    M.F.Tremlett c D.M.Young
                                                                    H.E.Watts st A.E.Wilson
                                                                    R.Smith c and b
                                                                    S.S.Rogers c D.M.Young
                                                                    J.Redman c C.A.Milton

592. Gloucestershire v Nottinghamshire, Bristol, August 27, 28, 29 (Nottinghamshire won by 130 runs)
did not bat   - 323-7d   24   6   60   1   F.W.Stocks c T.W.Graveney 311-6d
lbw b F.W.Stocks   19   122   27   7   89   2   R.J.Giles c A.E.Wilson   264-7d
                                                                    F.W.Stocks c G.M.Emmett

593. Gloucestershire v Northamptonshire, Gloucester, August 30, September 1, 2 (Match drawn)
not out   15   328-7d   9   0   48   0   324
did not bat   - 155-5   19   3   73   4   V.Broderick b   264-7d
                                                                    N.Oldfield c G.E.E.Lambert
                                                                    D.W.Barrick b
                                                                    A.E.Nutter c D.M.Young

SEASON'S AVERAGES

Batting and Fielding	M	I	NO	Runs	HS	Ave	50	Ct
Championship	13	11	2	110	19	12.22	-	5
Career	593	775	217	5234	71	9.37	4	312

Bowling	O	M	R	W	BB	Ave	5i	10m	Strike	RunR
Championship (6b)	424.2	113	1063	45	7-93	23.62	3	1	56.57	41.75
Career (6b)	22189.4	5898 ⎱	59116	2979	10-113	19.84	251	86	47.72	41.57
(8b)		1131 ⎰	211							

A note on grounds:
All references to Bristol other than where specifically stated otherwise refer to the County Ground, Nevill Road, references to Cheltenham, unless stated otherwise, refer to the Cheltenham College ground, and references to Gloucester, unless otherwise stated, refer to the Tuffley Avenue ground.

Season by Season (Batting and Fielding)

Season		M	I	NO	R	HS	Ave	50	Ct
1922		2	3	3	28	20*	-	-	-
1923		16	26	10	44	15	2.75	-	6
1924		9	11	5	15	5*	2.50	-	6
1925		11	16	6	78	30	7.80	-	5
1926		29	48	14	317	47	9.32	-	26
1927		18	24	11	147	29*	11.30	-	11
1929		31	37	13	203	27*	8.45	-	22
1930		31	35	5	191	24	6.36	-	13
1930/31	South Africa	7	6	0	53	25	8.83	-	1
1931		32	33	7	93	14	3.57	-	17
1932		29	40	16	373	71	15.54	1	20
1933		31	46	11	470	45	13.42	-	19
1934		25	36	8	241	30	8.60	-	19
1935		31	44	4	410	35	10.25	-	16
1936		29	36	7	376	67	12.96	1	17
1937		33	48	13	421	61*	12.02	1	21
1938		22	27	8	133	24	7.00	-	8
1938/39	South Africa	10	8	2	76	33	12.66	-	2
1939		29	33	11	215	56*	9.77	1	14
1946		29	33	10	198	22	8.60	-	17
1947		32	47	11	326	26	9.05	-	13
1948		27	35	8	259	28	9.59	-	11
1949		28	40	13	226	20	8.37	-	14
1950		28	34	12	168	29	7.63	-	5
1951		11	18	7	63	16	5.72	-	4
1952		13	11	2	110	19	12.22	-	5
Totals		593	775	217	5234	71	9.37	4	312

Season by Season (Bowling)

		O	M	R	W	BB	Ave	5wi	10wm	S/Rate	R/Rate
1922		18	5	48	1	1-48	48.00	-	-	108.00	44.44
1923		262.1	56	728	25	6-41	29.12	2	-	62.92	46.28
1924		141.5	26	415	22	6-23	18.86	2	-	38.68	48.76
1925		122	18	378	8	3-73	47.25	-	-	91.50	51.63
1926		797.2	162	2115	71	6-62	29.78	2	-	67.38	44.20
1927		465.5	75	1529	26	5-92	58.80	1	-	107.50	54.70
1929		1286.5	361	3015	184	9-21	16.38	16	6	41.96	39.04
1930		1402.4	435	2819	144	8-44	19.57	10	2	58.44	33.49
1930/31	(SA)	159.1	40	380	13	4-43	29.23	-	-	73.46	39.79
1931		1193.1	374	2636	141	8-79	18.69	8	2	50.77	36.82
1932		1316	343	3258	170	7-19	19.16	14	6	46.44	41.26
1933		1371.5	414	3187	183	8-77	17.41	18	7	44.97	38.71
1934		1185.2	314	3031	126	9-37	24.05	9	4	56.44	42.61
1935		1552.5	384	4073	200	8-139	20.36	18	6	46.58	44.21
1936		1425.4	423	3106	153	8-64	20.30	15	3	55.90	36.31
1937		1479.1	364	4158	248	10-113	16.76	32	13	35.78	46.85
1938		971.1	201	2625	114	8-62	23.02	10	4	51.11	45.04
1938/39	(8b) (SA)	311	72	817	31	6-38	26.35	1	-	80.25	32.83
1939	(8b)	820	139	2973	200	9-38	14.86	20	8	32.80	45.32
1946		1317.2	377	3095	177	9-82	17.48	12	6	44.65	39.15
1947		1450.2	344	4119	238	9-41	17.30	26	8	36.56	47.33
1948		1080.5	278	2687	125	7-50	21.49	10	2	51.86	41.44
1949		1188.2	326	3069	160	9-61	19.18	13	5	44.56	43.04
1950		1236.2	389	2739	137	8-37	19.99	9	3	54.14	36.92
1951		341.3	76	1053	37	4-42	28.45	-	-	55.37	51.39
1952		424.2	113	1063	45	7-93	23.62	3	1	56.57	41.75
Totals (6-ball)		22189.4	5898 }	59116	2979	10-113	19.84	251	86	47.72	41.57
(8-ball)		1131	211 }								

Five Wickets in an Innings (251)

For Gloucestershire - 245

Figures	Opponent	Venue	Year
5-19	v Surrey	Bristol	1923
6-41	v Lancashire	Gloucester	1923
5-58	v Sussex	Eastbourne	1924
6-23	v Glamorgan	Cheltenham (Victoria)	1924
5-123	v Hampshire	Gloucester	1926
6-62	v Essex	Bristol	1926
5-92	v Leicestershire	Hinckley	1927
7-25 } 6-95 }	v Middlesex	Lord's	1929
6-68	v South Africans	Bristol	1929
5-35 } 5-76 }	v Hampshire	Southampton	1929
8-117 } 5-37 }	v Worcestershire	Gloucester	1929
9-21	v Cambridge University	Cheltenham (Victoria)	1929
5-95	v Leicestershire	Leicester (Aylestone Rd)	1929
5-89 } 6-72 }	v Lancashire	Bristol	1929
8-89	v Leicestershire	Bristol	1929
7-65	v Glamorgan	Swansea	1929
5-66	v Glamorgan	Clifton	1929
6-85	v Sussex	Cheltenham	1929
7-46	v Hampshire	Cheltenham (Victoria)	1929
7-60	v Lancashire	Old Trafford	1930
5-67	v Surrey	Kennington Oval	1930
5-43	v Hampshire	Southampton	1930
5-66	v Essex	Chelmsford	1930
5-54	v Sussex	Gloucester	1930
5-79	v Hampshire	Gloucester	1930
7-100	v Leicestershire	Cheltenham	1930
5-71	v Derbyshire	Chesterfield	1930
5-52	v Australians	Bristol	1930
8-44	v Glamorgan	Swansea	1930
5-21	v Yorkshire	Bramall Lane	1931
5-92	v Lancashire	Bristol	1931
6-55	v Middlesex	Cheltenham (Victoria)	1931
8-79	v Derbyshire	Chesterfield	1931
5-58	v Hampshire	Southampton	1931
6-46 } 5-51 }	v Warwickshire	Gloucester	1931
5-44	v Middlesex	Lord's	1932
6-130	v Nottinghamshire	Bristol	1932
7-121	v Worcestershire	Worcester	1932
6-182	v Warwickshire	Gloucester	1932
6-39 } 5-70 }	v Surrey	Gloucester	1932
7-59	v Hampshire	Bournemouth	1932
5-102 } 7-19 }	v Middlesex	Clifton	1932
6-115	v All India	Bristol	1932
6-26	v Sussex	Cheltenham	1932
7-101	v Lancashire	Liverpool	1932
7-92 } 7-106 }	v Hampshire	Gloucester	1932
5-78 } 6-55 }	v Oxford University	The Parks	1933
5-114 } 6-71 }	v Kent	Bristol	1933
7-48 } 5-42 }	v Glamorgan	Pontypridd	1933

5-142	v Glamorgan	Gloucester	1933
8-77	v Yorkshire	Gloucester	1933
5-49 ⎱ 6-52 ⎰	v Derbyshire	Chesterfield	1933
7-54	v Middlesex	Bristol	1933
5-67	v Surrey	Bristol	1933
7-63	v Warwickshire	Edgbaston	1933
5-82	v Sussex	Gloucester	1933
6-67 ⎱ 6-73 ⎰	v Worcestershire	Cheltenham	1933
6-41	v Leicestershire	Cheltenham	1933
6-56	v Hampshire	Bournemouth	1933
8-132	v Middlesex	Lord's	1934
7-71	v Somerset	Bristol	1934
5-75	v Somerset	Bath	1934
9-37	v Leicestershire	Bristol	1934
5-90	v Derbyshire	Gloucester	1934
7-105	v Worcestershire	Dudley	1934
5-83 ⎱ 6-71 ⎰	v Sussex	Cheltenham	1934
5-101	v Yorkshire	Scarborough	1934
5-109	v Nottinghamshire	Trent Bridge	1935
7-147	v Kent	Bristol	1935
5-38 ⎱ 5-69 ⎰	v Somerset	Bristol	1935
6-36	v Glamorgan	Bristol	1935
5-25	v Worcestershire	Worcester	1935
6-62	v Derbyshire	Bristol	1935
5-76	v Hampshire	Bristol	1935
6-30	v Lancashire	Old Trafford	1935
5-99	v Yorkshire	Hull	1935
5-102 ⎱ 5-49 ⎰	v Kent	Canterbury	1935
8-139	v Middlesex	Cheltenham	1935
7-49	v Essex	Southend-on-Sea	1935
5-61	v Glamorgan	Cardiff	1935
6-98	v Nottinghamshire	Bristol	1935
5-36	v Leicestershire	Leicester (Aylestone Road)	1935
5-170	v Warwickshire	Gloucester	1935
6-110	v Oxford University	The Parks	1936
5-76	v Surrey	Kennington Oval	1936
5-147	v Nottinghamshire	Trent Bridge	1936
5-43	v Glamorgan	Bristol	1936
5-92	v Hampshire	Bristol	1936
7-55	v Warwickshire	Bristol	1936
5-61	v Glamorgan	Newport	1936
6-60	v Leicestershire	Gloucester	1936
6-67	v Yorkshire	Bramall Lane	1936
6-15 ⎱ 5-57 ⎰	v Lancashire	Preston	1936
5-70	v Essex	Bristol	1936
5-23	v Yorkshire	Bristol	1936
7-66	v Sussex	Cheltenham	1936
8-64	v Essex	Clacton-on-Sea	1936
6-65	v Somerset	Taunton	1937
5-73 ⎱ 5-115 ⎰	v Middlesex	Bristol	1937
6-57 ⎱ 7-85 ⎰	v Yorkshire	Headingley	1937
5-108	v Leicestershire	Gloucester	1937
7-84 ⎱ 5-42 ⎰	v Essex	Brentwood	1937
6-26	v Surrey	Kennington Oval	1937

Figures	Opponent	Venue	Year
6-26 / 6-67	v Kent	Cheltenham (Victoria)	1937
5-119	v Derbyshire	Buxton	1937
7-84 / 6-109	v Worcestershire	Dudley	1937
8-80 / 6-66	v Hampshire	Bristol	1937
5-82	v Warwickshire	Edgbaston	1937
6-58 / 5-22	v Essex	Bristol	1937
5-58 / 8-41	v Glamorgan	Newport	1937
6-116	v Somerset	Bristol	1937
6-68 / 10-113	v Worcestershire	Cheltenham	1937
7-104 / 5-41	v Derbyshire	Cheltenham	1937
7-65	v Lancashire	Gloucester	1937
6-74 / 8-73	v Nottinghamshire	Bristol	1937
7-182 / 5-94	v Middlesex	Lord's	1938
7-57 / 6-50	v Kent	Gillingham	1938
6-144	v Lancashire	Bristol	1938
5-33	v Glamorgan	Bristol	1938
5-61 / 7-26	v Hampshire	Cheltenham	1938
5-73 / 8-62	v Leicestershire	Bristol	1938
5-42	v Oxford University	The Parks	1939
9-55 / 7-44	v Worcestershire	Bristol	1939
5-76	v Yorkshire	Bradford	1939
5-83 / 6-68	v Middlesex	Lord's	1939
6-66	v Warwickshire	Bristol	1939
5-53	v Sussex	Worthing	1939
6-61 / 7-38	v Yorkshire	Bristol	1939
9-38 / 8-68	v Kent	Bristol	1939
7-91	v Surrey	Kennington Oval	1939
8-36	v Hampshire	Bristol	1939
7-77 / 5-65	v Hampshire	Bournemouth	1939
5-15 / 9-44	v Somerset	Bristol	1939
6-77 / 5-70	v Nottinghamshire	Trent Bridge	1939
6-59	v Oxford University	The Parks	1946
7-48	v Glamorgan	Bristol	1946
7-38 / 6-23	v Northamptonshire	Peterborough	1946
6-72	v Middlesex	Gloucester	1946
8-88 / 6-81	v Essex	Brentwood	1946
5-81	v Oxford University	Bristol	1946
5-65	v Leicestershire	Bristol	1946
7-59	v Middlesex	Lord's	1946
7-81	v Indians	Cheltenham	1946
9-82	v Surrey	Cheltenham	1946
6-90	v Oxford University	The Parks	1947
5-25	v Hampshire	Bristol	1947

Figures	Opponent	Venue	Year
9-41 } 6-40 }	v Nottinghamshire	Bristol	1947
6-35	v Yorkshire	Bristol	1947
8-26 } 7-108 }	v Leicestershire	Gloucester	1947
7-106	v Warwickshire	Edgbaston	1947
6-40	v Glamorgan	Swansea	1947
5-71 } 5-99 }	v Kent	Bristol	1947
7-55	v Surrey	Kennington Oval	1947
5-66 } 6-54 }	v Worcestershire	Gloucester	1947
5-44	v Northamptonshire	Gloucester	1947
5-66	v Leicestershire	Leicester (Grace Road)	1947
7-61 } 5-4 }	v Somerset	Bristol	1947
6-121	v Lancashire	Old Trafford	1947
6-116	v Yorkshire	Bradford	1947
7-70 } 8-86 }	v Middlesex	Cheltenham	1947
8-61	v Glamorgan	Cheltenham	1947
5-132	v Hampshire	Bournemouth	1947
5-106	v Essex	Bristol	1947
6-65	v Somerset	Taunton	1948
5-40 } 6-93 }	v Sussex	Bristol	1948
5-80	v Yorkshire	Bristol	1948
5-119	v Warwickshire	Bristol	1948
5-88	v Hampshire	Bournemouth	1948
5-61	v Northamptonshire	Cheltenham	1948
6-16	v Nottinghamshire	Cheltenham	1948
5-84	v Surrey	Cheltenham	1948
7-50	v Sussex	Eastbourne	1948
7-110	v Somerset	Taunton	1949
6-54 } 7-57 }	v Lancashire	Old Trafford	1949
6-46 } 9-61 }	v Derbyshire	Bristol	1949
5-131	v New Zealanders	Bristol	1949
7-53	v Kent	Bristol	1949
6-48	v Worcestershire	Gloucester	1949
8-70	v Warwickshire	Gloucester	1949
5-59	v Lancashire	Bristol	1949
5-133	v Northamptonshire	Northampton	1949
6-55 } 5-83 }	v Yorkshire	Huddersfield	1949
6-45	v Warwickshire	Gloucester	1950
5-31	v Glamorgan	Gloucester	1950
7-42	v Derbyshire	Bristol	1950
5-67	v Hampshire	Bristol	1950
5-58 } 8-37 }	v Sussex	Worthing	1950
6-59	v Warwickshire	Edgbaston	1950
5-50	v Somerset	Bristol	1950
6-65	v Hampshire	Bournemouth	1950
5-63	v Middlesex	Gloucester	1952
5-79	v Hampshire	Bristol	1952
7-93	v Somerset	Bristol	1952

For Other Teams

6-72	MCC South African Team v Rest of England	Folkestone	1931
6-29	ENGLAND v NEW ZEALAND	Old Trafford	1937
6-95 ⎫	Over Thirty v Under Thirty	Folkestone	1937
7-122 ⎭			
6-38	MCC v Rhodesia	Salisbury	1938/39
5-53	South of England v Sir Pelham Warner's XI	Hastings	1947

Ten Wickets in a Match (86)

For Gloucestershire - 85

7-25 and 6-95	v Middlesex	Lord's	1929
5-35 and 5-76	v Hampshire	Southampton	1929
8-117 and 5-37	v Worcestershire	Gloucester	1929
5-89 and 6-72	v Lancashire	Bristol	1929
8-89 and 4-46	v Leicestershire	Bristol	1929
4-78 and 7-46	v Hampshire	Cheltenham (Victoria)	1929
3-42 and 7-100	v Leicestershire	Cheltenham	1930
8-44 and 4-53	v Glamorgan	Swansea	1930
8-79 and 3-53	v Derbyshire	Chesterfield	1931
6-46 and 5-51	v Warwickshire	Gloucester	1931
6-182 and 4-72	v Warwickshire	Gloucester	1932
6-39 and 5-70	v Surrey	Gloucester	1932
5-102 and 7-19	v Middlesex	Clifton	1932
4-58 and 6-115	v All India	Bristol	1932
7-101 and 3-59	v Lancashire	Liverpool	1932
7-92 and 7-106	v Hampshire	Gloucester	1932
5-78 and 6-55	v Oxford University	The Parks	1933
5-114 and 6-71	v Kent	Bristol	1933
7-48 and 5-42	v Glamorgan	Pontypridd	1933
5-49 and 6-52	v Derbyshire	Chesterfield	1933
4-42 and 7-63	v Warwickshire	Edgbaston	1933
6-67 and 6-73	v Worcestershire	Cheltenham	1933
6-56 and 4-8	v Hampshire	Bournemouth	1933
8-132 and 2-44	v Middlesex	Lord's	1934
4-54 and 7-71	v Somerset	Bristol	1934
1-40 and 9-37	v Leicestershire	Bristol	1934
5-83 and 6-71	v Sussex	Cheltenham	1934
7-147 and 4-40	v Kent	Bristol	1935
5-38 and 5-69	v Somerset	Bristol	1935
6-62 and 4-60	v Derbyshire	Bristol	1935
5-102 and 5-49	v Kent	Canterbury	1935
8-139 and 2-86	v Middlesex	Cheltenham	1935
4-132 and 7-49	v Essex	Southend-on-Sea	1935
6-110 and 4-83	v Oxford University	The Parks	1936
4-57 and 7-55	v Warwickshire	Bristol	1936
6-15 and 5-57	v Lancashire	Preston	1936
5-73 and 5-115	v Middlesex	Bristol	1937
6-57 and 7-85	v Yorkshire	Headingley	1937
7-84 and 5-42	v Essex	Brentwood	1937
6-26 and 6-67	v Kent	Cheltenham (Victoria)	1937
7-84 and 6-109	v Worcestershire	Dudley	1937
8-80 and 6-66	v Hampshire	Bristol	1937
6-58 and 5-22	v Essex	Bristol	1937
5-58 and 8-41	v Glamorgan	Newport	1937
6-68 and 10-113	v Worcestershire	Cheltenham	1937
7-104 and 5-41	v Derbyshire	Cheltenham	1937
4-106 and 7-65	v Lancashire	Gloucester	1937
6-74 and 8-73	v Nottinghamshire	Bristol	1937
7-182 and 5-94	v Middlesex	Lord's	1938
7-57 and 6-50	v Kent	Gillingham	1938
5-61 and 7-26	v Hampshire	Cheltenham	1938
5-73 and 8-62	v Leicestershire	Bristol	1938

9-55 and 7-44	v Worcestershire	Bristol	1939
5-83 and 6-68	v Middlesex	Lord's	1939
6-61 and 7-38	v Yorkshire	Bristol	1939
9-38 and 8-68	v Kent	Bristol	1939
4-36 and 8-36	v Hampshire	Bristol	1939
7-77 and 5-65	v Hampshire	Bournemouth	1939
5-15 and 9-44	v Somerset	Bristol	1939
6-77 and 5-70	v Nottinghamshire	Trent Bridge	1939
4-27 and 7-48	v Glamorgan	Bristol	1946
7-38 and 6-23	v Northamptonshire	Peterborough	1946
8-88 and 6-81	v Essex	Brentwood	1946
7-59 and 3-59	v Middlesex	Lord's	1946
7-81 and 4-66	v Indians	Cheltenham	1946
4-45 and 9-82	v Surrey	Cheltenham	1946
9-41 and 6-40	v Nottinghamshire	Bristol	1947
8-26 and 7-108	v Leicestershire	Gloucester	1947
7-106 and 4-77	v Warwickshire	Edgbaston	1947
5-71 and 5-99	v Kent	Bristol	1947
7-55 and 4-113	v Surrey	Kennington Oval	1947
5-66 and 6-54	v Worcestershire	Gloucester	1947
7-61 and 5-4	v Somerset	Bristol	1947
7-70 and 8-86	v Middlesex	Cheltenham	1947
5-40 and 6-93	v Sussex	Bristol	1948
4-115 and 7-50	v Sussex	Eastbourne	1948
6-54 and 7-57	v Lancashire	Old Trafford	1949
6-46 and 9-61	v Derbyshire	Bristol	1949
7-53 and 4-88	v Kent	Bristol	1949
2-86 and 8-70	v Warwickshire	Gloucester	1949
6-55 and 5-83	v Yorkshire	Huddersfield	1949
4-100 and 7-42	v Derbyshire	Bristol	1950
5-58 and 8-37	v Sussex	Worthing	1950
6-65 and 4-80	v Hampshire	Bournemouth	1950
3-16 and 7-93	v Somerset	Bristol	1952

For Other Teams

6-95 and 7-122	Over Thirty v Under Thirty	Folkestone	1937

Test Cricket (Batting and Fielding)

Season		M	I	NO	R	HS	Ave	50	Ct
1930	v Australia	1	-	-	-	-	-	-	-
1937	v New Zealand	2	2	2	5	4*	-	-	1
1938/39	v South Africa	3	2	1	8	8	8.00	-	1
1939	v West Indies	2	1	-	0	0	0.00	-	1
Total		**8**	**5**	**3**	**13**	**8**	**6.50**	**-**	**3**

Test Cricket (Bowling)

		O	M	R	W	BB	Ave	5wi	10wm	S/Rate	R/Rate
1930	v Aus	32.1	14	49	2	2-49	24.50	-	-	96.50	25.38
1937	v NZ	60.4	20	143	8	6-29	17.87	1	-	45.50	39.28
1938/39	(8b) v SA	105	26	282	8	3-54	35.25	-	-	105.00	33.57
1939	(8b) v WI	20.6	1	114	4	2-43	28.50	-	-	41.50	68.67
Total	**(6b)**	**92.5**	**34}**	**588**	**22**	**6-29**	**26.72**	**1**	**-**	**71.04**	**37.61**
	(8b)	**125.6**	**27}**								

Test Match Performances on Each Ground (Batting and Fielding)

	M	I	NO	R	HS	Ave	50	Ct
In England								
Kennington Oval	2	1	0	0	0	0.00	-	1
Old Trafford	3	2	2	5	4*	-	-	1
Totals	5	3	2	5	4*	5.00	-	2
In South Africa								
Cape Town	1	-	-	-	-	-	-	-
Johannesburg	2	2	1	8	8	8.00	-	1
Totals	3	2	1	8	8	8.00	-	1

Test Match Performances on Each Ground (Bowling)

	O	M	R	W	BB	Ave	5wi	10wm	S/Rate	R/Rate
In England										
Kennington Oval (6b)	28	10 ⎫	122	3	2-41	40.66	-	-	111.33	36.52
(8b)	20.6	2 ⎭								
Old Trafford (6b)	64.5	18 ⎫	126	8	6-29	15.75	1	-	57.37	27.45
(8b)	8.6	1 ⎭								
Totals (6b)	92.5	28 ⎫	248	11	6-29	22.54	1	-	72.09	31.27
(8b)	29.4	3 ⎭								
In South Africa – 8 ball overs										
Cape Town	49	16	132	4	3-64	33.00	-	-	98.00	33.67
Johannesburg	56	10	150	4	3-54	37.50	-	-	112.00	33.48
Totals	105	26	282	8	3-54	35.25	-	-	105.00	33.57

Season by Season for Gloucestershire (Batting and Fielding)

Season	M	I	NO	R	HS	Ave	50	Ct
1922	2	3	3	28	20*	-	-	-
1923	16	26	10	44	15	2.75	-	6
1924	9	11	5	15	5*	2.50	-	6
1925	11	16	6	78	30	7.80	-	5
1926	29	48	14	317	47	9.32	-	26
1927	18	24	11	147	29*	11.30	-	11
1929	28	33	11	157	27*	7.13	-	21
1930	29	35	5	191	24	6.36	-	12
1931	30	32	7	92	14	3.68	-	16
1932	29	40	16	373	71	15.54	1	20
1933	31	46	11	470	45	13.42	-	19
1934	25	36	8	241	30	8.60	-	19
1935	31	44	4	410	35	10.25	-	16
1936	29	36	7	376	67	12.96	1	17
1937	29	44	10	416	61*	12.23	1	19
1938	21	26	7	133	24	7.00	-	8
1939	27	32	11	215	56*	10.23	1	12
1946	28	32	10	194	22	8.81	-	17
1947	29	41	9	303	26	9.46	-	12
1948	27	35	8	259	28	9.59	-	11
1949	28	40	13	226	20	8.37	-	14
1950	28	34	12	168	29	7.63	-	5
1951	11	18	7	63	16	5.72	-	4
1952	13	11	2	110	19	12.22	-	5
Totals	558	743	207	5026	71	9.37	4	301

Season by Season for Gloucestershire (Bowling)

		O	M	R	W	BB	Ave	5wi	10wm	S/Rate	R/Rate
1922		18	5	48	1	1-48	48.00	-	-	108.00	44.44
1923		262.1	56	728	25	6-41	29.12	2	-	62.92	46.28
1924		141.5	26	415	22	6-23	18.86	2	-	38.68	48.76
1925		122	18	378	8	3-73	47.25	-	-	91.50	51.63
1926		797.2	162	2115	71	6-62	29.78	2	-	67.38	44.20
1927		465.5	75	1529	26	5-92	58.80	1	-	107.50	54.70
1929		1172.5	337	2722	175	9-21	15.55	16	6	40.21	38.68
1930		1336.3	410	2723	141	8-77	19.31	10	2	56.87	33.95
1931		1140.5	362	2449	132	8-79	18.55	7	2	51.85	35.77
1932		1316	343	3258	170	7-19	19.16	14	6	46.44	41.26
1933		1371.5	414	3187	183	8-54	17.41	18	7	44.97	38.71
1934		1185.2	314	3031	126	9-37	24.05	9	4	56.44	42.61
1935		1552.5	384	4073	200	8-139	20.36	18	6	46.58	44.21
1936		1425.4	423	3106	153	8-64	20.30	15	3	55.90	36.31
1937		1336	330	3730	222	10-113	16.80	29	12	36.10	46.53
1938		936.4	192	2526	109	8-62	23.17	10	4	51.55	44.94
1939	(8b)	799.2	137	2859	196	9-38	14.58	20	8	32.62	44.71
1946		1273.2	371	2936	176	9-82	16.68	12	6	43.40	38.42
1947		1326.1	323	3636	222	9-45	16.37	25	8	35.83	45.70
1948		1080.3	278	2687	125	7-50	21.49	10	2	51.86	41.44
1949		1187.2	326	3069	160	9-61	19.18	13	5	44.56	43.04
1950		1236.2	389	2739	137	8-37	19.99	9	3	54.14	36.92
1951		341.3	76	1053	37	4-42	28.45	-	-	55.37	51.39
1952		424.2	113	1063	45	7-93	23.62	3	1	56.57	41.75
Totals	(6b)	21452.1	5727⎫	56060	2862	10-113	19.58	245	85	47.20	41.49
	(8b)	799.2	137⎭								

For Gloucestershire Against Each Opponent (Batting and Fielding)

	M	I	NO	R	HS	Ave	50	Ct
Derbyshire - Home	17	24	7	168	30	9.88	-	13
Derbyshire - Away	16	25	2	184	29	8.00	-	13
Total v Derbyshire	33	49	9	352	30	8.80	-	26
Essex - Home	17	21	7	181	47	12.92	-	7
Essex - Away	16	24	3	296	71	14.09	1	6
Total v Essex	33	45	10	477	71	13.62	1	13
Glamorgan - Home	17	23	8	112	15*	7.46	-	20
Glamorgan - Away	15	15	1	133	23	9.50	-	8
Total v Glamorgan	32	38	9	245	23	8.44	-	28
Hampshire - Home	22	30	9	176	22	8.38	-	19
Hampshire - Away	20	21	5	192	30*	12.00	-	8
Total v Hampshire	42	51	14	368	30*	9.94	-	27
Kent - Home	16	26	7	175	31*	9.21	-	9
Kent - Away	15	24	6	79	17	4.38	-	10
Total v Kent	31	50	13	254	31*	6.86	-	19
Lancashire - Home	19	27	10	259	45	15.23	-	6
Lancashire - Away	18	24	4	205	29	10.25	-	8
Total v Lancashire	37	51	14	464	45	12.54	-	14
Leicestershire - Home	15	21	5	122	30	7.62	-	16
Leicestershire - Away	13	18	3	98	27	6.53	-	10
Total v Leicestershire	28	39	8	220	30	7.09	-	26
Middlesex - Home	16	25	7	195	27	10.83	-	9
Middlesex - Away	17	24	8	96	16	6.00	-	12
Total v Middlesex	33	49	15	291	27	8.55	-	21
Northamptonshire - Home	10	10	4	28	15*	4.66	-	-
Northamptonshire - Away	8	8	3	22	6	4.40	-	4
Total v Northamptonshire	18	18	7	50	15*	4.54	-	4
Nottinghamshire - Home	14	17	7	124	29*	12.40	-	10

Nottinghamshire - Away	15	19	6	180	35*	13.84	-	7
Total v Nottinghamshire	29	36	13	304	35*	13.21	-	17
Somerset - Home	17	18	5	116	56*	8.92	1	7
Somerset - Away	17	23	13	229	61*	22.90	1	11
Total v Somerset	34	41	18	345	61*	15.00	2	18
Surrey - Home	14	17	5	64	18*	5.35	-	8
Surrey - Away	19	27	8	119	28	6.26	-	6
Total v Surrey	33	44	13	183	28	5.90	-	14
Sussex - Home	16	21	8	147	19	11.30	-	4
Sussex - Away	21	30	8	235	67	10.68	1	6
Total v Sussex	37	51	16	382	67	10.91	1	10
Warwickshire - Home	15	18	7	90	19	8.18	-	11
Warwickshire - Away	16	23	4	135	24	7.10	-	5
Total v Warwickshire	31	41	11	225	24	7.50	-	16
Worcestershire - Home	21	24	8	132	29	8.25	-	8
Worcestershire - Away	16	19	7	147	34	12.25	-	5
Total v Worcestershire	37	43	15	279	34	9.96	-	13
Yorkshire - Home	14	20	7	91	27*	7.00	-	7
Yorkshire - Away	18	30	4	189	35	7.26	-	11
Total v Yorkshire	32	50	11	280	35	7.17	-	18
All India	1	2	0	19	14	9.50	-	1
Australians	4	7	2	26	10*	5.20	-	-
Indians	1	1	0	12	12	12.00	-	-
New Zealanders	5	7	2	11	5*	2.20	-	1
South Africans	3	5	0	4	4	0.80	-	2
West Indians	2	2	1	16	13	16.00	-	5
Cambridge University	4	3	2	27	18*	27.00	-	1
Oxford University	18	20	4	192	45	12.00	-	7
OVERALL TOTALS	**558**	**743**	**207**	**5026**	**71**	**9.37**	**4**	**301**

For Gloucestershire Against Each Opponent (Bowling)

	O	M	R	W	BB	Ave	5wi	10wm	S/Rate	R/Rate
Derbyshire - Home										
(6b)	696.3	186 ⎫	1711	89	9-61	19.22	7	4	48.12	39.94
(8b)	13	1 ⎭								
Derbyshire - Away										
(6b)	564.3	160 ⎫	1345	72	8-79	18.68	5	2	49.48	37.74
(8b)	22	3 ⎭								
Total v Derbyshire										
(6b)	1261	346 ⎫	3056	161	9-61	18.98	12	6	48.73	38.94
(8b)	35	4 ⎭								
Essex - Home										
(6b)	592.2	150 ⎫	1458	71	6-53	20.53	5	1	52.42	39.17
(8b)	21	5 ⎭								
Essex - Away										
(6b)	611.5	158 ⎫	1693	88	8-64	19.23	7	3	44.39	43.33
(8b)	30	7 ⎭								
Total v Essex										
(6b)	1203.3	308 ⎫	3151	159	8-64	19.81	12	4	47.98	41.30
(8b)	51	12 ⎭								
Glamorgan - Home										
(6b)	587	169 ⎫	1342	89	8-61	15.07	9	1	41.84	36.03
(8b)	25.2	3 ⎭								
Glamorgan - Away										
(6b)	647.5	213 ⎫	1528	97	8-41	15.75	9	3	45.08	34.94
(8b)	60.6	14 ⎭								
Total v Glamorgan										
(6b)	1234.5	382 ⎫	2870	186	8-41	15.43	18	4	43.53	35.44
(8b)	86	17 ⎭								

Hampshire - Home										
	(6b)	890.4	225 }	2337	143	8-36	16.34	15	5	38.97	41.93
	(8b)	28.5	9 }								
Hampshire - Away										
	(6b)	852.2	239 }	2145	121	7-59	17.72	11	4	44.69	39.66
	(8b)	36.6	4 }								
Total v Hampshire										
	(6b)	1743	464 }	4482	264	8-36	16.97	26	9	41.59	40.81
	(8b)	65.3	13 }								
Kent - Home										
	(6b)	685.1	170 }	1900	106	9-38	17.92	10	6	41.17	43.52
	(8b)	31.6	3 }								
Kent - Away										
	(6b)	512.2	122 }	1525	75	7-52	20.33	4	2	44.32	45.87
	(8b)	31.2	1 }								
Total v Kent										
	(6b)	1197.3	292 }	3425	181	9-38	18.92	14	8	42.48	44.54
	(8b)	63	4 }								
Lancashire - Home										
	(6b)	861	230 }	2054	84	7-65	24.45	7	2	64.45	37.93
	(8b)	31	9 }								
Lancashire - Away										
	(6b)	602	184	1341	74	7-57	18.12	8	3	48.81	37.12
Total v Lancashire										
	(6b)	1463	414 }	3395	158	7-57	21.48	15	5	57.12	37.61
	(8b)	31	9 }								
Leicestershire - Home										
	(6b)	634.2	173	1405	96	9-37	14.63	11	5	39.64	36.91
Leicestershire - Away										
	(6b)	561.4	150	1240	59	5-36	21.01	4	-	57.11	36.79
Total v Leicestershire										
	(6b)	1196	323	2645	155	9-37	17.06	15	5	46.29	36.85
Middlesex - Home										
	(6b)	642.3	130	1904	99	8-86	19.23	11	4	38.93	49.39
Middlesex - Away										
	(6b)	594.1	122 }	1819	98	8-132	18.56	9	5	39.82	46.60
	(8b)	42.2	1 }								
Total v Middlesex										
	(6b)	1236.4	252 }	3723	197	8-86	18.89	20	9	39.38	47.98
	(8b)	42.2	1 }								
Northamptonshire - Home										
	(6b)	358.3	101	847	48	5-44	17.64	2	-	44.81	39.37
Northamptonshire - Away										
	(6b)	229.4	73	519	36	7-38	14.41	3	1	38.27	37.66
Total v Northamptonshire										
	(6b)	588.1	174	1366	84	7-38	16.26	5	1	42.01	38.70
Nottinghamshire - Home										
	(6b)	535.4	149	1371	76	9-41	18.03	7	2	42.28	42.65
Nottinghamshire - Away										
	(6b)	629	144 }	1820	63	6-77	28.88	4	1	63.14	45.75
	(8b)	25.4	2 }								
Total v Nottinghamshire										
	(6b)	1164.4	293 }	3191	139	9-41	22.95	11	3	51.74	44.36
	(8b)	25.4	2 }								
Somerset - Home										
	(6b)	699.1	229 }	1609	100	9-44	16.09	10	5	43.84	36.70
	(8b)	23.5	7 }								
Somerset - Away										
	(6b)	629.3	191 }	1843	68	7-110	27.10	4	-	60.33	44.91
	(8b)	40.6	10 }								
Total v Somerset										
	(6b)	1328.4	420 }	3452	168	9-44	20.54	14	5	50.51	40.67
	(8b)	64.3	17 }								

Team		Overs	Mdns	Runs	Wkts	Best	Avge	5wi	10wm	S/R	RpO
Surrey - Home	(6b)	539.4	145 ⎫	1397	78	9-82	17.91	6	2	43.65	41.02
	(8b)	20.7	4 ⎭								
Surrey - Away	(6b)	726.4	206 ⎫	1974	81	7-55	24.37	5	1	57.60	42.30
	(8b)	38.2	6 ⎭								
Total v Surrey	(6b)	1266.2	351 ⎫	3371	159	9-82	21.20	11	3	50.76	41.76
	(8b)	59.1	10 ⎭								
Sussex - Home	(6b)	717.4	183	1722	95	7-66	18.12	9	2	45.32	39.99
Sussex - Away	(6b)	723.4	198 ⎫	2032	73	8-37	27.83	5	2	63.13	44.08
	(8b)	33.3	7 ⎭								
Total v Sussex	(6b)	1441.2	381 ⎫	3754	168	8-37	22.34	14	4	53.06	42.10
	(8b)	33.3	7 ⎭								
Warwickshire - Home	(6b)	656.3	169 ⎫	1788	88	8-70	20.31	9	4	47.54	42.73
	(8b)	30.5	1 ⎭								
Warwickshire - Away	(6b)	571.4	136 ⎫	1643	69	7-63	23.81	4	2	52.84	45.06
	(8b)	27	7 ⎭								
Total v Warwickshire	(6b)	1228.1	305 ⎫	3431	157	8-70	21.85	13	6	49.87	43.81
	(8b)	57.5	8 ⎭								
Worcestershire - Home	(6b)	670.1	188 ⎫	1776	116	10-113	15.31	11	5	36.47	41.97
	(8b)	26.2	6 ⎭								
Worcestershire - Away	(6b)	667.5	198 ⎫	1730	75	7-84	23.06	5	1	56.38	40.90
	(8b)	27.6	4 ⎭								
Total v Worcestershire	(6b)	1338	386 ⎫	3506	191	10-113	18.35	16	6	44.29	41.44
	(8b)	54	10 ⎭								
Yorkshire - Home	(6b)	504.1	129 ⎫	1342	66	8-77	20.33	6	1	51.40	39.55
	(8b)	46	12 ⎭								
Yorkshire - Away	(6b)	726.1	195 ⎫	1960	85	7-85	23.05	10	2	53.98	42.71
	(8b)	29	4 ⎭								
Total v Yorkshire	(6b)	1230.2	324 ⎫	3302	151	8-77	21.86	16	3	52.86	41.36
	(8b)	75	16 ⎭								
All India	(6b)	62.5	14	173	10	6-115	17.30	1	1	37.70	45.88
Australians	(6b)	169.1	44	443	10	5-52	44.30	1	-	101.50	43.64
Indians	(6b)	45	6	147	11	7-81	13.36	1	1	24.54	54.44
New Zealanders	(6b)	169.2	39	508	24	5-131	21.16	1	-	42.33	50.00
South Africans	(6b)	156.1	37	418	19	6-68	22.00	1	-	49.31	44.61
West Indians	(6b)	10	0 ⎫	143	8	3-45	17.87	-	-	34.87	51.25
	(8b)	27.3	3 ⎭								
Cambridge University	(6b)	126.5	43	263	16	9-21	16.43	1	-	47.56	34.55
Oxford University	(6b)	591.4	125 ⎫	1845	86	6-55	21.45	7	2	44.00	48.75
	(8b)	29.2	6 ⎭								

OVERALL TOTALS

	(6b)	21452.1	5727 ⎫	56060	2862	10-113	19.58	245	85	47.20	41.49
	(8b)	799.2	137 ⎭								

For Other Teams Against Each Opponent (Batting and Fielding)

	M	I	NO	R	HS	Ave	50	Ct
In England								
Players v Gentlemen								
Lord's	2	2	1	5	5*	5.00	-	-
Folkestone	1	-	-	-	-	-	-	1
Scarborough	1	1	1	0	0*	-	-	-
Totals	4	3	2	5	5*	5.00	-	1
Test Trial – Rest of England v England								
	1	1	0	15	15	15.00	-	1
Rest of England v Champion County								
v Nottinghamshire	1	2	1	26	13*	26.00	-	-
v Middlesex	1	2	0	22	14	11.00	-	-
MCC South African XI v Lord Hawke's XI								
	1	-	-	-	-	-	-	1
MCC South African Team v Rest of England								
	1	1	0	1	1	1.00	-	-
South of England								
v Indians	1	1	0	4	4	4.00	-	-
v South Africans	1	2	2	1	1*	-	-	-
v Sir Pelham Warner's XI	1	2	0	0	0	0.00	-	1
Under Thirty v Over Thirty	1	1	1	0	0*	-	-	2
In South Africa								
For MCC								
Border	1	1	1	14	14*	-	-	-
Combined Transvaal	1	1	0	1	1	1.00	-	-
Cape Province	1	-	-	-	-	-	-	-
Eastern Province	1	1	0	0	0	0.00	-	-
Griqualand West	2	2	0	11	10	5.50	-	2
Natal	2	2	0	29	25	14.50	-	-
North Eastern Transvaal	1	-	-	-	-	-	-	-
Rhodesia	1	1	0	33	33	33.00	-	-
Transvaal	2	2	0	16	13	8.00	-	-
Western Province	2	2	0	17	16	8.50	-	-
Totals	14	12	1	121	33	11.00	-	2

For Other Teams Against Each Opponent (Bowling)

	O	M	R	W	BB	Ave	5wi	10wm	S/Rate	R/Rate
In England										
Players v Gentlemen										
Lord's	54.5	8	160	7	3-58	22.85	-	-	47.00	48.63
Folkestone	4	2	20	1	1-20	20.00	-	-	24.00	83.33
Scarborough	34.3	9	99	5	4-58	19.80	-	-	41.40	47.82
Totals	93.2	19	279	13	4-58	21.46	-	-	43.07	49.82
Test Trial – Rest of England v England										
	45	12	93	4	3-36	23.25	-	-	67.50	34.44
Rest of England v Champion County										
v Nottinghamshire	37	7	108	3	3-46	36.00	-	-	74.00	48.64
v Middlesex	46.3	6	179	4	4-179	44.75	-	-	69.75	64.15
MCC South African XI v Lord Hawke's XI										
	34	11	47	1	1-47	47.00	-	-	204.00	23.03
MCC South African Team v Rest of England										
	48.2	10	167	8	6-72	20.87	1	-	36.25	57.58

South of England											
v Indians		44	6	159	1	1-65	159.00	-	-	264.00	60.22
v South Africans		38	7	149	3	2-136	49.66	-	-	76.00	65.35
v Sir Pelham Warner's XI		39.4	8	155	9	5-53	17.22	1	-	26.44	65.12
Under Thirty v Over Thirty		59.4	11	217	13	7-122	16.69	2	1	27.53	60.61
In South Africa											
For MCC											
Border	(8b)	18	10	33	1	1-19	33.00	-	-	144.00	22.91
Combined Transvaal	(8b)	37	4	131	5	4-71	26.20	-	-	59.20	44.25
East London	(6b)	36	11	72	7	4-43	10.28	-	-	30.85	33.33
Eastern Province	(6b)	15	1	31	1	1-31	31.00	-	-	90.00	34.44
Griqualand West	(6b)	25.1	7 }	162	6	3-66	27.00	-	-	70.50	38.29
	(8b)	34	8								
Natal	(6b)	40	12	90	0	-	-	-	-	-	37.50
North Eastern Transvaal	(8b)	19	4	60	4	3-49	15.00	-	-	38.00	39.47
Rhodesia	(8b)	29	6	60	8	6-38	7.50	1	-	29.00	25.86
Transvaal	(6b)	29	5 }	166	2	2-71	83.00	-	-	247.00	33.60
	(8b)	40	5								
Western Province	(6b)	14	4 }	110	2	1-13	55.00	-	-	158.00	34.81
	(8b)	29	9								
Totals	(6b)	159.1	40 }	915	25	6-38	36.60	1	-	104.12	35.15
	(8b)	206	46								

Performances on Each Ground (Batting and Fielding)

	M	I	NO	R	HS	Ave	50	Ct
In England								
Bath	3	5	3	45	37*	22.50	-	2
Bournemouth	7	7	1	71	24	11.83	-	2
Bradford	4	7	0	27	11	3.85	-	1
Bramall Lane	3	4	1	19	13	6.33	-	-
Brentwood	3	3	0	23	19	7.66	-	2
Bristol (County Ground)	138	175	51	1121	56*	9.04	1	75
Bristol (Greenbank)	5	7	6	59	29*	59.00	-	3
Burton-on-Trent	2	3	0	5	5	1.66	-	3
Buxton	1	2	0	20	18	10.00	-	-
Canterbury	3	4	1	21	17	7.00	-	2
Cardiff	3	4	1	48	23	16.00	-	-
Chelmsford	1	1	1	4	4*	-	-	-
Cheltenham College	51	76	25	372	27	7.29	-	26
Cheltenham (Victoria)	14	17	5	150	31*	12.50	-	14
Chesterfield	7	11	2	79	21	8.77	-	7
Chichester	1	1	1	2	2*	-	-	-
Clacton-on-Sea	2	4	0	33	17	8.25	-	1
Clifton College	7	9	1	30	14	3.75	-	7
Colchester	1	1	1	8	8*	-	-	-
Coventry	1	2	0	1	1	0.50	-	-
Derby	6	9	0	80	29	8.88	-	3
Dewsbury	1	2	0	17	16	8.50	-	-
Dover	1	2	0	15	9	7.50	-	-
Dudley	3	4	1	30	16	10.00	-	2
Eastbourne	3	2	0	74	67	37.00	1	1
Ebbw Vale	2	2	0	19	18	9.50	-	-
Edgbaston	14	20	4	134	24	8.37	-	4

Ground								
Fenner's	1	1	0	8	8	8.00	-	-
Folkestone	4	4	1	5	4	1.66	-	3
Gillingham	1	1	0	0	0	0.00	-	2
Gloucester Spa	4	5	3	33	20*	16.50	-	-
Gloucester (Tuffley Avenue)	62	80	27	549	30	10.35	-	40
Gravesend	3	5	2	7	3*	2.33	-	3
Harrogate	1	2	0	17	17	8.50	-	2
Hastings	3	5	2	5	4	1.66	-	1
Headingley	2	4	0	11	5	2.75	-	2
Hinckley	1	2	1	3	3*	3.00	-	-
Horsham	3	5	2	16	8*	5.33	-	2
Hove	12	20	5	136	19	9.06	-	2
Huddersfield	1	2	0	16	15	8.00	-	-
Hull	4	6	1	48	35	9.60	-	2
Ilford	1	2	0	31	27	15.50	-	1
Kennington Oval	23	32	9	167	28	7.26	-	7
Kettering	2	1	0	0	0	0.00	-	2
Leicester (Aylestone Road)	9	13	1	91	27	7.58	-	9
Leicester (Grace Road)	3	3	1	4	4*	2.00	-	1
Leyton	3	5	0	11	6	2.20	-	-
Liverpool	2	3	0	38	19	12.66	-	4
Llanelli	1	1	0	5	5	5.00	-	-
Lord's	20	27	9	116	16	6.44	-	13
Maidstone	5	9	3	32	10	5.33	-	3
Neath	1	1	0	0	0	0.00	-	1
Newport	3	2	0	30	21	15.00	-	2
Northampton	5	6	3	17	6	5.66	-	2
Nuneaton	1	1	0	0	0	0.00	-	1
Old Trafford	18	21	6	160	29	10.66	-	5
The Parks	16	19	4	170	45	11.33	-	6
Peterborough	1	1	0	5	5	5.00	-	-
Pontypridd	1	1	0	2	2	2.00	-	2
Portsmouth	4	3	1	66	30*	33.00	-	2
Preston	1	2	0	12	10	6.00	-	-
Scarborough	4	4	3	29	14*	29.00	-	5
Southampton	9	11	3	55	16*	6.87	-	4
Southend-on-Sea	2	4	1	131	71	43.66	1	1
Stourbridge	2	3	1	14	10*	7.00	-	1
Swansea	4	4	0	29	13	7.25	-	3
Taunton	13	18	10	184	61*	23.00	1	8
Trent Bridge	15	19	6	180	35*	13.84	-	7
Tunbridge Wells	1	1	0	0	0	0.00	-	-
Weston-super-Mare	1	-	-	-	-	-	-	1
Westcliff-on-Sea	3	4	0	55	26	13.75	-	1
Worcester	11	12	5	103	34	14.71	-	2
Worthing	2	2	0	7	4	3.50	-	1
Total	576	761	215	5115	71	9.36	4	309
In South Africa								
Cape Town	3	2	0	17	16	8.50	-	-
Durban	1	1	0	25	25	25.60	-	-
East London	2	1	1	14	14*	-	-	-
Johannesburg	5	5	1	25	13	6.25	-	1
Kimberley	2	2	0	11	10	5.50	-	2
Pietermaritzburg	1	1	0	4	4	4.00	-	-
Port Elizabeth	1	1	0	0	0	0.00	-	-
Pretoria	1	-	-	-	-	-	-	-
Salisbury	1	1	0	33	33	33.00	-	-
Totals	17	14	2	129	33	10.75	-	3
OVERALL TOTALS	**593**	**775**	**217**	**5234**	**71**	**9.37**	**4**	**312**

Performances on Each Ground (Bowling)

		O	M	R	W	BB	Ave	5wi	10wm	S/Rate	R/Rate
In England											
Bath	(6b)	118.4	37	280	12	5-75	23.33	1	-	59.33	39.32
Bournemouth	(6b)	273.5	71 ⎫	780	55	7-59	14.18	7	3	35.21	40.26
	(8b)	36.6	4 ⎭								
Bradford	(6b)	161.3	40 ⎫	591	20	6-116	29.55	2	-	60.05	49.20
	(8b)	29	4 ⎭								
Bramall Lane	(6b)	98	31	193	14	6-67	13.78	2	-	42.00	32.82
Brentwood	(6b)	143.3	32	366	27	8-88	13.55	4	2	31.88	42.50
Bristol (County Ground)											
	(6b)	5874.1	1585 ⎫	14629	811	9-37	18.03	76	28	45.55	39.59
	(8b)	212.1	39 ⎭								
Bristol (Greenbank)											
	(6b)	192	42	556	10	3-67	55.60	-	-	115.20	48.26
Burton-on-Trent											
	(6b)	84.1	15	197	5	4-97	39.40	-	-	101.00	39.09
Buxton	(6b)	39.2	9	119	5	5-119	23.80	1	-	47.20	50.42
Canterbury	(6b)	136.4	28	373	19	5-49	19.63	2	1	43.15	45.48
Cardiff	(6b)	181	58	368	14	5-61	26.28	1	-	77.57	33.88
Chelmsford	(6b)	49.1	6	119	8	5-66	14.87	1	-	36.87	40.33
Cheltenham College											
	(6b)	1743	427 ⎫	4728	269	10-113	17.57	24	10	40.07	43.85
	(8b)	40.3	4 ⎭								
Cheltenham (Victoria)											
	(6b)	387.5	106	963	71	9-21	13.56	6	2	32.77	41.38
Chesterfield	(6b)	270.5	82 ⎫	632	39	8-79	16.20	4	2	46.17	35.09
	(8b)	22	3 ⎭								
Chichester	(6b)	36	3	154	2	2-154	77.00	-	-	108.00	71.29
Clacton-on-Sea	(6b)	58.4	12	197	13	8-64	15.15	1	-	27.07	55.96
Clifton College											
	(6b)	282.4	79	640	43	7-19	14.88	4	2	39.44	37.73
Colchester	(6b)	46	16	78	4	3-33	19.50	-	-	69.00	28.26
Coventry	(6b)	20.2	4	82	1	1-33	82.00	-	-	122.00	67.21
Derby	(6b)	170.1	54	397	23	4-42	17.26	-	-	44.39	38.88
Dewsbury	(6b)	29	5	79	3	3-79	26.33	-	-	58.00	45.40
Dover	(6b)	31.3	2	175	1	1-77	175.00	-	-	189.00	92.59
Dudley	(6b)	181.1	46	515	23	7-84	22.39	3	1	47.26	47.37
Eastbourne	(6b)	146.3	36	460	20	7-50	23.00	2	1	43.95	52.33
Ebbw Vale	(6b)	32	6	78	3	3-59	26.33	-	-	64.00	40.62
Edgbaston	(6b)	490.2	123 ⎫	1350	60	7-63	22.50	4	2	52.63	42.74
	(8b)	27	7 ⎭								
Fenner's	(6b)	33	11	63	3	3-63	21.00	-	-	66.00	31.81
Folkestone	(6b)	141	27	511	23	7-122	22.21	3	1	36.78	60.40
Gillingham	(6b)	41.3	7	107	13	7-57	8.23	2	1	19.15	42.97
Gloucester Spa	(6b)	18	5	48	1	1-48	48.00	-	-	108.00	44.44
Gloucester (Tuffley Avenue)											
	(6b)	2530.5	665 ⎫	6589	343	8-26	19.20	32	9	45.97	41.78
	(8b)	72.7	18 ⎭								
Gravesend	(6b)	137.3	43	287	18	4-33	15.94	-	-	45.83	34.78
Harrogate	(6b)	14	3	50	1	1-50	50.00	-	-	84.00	59.52
Hastings	(6b)	121.4	21	463	13	5-53	35.61	1	-	56.15	63.42
Headingley	(6b)	99	28	225	15	7-85	15.00	2	1	39.60	37.87
Hinckley	(6b)	50.1	8	180	5	5-92	36.00	1	-	60.20	59.80
Horsham	(6b)	90.1	14	270	6	3-59	45.00	-	-	90.16	49.94
Hove	(6b)	388	114	914	23	4-78	39.73	-	-	101.21	39.26
Huddersfield	(6b)	56.1	14	138	11	6-55	12.54	2	1	30.63	40.94
Hull	(6b)	155	40	389	10	5-99	38.90	1	-	93.00	41.82
Ilford	(6b)	32	5	92	2	2-92	46.00	-	-	96.00	47.91
Kennington Oval											
	(6b)	838.1	229 ⎫	2383	91	7-55	26.18	5	1	59.68	43.87
	(8b)	50.2	7 ⎭								

Ground		Overs	Mdns	Runs	Wkts	Best	Avge	5wI	10wM		
Kettering	(6b)	92.2	38	150	6	3-50	25.00	-	-	92.33	27.07
Leicester (Aylestone Road)											
	(6b)	371.2	95	791	34	5-36	23.26	2	-	65.52	35.50
Leicester (Grace Road)											
	(6b)	140.1	47	269	20	5-66	13.45	1	-	42.05	31.98
Leyton	(6b)	67	24	126	5	3-13	25.20	-	-	80.40	31.34
Liverpool	(6b)	100.5	40	164	10	7-101	16.40	1	1	60.50	27.10
Llanelli	(6b)	42	12	97	4	4-97	24.25	-	-	63.00	38.49
Lord's	(6b)	694	142 ⎫	2072	109	8-132	19.00	9	5	41.30	46.02
	(8b)	42.2	1 ⎭								
Maidstone	(6b)	122.1	36 ⎫	439	19	4-70	23.10	-	-	51.73	44.65
	(8b)	31.2	1 ⎭								
Neath	(6b)	50.3	16	140	6	4-51	23.33	-	-	50.50	46.20
Newport	(6b)	112	40 ⎫	359	26	8-41	13.80	3	1	44.53	31.00
	(8b)	60.6	14 ⎭								
Northampton	(6b)	108.2	29	308	17	5-133	18.11	1	-	38.23	47.38
Nuneaton	(6b)	61	9	211	8	4-101	26.37	-	-	45.75	57.65
Old Trafford	(6b)	504	137 ⎫	1289	64	7-57	20.14	6	1	48.34	41.66
	(8b)	8.6	1 ⎭								
The Parks	(6b)	540.3	117 ⎫	1687	77	6-55	21.90	6	2	45.15	48.51
	(8b)	29.2	6 ⎭								
Peterborough	(6b)	29	6	61	13	7-38	4.69	2	1	13.38	35.05
Pontypridd	(6b)	34.2	10	90	12	7-48	7.50	2	1	17.16	43.68
Portsmouth	(6b)	213.2	66	509	19	4-99	26.78	-	-	67.36	39.76
Preston	(6b)	62	31	72	11	6-54	6.54	2	1	33.81	19.35
Scarborough	(6b)	182	54	441	17	5-101	25.94	1	-	64.23	40.38
Southampton	(6b)	365.1	102	856	47	5-35	18.21	4	1	46.61	39.06
Southend-on-Sea											
	(6b)	100.2	24	292	14	7-49	20.85	1	1	43.00	48.50
Stourbridge	(6b)	69.5	20	147	9	4-26	16.33	-	-	46.55	35.08
Swansea	(6b)	196	71	396	32	8-44	12.37	3	1	36.75	33.67
Taunton	(6b)	487.1	142 ⎫	1506	53	7-110	28.41	3	-	61.30	46.35
	(8b)	40.6	10 ⎭								
Trent Bridge	(6b)	629	144 ⎫	1820	63	6-77	28.88	4	1	63.14	45.75
	(8b)	25.4	2 ⎭								
Tunbridge Wells											
	(6b)	14	2	37	4	4-37	9.25	-	-	21.00	44.04
Westcliff-on-Sea											
	(6b)	114.3	39 ⎫	423	15	4-92	28.20	-	-	61.80	45.63
	(8b)	30	7 ⎭								
Weston-super-Mare											
	(6b)	23.4	12	57	3	3-57	19.00	-	-	47.33	40.14
Worcester	(6b)	416.5	133 ⎫	1068	43	7-121	24.83	2	-	63.32	39.22
	(8b)	27.6	4 ⎭								
Worthing	(6b)	63	31 ⎫	234	22	8-37	10.63	3	1	29.31	36.27
	(8b)	33.3	7 ⎭								
Totals	(6b)	22030.3	5858 ⎫	57919	2935	10-113	19.73	250	86	47.27	41.74
	(8b)	820	139 ⎭								
In South Africa											
Cape Town	(6b)	14	4 ⎫	242	6	3-64	40.33	-	-	118.00	34.18
	(8b)	78	23 ⎭								
Durban	(6b)	29	8	62	0	-	-	-	-	-	35.63
East London	(6b)	36	11 ⎫	105	8	4-43	13.12	-	-	45.00	29.16
	(8b)	18	10 ⎭								
Johannesburg	(6b)	29	5 ⎫	447	11	4-71	40.63	-	-	112.54	36.10
	(8b)	133	19 ⎭								
Kimberley	(6b)	25.1	7 ⎫	162	6	3-66	27.00	-	-	70.50	38.29
	(8b)	34	8 ⎭								
Pietermaritzburg (6b)											
		11	4	28	0	-	-	-	-	-	42.42
Port Elizabeth	(6b)	15	1	31	1	1-31	31.00	-	-	90.00	34.44
Pretoria	(8b)	19	4	60	4	3-49	15.00	-	-	38.00	39.47

Salisbury	(8b)	29	6	60	8	6-38	7.50	1	-	29.00	25.86
Totals	(6b)	159.1	40 ⎫	1197	40	6-38	27.20	1	-	56.54	34.76
	(8b)	311	72 ⎭								

OVERALL TOTALS

	(6b)	22189.4	5898 ⎫	59116	2979	10-113	19.84	251	86	47.72	41.57
	(8b)	1131	211 ⎭								

Modes of Dismissal

Caught	268	(34.58%)
Bowled	222	(28.65%)
L.B.W	24	(3.10%)
Stumped	17	(2.19%)
Run out	25	(3.23%)
Not out	217	(28.00%)
Hit wicket	2	(0.25%)
Total	**775**	

Bowlers Who Took Goddard's Wicket on Most Occasions

14	A.P.Freeman (Kent)
11	G.Geary (Leicestershire)
10	M.S.Nichols (Essex)
7	W.E.Astill (Leicestershire), W.H.Copson (Derbyshire), R.Howorth (Worcestershire), J.Mercer (Glamorgan)

How Goddard Took His Wickets

Batsmen dismissed

Caught	1464	(49.14%)
Bowled	900	(30.21%)
L.B.W.	516	(17.32%)
Stumped	93	(3.12%)
Hit wicket	6	(0.20%)
Total	**2979**	

Batsmen dismissed most frequently

19	D.Davies (Glamorgan), D.E.Davies (Glamorgan)
18	T.P.B.Smith (Essex), L.F.Townsend (Derbyshire)
17	C.P.Mead (Hampshire), L.J.Todd (Kent)
16	L.E.G.Ames (Kent), J.Langridge (Sussex), R.T.D.Perks (Worcestershire)
15	G.Lavis (Glamorgan), N.T.McCorkell (Hampshire), A.E.Pothecary (Hampshire), R.W.V.Robins (Middlesex)

Principal catchers off Goddard's bowling

116	W.R.Hammond
114	J.F.Crapp
97	C.J.Barnett
93	B.O.Allen
86	W.L.Neale
69	B.H.Lyon
53	R.A.Sinfield
51	E.J.Stephens
50	A.E.Wilson*

* Wilson also made 48 of the 93 stumpings off Goddard's bowling

Goddard also held 129 catches off his own bowling.

Miscellaneous Records

Hat Tricks – Six
For Gloucestershire
1st inns   v Sussex at Eastbourne 1924
            (A.H.H.Gilligan b, W.L.Cornford c H.Smith, T.E.R.Cook c G.E.Dennett)
1st inns   v Glamorgan at Swansea 1930
            (W.E.Jones c F.J.Seabrook, J.Mercer b, F.P.Ryan c C.C.R.Dacre)
1st inns   v Glamorgan at Swansea 1947
            (W.E.Jones lbw, H.G.Davies b, G.Lavis st A.E.Wilson)
2nd inns   v Somerset at Bristol 1947
            (R.J.O.Meyer lbw, G.R.Langdale b, A.W.Wellard c G.W.Parker)
For England
1st inns   v South Africa at Johannesburg 1938/39
            (A.D.Nourse c and b, N.Gordon st L.E.G.Ames, W.W.Wade b)
For MCC
1st inns   v Rhodesia at Salisbury 1938/39
            (D.S.Tomlinson lbw, M.Napier b, P.N.F.Mansell b)

Best Bowling Analysis in an Innings

10-113	v Worcestershire	Cheltenham College	1937
9-21	v Cambridge University	Cheltenham Victoria	1929
9-37	v Leicestershire	Bristol	1934
9-38	v Kent	Bristol	1939
9-41	v Nottinghamshire	Bristol	1947
9-44	v Somerset	Bristol	1939
9-55	v Worcestershire	Bristol	1939
9-61	v Derbyshire	Bristol	1949
9-82	v Surrey	Cheltenham College	1946

Best Bowling Analysis in a Match

17-106	v Kent	Bristol	1939
16-99	v Worcestershire	Bristol	1939
16-181	v Worcestershire	Cheltenham College	1937
15-81	v Nottinghamshire	Bristol	1947
15-107	v Derbyshire	Bristol	1949
15-134	v Leicestershire	Gloucester Tuffley	1947
15-156	v Middlesex	Cheltenham College	1947

Most Balls Bowled in an Innings

390	65-12-144-6 v Lancashire	Bristol	1938

Most Balls Bowled in a Match

593	98.5-40-160-10 v Lancashire	Liverpool	1932

Most Runs conceded in an Innings

0-186	v Australians	Bristol	1948

Most Runs conceded in a Match

12-276	v Middlesex	Lord's	1938

Most wickets in a season for Gloucestershire
222 in seasons 1937 and 1947 (County Records)

Most balls bowled in a season for Gloucestershire
9318 in 1935
Goddard conceded 4073 runs that season for Gloucestershire, the highest number of runs ever conceded in a season by a Gloucestershire bowler.

Lowest bowling average in a season for Gloucestershire
14.58   in 1939   2858 runs   196 wickets

Goddard lies eighth in the all-time list of catchers for Gloucestershire with a total of 300.